Ancient Egyptians

PEOPLE OF THE PYRAMIDS

Ancient Egyptians

PEOPLE OF THE PYRAMIDS

ROSALIE F. AND CHARLES F. BAKER III

OXFORD

UNIVERSITY PRESS

In loving appreciation of
Joseph and Rose Ferreira

OXFORD
UNIVERSITY PRESS

Oxford New York

Athens Auckland Bangkok Bogotá Buenos Aires Cape Town
Chennai Dar es Salaam Delhi Florence Hong Kong Istanbul Karachi
Kolkata Kuala Lumpur Madrid Melbourne Mexico City Mumbai Nairobi
Paris Sao Paulo Shanghai Singapore Taipei Tokyo Toronto Warsaw
with associated companies in Berlin Ibadan

Copyright © 2001 by Rosalie F. and Charles F. Baker III

Published by Oxford University Press, Inc.
198 Madison Avenue, New York, New York 10016

Oxford is a registered trademark of Oxford University Press

Library of Congress Cataloging in-Publication Data

Baker, Rosalie F.
Ancient Egyptians : people of the pyramids /
Rosalie F. and Charles F. Baker.
p. cm. – (Oxford profiles)
Includes bibliographical references and index.
ISBN 0-19-512221-6
1. Egypt—History—To 332 B.C.—
Biography. I. Baker, Charles F. II. Title. III. Series.
DT83.B25 2001
920.032—dc21   2001021209

135798642
Printed in the United States of America
on acid-free paper

On the cover: Djoser's Step Pyramid; *inset* (clockwise from top left)
Menkaure, Hatshepsut, Senwosret III

Frontispiece: Nackht, a scribe and priest during the reign of Thutmose IV
(18th Dynasty), commissioned this hunting scene for the wall of his
tomb. Nackht aims his throw-stick (similar to a boomerang) at a fowl
while his family watches.

Design: Sandy Kaufman
Layout: Loraine Machlin
Picture research: Patricia Burns

Contents

Preface

Ancient Egyptian civilization has fascinated people for centuries. Even today, archaeological discoveries in Egypt become headline items throughout the world. What is it about these ancient people that so intrigues us? Is it the massiveness of the tombs and temples they built? The elaborate preparations they made to enjoy the next world? The enduring nature of their system of government? Certainly there is no one answer.

Unfortunately, the stories of the people who nurtured this civilization are incomplete, because few records of their feelings and ideas have been uncovered thus far. The vast majority of written materials to survive have been found inscribed on temple and tomb walls, stelae (monumental stone pillars), and boundary markers. Whereas the dry, hot sand of the lands beyond the Nile acts as a natural preserver, the humidity of the riverbanks and the Delta region is destructive. As a result, the tomb complexes and religious structures, built traditionally away from the Nile, have survived. The villages, towns, and cities that lay along the riverbanks have not lasted, so we lack substantial documentation of the home and working lives of the ancient Egyptians. Several chance finds, such as letters written on papyrus, notes scribbled on broken pieces of clay, and the like have helped broaden our understanding of ancient Egypt.

Because the Egyptians left no dictionaries or detailed explanations of their beliefs, Egyptologists are sometimes unable to understand the significance of words and phrases they have been able to translate. By comparing a variety of sources and texts, some conclusions may be drawn. But Egyptologists do not always agree on translations or on the meaning of specific passages. Nor do they always agree on dates or even the transliteration of Egyptian names.

We have tried to follow the consensus of opinion among Egyptologists. As regards dates, we have used those suggested by respected Egyptologist William J. Murnane in his book, *The Penguin Guide to Ancient Egypt* (1996). The transliteration of Egyptian names generally follows Murnane's transliterations. For translations of historical documents, we are principally indebted to James Henry Breasted's universally accepted four-volume work, *Ancient Records of Egypt* (1906).

Each profile combines personal information with details of Egyptian life and customs. In order not to repeat traditional rituals such as the mummification process and the "Opening of the Mouth" ceremony, each of these topics is treated once in detail and referred to briefly in other biographies. Detailed explanations can be found by looking up the ritual in the index.

The full biographies begin with Djoser, the ruler whose Step Pyramid set the standard for pyramid building. They end with Ramesses III, the last of the great kings. The names of some characters are familiar: Khufu, who built the Great Pyramid; the beautiful Nefertiti; and Ramesses the Great. Others are not so well known: Ptahhotep, for example, whose maxims are timeless. Each of the book's five parts ends with a section called More Ancient Egyptians to Remember. Profiles of Menes, the ruler credited with unifying Upper and Lower Egypt, and of Manetho, the historian whose list of kings became the standard in Egyptology, can be found in this section of the first and last parts respectively.

To help you locate the places mentioned in this book, three maps are included. Suggested readings appear at the end of most profiles. At the back of the book, a more general list of Further Reading and Websites will guide you as you delve deeper into the rich civilization of the ancient Egyptians.

Rosalie F. and Charles F. Baker
New Bedford, Massachusetts

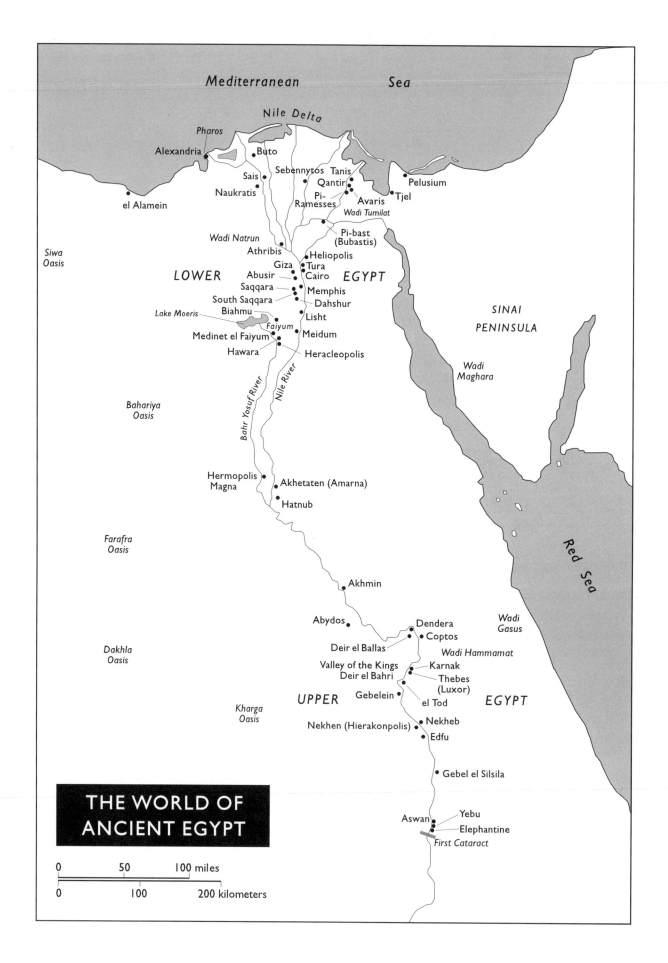

Mediterranean Sea

Nile Delta

Pharos
Alexandria
Buto
Sais
Naukratis
el Alamein

Sebennytos
Tanis
Qantir
Pi-Ramesses
Avaris
Wadi Tumilat
Pelusium
Tjel

Siwa Oasis

Pi-bast (Bubastis)
Wadi Natrun
Athribis
Heliopolis
Giza
Tura
LOWER
Abusir
Cairo
EGYPT
Saqqara
Memphis
South Saqqara
Dahshur
Lake Moeris
Biahmu
Lisht
Faiyum
Medinet el Faiyum
Meidum
Hawara
Heracleopolis

SINAI
PENINSULA

Wadi Maghara

Bahariya Oasis

Bahr Yosuf River
Nile River

Farafra Oasis

Hermopolis Magna
Akhetaten (Amarna)
Hatnub

Red Sea

Dakhla Oasis

Akhmin

Abydos
Dendera
Coptos
Deir el Ballas
Wadi Gasus

Wadi Hammamat

Valley of the Kings
Karnak
Deir el Bahri
Thebes (Luxor)
Gebelein
el Tod
UPPER
EGYPT
Kharga Oasis

Nekhen (Hierakonpolis)
Nekheb
Edfu

Gebel el Silsila

Aswan
Yebu
Elephantine
First Cataract

THE WORLD OF
ANCIENT EGYPT

0   50   100 miles
0   100   200 kilometers

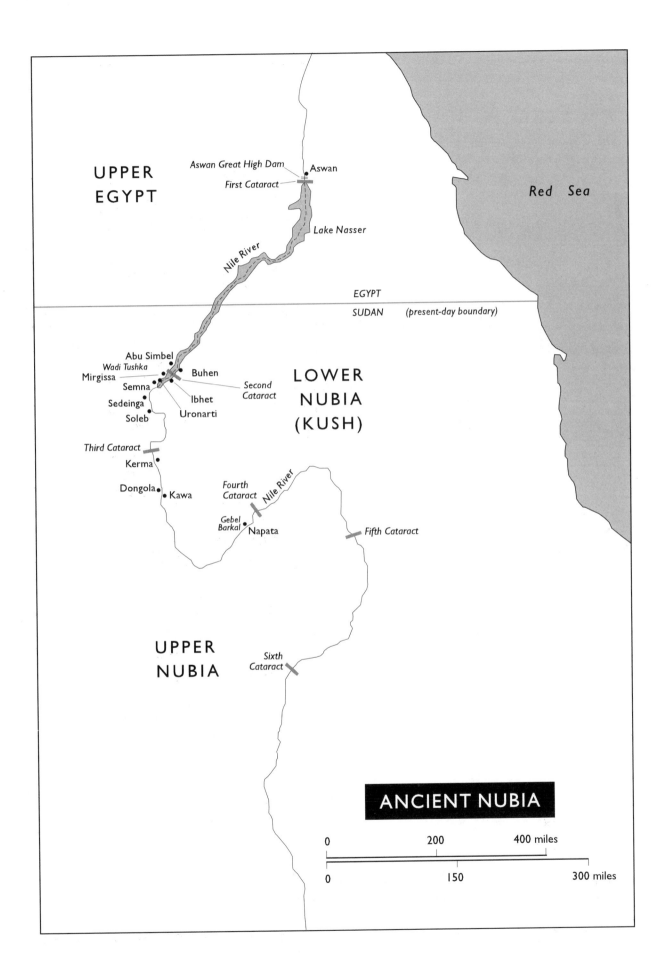

UPPER
EGYPT

Aswan Great High Dam • Aswan

First Cataract

Red Sea

Lake Nasser

Nile River

EGYPT

SUDAN   (present-day boundary)

Abu Simbel
Wadi Tushka
Mirgissa   • Buhen
Semna
Sedeinga   Ibhet   Second
Soleb   Uronarti   Cataract

LOWER
NUBIA
(KUSH)

Third Cataract
Kerma

Dongola • Kawa   Fourth   Nile River
                    Cataract
            Gebel
            Barkal • Napata   Fifth Cataract

UPPER
NUBIA   Sixth
                    Cataract

ANCIENT NUBIA

0   200   400 miles

0   150   300 miles

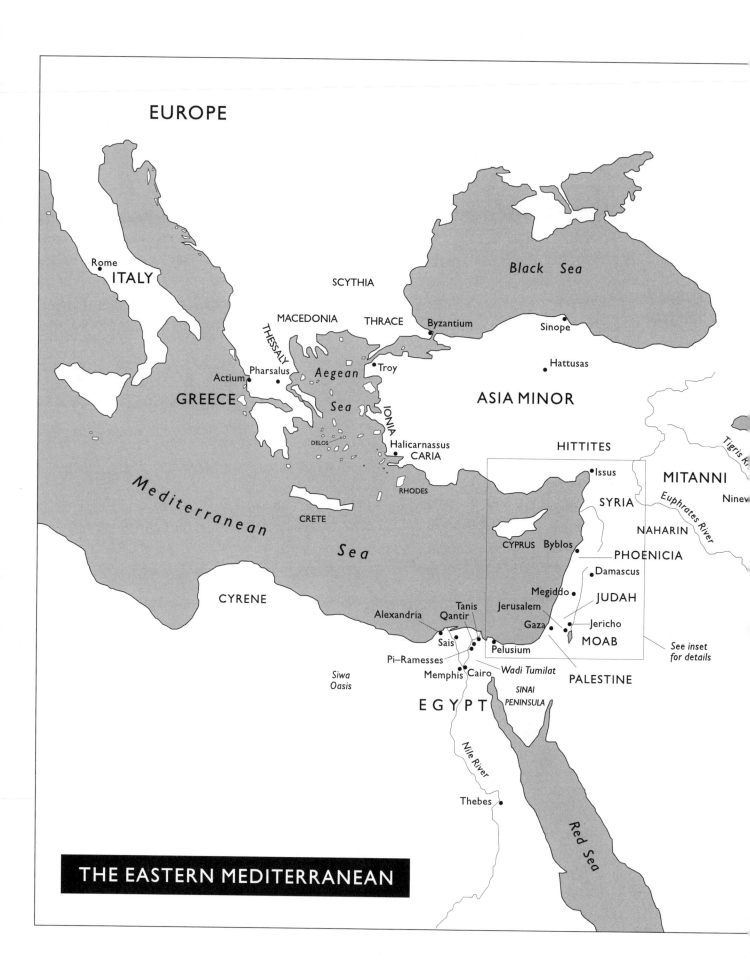

EUROPE

Rome •
ITALY

Black Sea

SCYTHIA

MACEDONIA   THRACE   Byzantium •
THESSALY   Sinope •

Actium •   Pharsalus •   *Aegean*   Troy •   Hattusas •
GREECE   *Sea*   ASIA MINOR

IONIA
DELOS   HITTITES   Issus •
Halicarnassus •   MITANNI
CARIA   Ninev
SYRIA   *Euphrates River*
Mediterranean   RHODES   NAHARIN

CRETE   CYPRUS   Byblos •   PHOENICIA   *Tigris R.*

Sea   Damascus •

CYRENE   Megiddo •   JUDAH
Tanis   Jerusalem •
Alexandria •   Qantir   Gaza •   Jericho •   See inset
Sais •   •   MOAB   for details
Pi–Ramesses   Pelusium   PALESTINE
Siwa   Memphis Cairo   *Wadi Tumilat*
Oasis   •   SINAI
E G Y P T   PENINSULA

Nile River

Thebes •

Red Sea

THE EASTERN MEDITERRANEAN

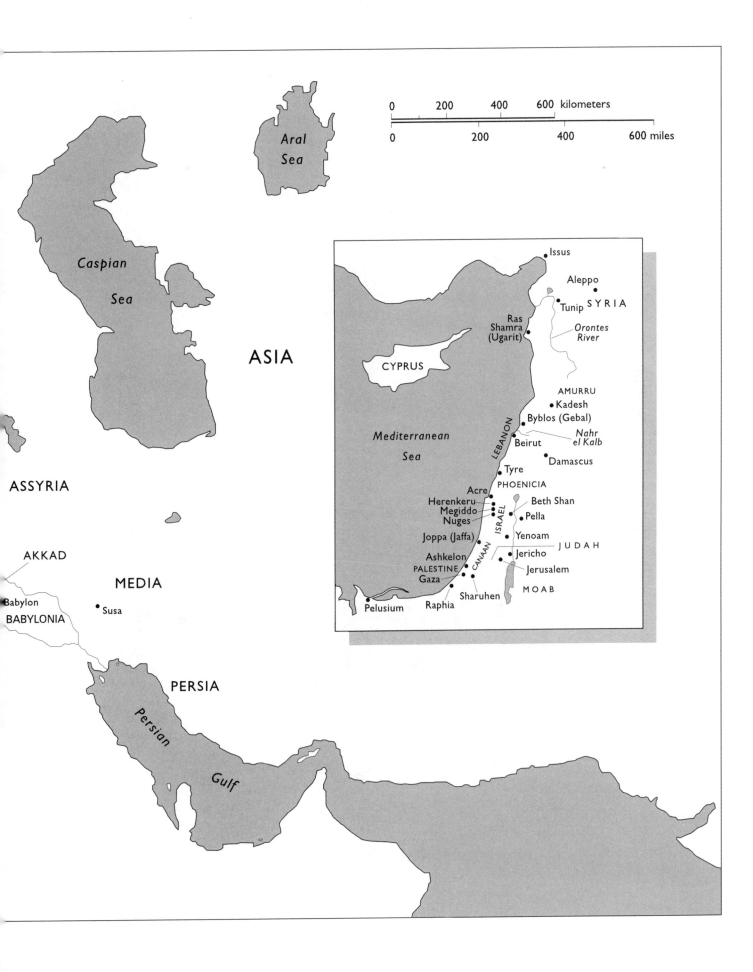

Aral
Sea

Caspian
Sea

ASIA

ASSYRIA

AKKAD

MEDIA

Babylon
BABYLONIA

Susa

PERSIA

Persian
Gulf

0   200   400   600   kilometers

0   200   400   600 miles

Issus

Aleppo

Tunip   SYRIA

Ras
Shamra
(Ugarit)

Orontes
River

CYPRUS

AMURRU

Kadesh

Byblos (Gebal)

Nahr
el Kalb

Mediterranean
Sea

Beirut

Damascus

Tyre

PHOENICIA

Acre

Beth Shan

Herenkeru

Megiddo

Pella

Nuges

Joppa (Jaffa)

Yenoam

JUDAH

Ashkelon

Jericho

PALESTINE

Jerusalem

Gaza

MOAB

Sharuhen

Pelusium

Raphia

LEBANON

ISRAEL

CANAAN

For more than 25 years, a special crew worked to restore Khufu's cedarwood boat.

1 Tradition and Grandeur (Old Kingdom, about 2686–2181 B.C.)

The fifth-century B.C. Greek historian and traveler Herodotus captured the essence of the country when he wrote, "Egypt is the gift of the Nile." The story of Egypt and the Egyptians cannot be treated independently from the geography of the Nile. The Nile River basin—the land drained by the Nile River and its tributaries—includes about one-tenth of the entire continent of Africa. Rising first in the highlands of Burundi, the Nile flows north to Lake Victoria, north again to the Sudan, then northeast into Ethiopia, back into the Sudan, and finally north into Egypt. Approximately 100 miles before the Nile reaches the Mediterranean Sea, it fans out into several branches that stream across the rich, fertile area known as the Nile Delta.

Along the route, its name changes several times. It begins as the Kagera River, then changes to the Victoria Nile, the Albert Nile, the Mountain Nile, and the White Nile. The last joins with the Blue Nile, which rises in the highlands of central Ethiopia, and together they become the Nile, proper. Many other rivers, large and small, join with the Nile along a course that extends for more than 4,000 miles, making the Nile the longest river in the world.

For the Egyptians, past and present, the Nile represents life. The early Egyptians dug channels that brought the waters of the Nile into the barren desert. This system of irrigation, still used today, created fertile strips where farmers planted and harvested their crops. In time, the river became a highway that allowed for the transportation of goods, materials, and people.

Yet the river was not always hospitable to those living along its banks. They could count on its waters to rise every year, but they could not predict how high. A below-normal rise threatened drought and famine. If the waters rose too high, floods and widespread destruction resulted. But the unchanging fact of life that the Nile would rise gave the people a sense of unity, stability, and confidence that came to be reflected in their beliefs and customs.

The early Egyptians ascribed the flooding to deities whom they believed favored them with an abundance of natural resources. To show their appreciation for such gifts, the Egyptians developed special symbols and rituals to honor these supernatural individuals. A set of religious beliefs gradually evolved, with one of the principal deities being the sun god Re. The Egyptians often introduced animal figures in their symbolism and even represented their deities with animal heads.

To be sure, the respect the Egyptians paid nature was merited, for it was nature that isolated and protected them, and it was nature that could destroy them. To the west and east of the narrow strip of land that bordered the Nile lay the dry and forbidding desert. To the south lay more desert and six treacherous cataracts (scattered groups of rocks along the Nile that make navigation almost impossible at the Fourth, Second, and First Cataracts). To the north was the Mediterranean Sea.

In fact, nature and the Nile were so much a part of Egyptian thinking that the people used both to orient themselves. "To go downstream" meant to go north, since the Nile flows north to the Mediterranean. "To go upstream" meant to go south, toward the source of the Nile. The Egyptians called the fertile strip of black mud directly abutting the river *Kmt* (pronounced Kemet), or "black land." The dry desert areas that lay just beyond the *Kmt* and gave the landscape a reddish tinge they called *Dsrt* (pronounced Deshret), or "red land."

According to surviving ancient Egyptian accounts, sometime between 3400 and 3100 B.C., two independent kingdoms emerged. The delta area to the north was known as Lower Egypt, and its king wore a red crown that had a distinctive coil. The bee and the papyrus plant were its symbols, and Edjo, the cobra goddess, its patron deity. The land that bordered the Nile between the delta and the First Cataract to the south was called Upper Egypt. Its king wore a tall bulb-shaped white crown. The sedge and the lotus flower were its symbols, and Nekhbet, the vulture goddess, its patron deity.

Part 1 of *Ancient Egyptians* profiles men and women who established the traditions that endured for centuries and built the monuments that have come to symbolize the spirit of this magnificent civilization.

Djoser

CREATOR OF
A TRADITION

t some time around 2686 B.C., the rulers
of Upper and Lower Egypt united the two
areas. An era of prosperity followed, and
leaders such as Djoser emerged. Unfortunately, only a few brief inscriptions and re-
liefs carved on rocks have survived to tell us about this era.
Egyptologists have been unable to confirm the king list for
this period, which has come to be known as the 3rd Dynasty.
Some sources consider Djoser the founder of the dynasty;
others suggest that either Nebka or Sanakht might have
been the first leader. Still others believe that Nebka and
Sanakht are the same person. The identity of Djoser's parents is also in question. Some believe his mother was Queen
Nimaathap, the wife of Khasekhemwy, the last ruler of the
2nd Dynasty.

According to records uncovered in the Sinai Peninsula,
just east of Egypt, Djoser and his predecessors sent expeditions to the area to find turquoise mines. As a result of such
ventures, the Egyptians came to control the local Bedouin

Following custom, Djoser ordered this life-size statue of himself
placed in his tomb's *serdab,* a small sealed chamber. The realistic
reproduction would receive offerings throughout eternity.

Djoser (left) makes an offering to the god Khnum for ending a seven-year famine, in this relief above the king's decree of thanksgiving. Archaeologists found this stela on the island of Sehel in the cataract region of the Nile. It dates to the reign of the Ptolemies, more than 2,400 years after Djoser ruled.

gods of creation, birth, and death, he was still considered a god.

Djoser accepted his divinity as fact, but he was well aware of his limitations. His body was mortal and would die. Only the essence that made him a god-king was immortal; upon his death, this part of him would enter the heavens and share in the eternal life of the gods. Immortality was a king's privilege. Djoser's royal name (the name he assumed when he became king), Netjerykhet, meaning "godlike of body" reflected this belief. The sky god Horus was manifest on Earth as the king. Interestingly enough, the name Djoser was first associated with the name Netjerykhet in records written 1,000 years after Djoser lived. Egyptologists believe that Djoser, which means "holy one," was his birth name.

Djoser gave the architects of his burial complex a simple order: Build a tomb worthy of a god-king. Egyptians believed that those buried near the royal tomb might be able to share in the king's afterlife, and it soon followed that the highest honor any Egyptian could receive was permission to build his tomb in the shadow of the king's. Concern about the afterlife also motivated Egyptian workers and artisans. They believed that, if their work pleased the king on Earth, they might be allowed to serve him in his afterlife.

The tomb site would require enough open area around it so that others might be buried near Djoser and so the tomb could be stocked with everything he might need in the next life. A few high-ranking officials, nobles, and kings had substantial tombs at a rocky plateau called Saqqara, which lay just to the west of the royal palace in White Wall (later Memphis). Djoser's immediate predecessors had preferred the royal

tribes. Further expansion and conquest did not seem important to the rulers of the lands along the Nile. They considered their land truly blessed by the gods and gave thanks that, every year, the waters of the great river deposited a life-giving bounty of silt along the riverbanks. The Egyptians thought their rulers were mortal incarnations of divine power. Although an earthly king could not be deemed equal to the great

Djoser

POSITION

King of Egypt

ACTIVE DATES

About 2668–49 B.C.

ACCOMPLISHMENTS

Highly skilled at governing; his ability to lead kept Upper and Lower Egypt a unified, peaceful nation; ordered the building of a tomb complex—the so-called Step Pyramid—that was radically different in design from those of his predecessors and that set the precedent for future pyramids

[P]lants, herbs, and trees shall bend beneath [the weight of] their produce . . . . Starvation will end, and the emptiness of the granaries shall come to an end.

—Khnum's words to Djoser in a dream, inscribed at Sehel

cemetery at Abydos in Upper Egypt, more than 200 miles from White Wall. Djoser elected not to have his tomb there; instead, he chose Saqqara.

Djoser followed a newer tradition when he selected a site on the west bank of the Nile. In recent generations, the Egyptians had come to associate their kings with both Horus and Re. Because Re brought life and prosperity to the lands along the Nile, it seemed only fitting that Egypt's kings should be related to him. Burial on the west bank also seemed appropriate because the sun set, or left the earth every day, in the west. According to the Egyptians, a king buried on the west bank could join Re more easily. The two could then travel along the dark nightly journey and "come alive" again at daybreak.

Djoser's burial chamber, like those of his predecessors, lay deep within the tomb—approximately 94 feet below ground level. Workers carefully lined this chamber with specially cut pink granite casing slabs and then cut a hole in one side so that Djoser's corpse could be placed in the chamber. As a seal for the hole, workers carved a granite plug that weighed three tons.

These preparations had one purpose: to protect Djoser for eternity by providing his *ka* (life force) with a suitable home. But preparing a beautifully constructed, sealed burial chamber as a suitable home for the *ka* was only the

first step in a long process of readying a king's tomb for his human body. Because the human body decays quickly, arrangements had to be made for its preservation. In Djoser's time, mummification was the accepted method of caring for a dead king's body. When the French Egyptologist Jean-Philippe Lauer cleared Djoser's burial chamber in 1934, he found a mummified left foot. Further investigation proved that the tomb had been robbed of its contents in antiquity. Many Egyptologists believe it is Djoser's.

Djoser also made sure that his tomb site had a proper place for food offerings. In general, tomb structures had a chamber called the *serdab* (a walled room with no doors). Djoser's *serdab* housed a life-size seated statue of him, dressed in a long white cloak and wearing the royal striped head cloth over a large bushy wig that reached across his shoulders onto his chest and back. The sculptor gave Djoser's statue a stern face, prominent cheekbones, thick lips, and a heavy jawline. The sculptor also carved the traditional "royal beard." Rectangular in shape, it extended from Djoser's chin to his right arm, which reached across his chest and touched his left upper arm. Djoser's left hand rested, palm down, on his thigh. Drilled into one stone wall of the *serdab* were two holes so that Djoser could "look" with his rock-crystal eyes and "see" the offerings left for him during the funeral. Robbers later gouged out the eyes, and time wore away the brilliant colors of the tomb workers' paint, but the statue still catches the attention of all who visit Egypt's Cairo Museum. (Today, a copy sits in Djoser's *serdab*.)

Within the tomb and around the burial chamber, Djoser and his architects had workers cut several shafts and passageways—a few led to the burial chamber, others led to small rooms. Some of the walls were inlaid with bright blue glazed tiles that were rectangular in shape to imitate the colored reed mats hanging in the palace. Other walls were painted with scenes showing Djoser performing royal rituals. In one, he wears the red crown of Lower Egypt; in another, he wears the white crown of Upper Egypt. According to Egyptian belief, representing the ruler's image and name throughout the tomb area ensured the survival of his spirit in the afterlife.

Life must have fairly bustled as work proceeded on Djoser's burial complex. Originally, Djoser had approved the traditional *mastaba*-type tomb for his own. In modern times, *mastaba*, an Arabic word meaning "bench," has been used to refer to the mud-brick superstructure the ancient Egyptians placed over a burial pit in the sand. This superstructure not only prevented the wind from blowing sand away from the tomb and exposing the body, it also protected the possessions that had been placed alongside the deceased for use in the afterlife. As the centuries passed, Egyptian rulers built larger and larger

mastabas, adding separate burial chambers and rooms to house these various objects. They began to decorate the rooms to imitate the dead person's earthly home and to erect small tombs for those who had helped the deceased in this life.

Because Djoser wanted everything that might be of service to him in the afterlife placed in the rooms about his mummified body, he planned to have artisans paint the walls with representations of these objects, as well as with images of his servants and of food. Religious beliefs of the time told him that prayer and the special rituals performed by those who remained on Earth would make these images come alive and sustain him in death.

A traditional *mastaba* would be too small to accommodate what Djoser would need in the afterlife. In addition to a larger structure, he would also need an architect who was innovative, someone who was not afraid to work with new materials or to test the strength and durability of stone. The traditional mud bricks would not be suitable because mud-brick structures could be only so tall before they would collapse on themselves. To undertake the task, Djoser chose Imhotep, an architect who was willing to test new theories.

As work progressed on the tomb, workers paid particular attention to the Heb-Sed court just south of the pyramid. In Djoser's time, Heb-Sed celebrations lasted five days. Held at specific intervals (which varied over the centuries), the festival reaffirmed a king's ability to rule. The principal event involved the king running around a special courtyard in the presence of his subjects to show that his physical powers were still in order. For the race, the king wore a special short white garment that completely covered his torso and arms—the same type of garment that Djoser's *serdab* statue wore. According to Egyptian belief, Djoser's *ka* would continue to perform this ritual ceremony in the afterlife. Exactly how many times Djoser performed the jubilee ritual in this life is not known. It could not have been many, considering that sources say he died in the 19th year of his reign.

In death, he continued to be honored and remembered. Some 2,400 years after Djoser ruled Egypt, an artisan carved into a large rounded block of granite at Sehel, near the First Cataract, an inscription that explained why the area just south of the island of Elephantine was sacred to the god Khnum. (In Egyptian mythology, Khnum created the first human out of straw and clay and fashioned him on a potter's wheel.) The inscription said that Djoser granted Khnum the land as a thanksgiving offering for ending a seven-year famine.

According to the inscription, Djoser had not worshiped Khnum properly, and so the god had stopped the Nile's waters from flooding the Two Lands (that is, Upper and Lower Egypt) for seven years. As reports of widespread famine reached the palace, Djoser sent a message to Madir, the governor at Elephantine:

> Year 18 of the king of Upper and Lower Egypt, Netjerykhet [the 18th year of Djoser's reign] . . .

This is to inform you that I am distressed as I sit on the Great Throne, and I feel for those who dwell in the palace, because the waters of the Nile have not risen to their proper height for seven years. Grain is very scarce, there are no garden vegetables at all, and extremely little remains of everything that was used for food. Every man has robbed his neighbor. No one can walk anymore. The children are wailing; the young people barely move along. The hearts of the old men are broken down with despair. . . . The officials, too, are in need and the temples hold nothing but air. . . . I asked Imhotep, the Chief Lector Priest:

> "Where is the birthplace of the Nile? What deity rules there?"

According to the inscription, Imhotep read the king's message and began studying about the Nile. He reported his findings to Djoser, who said:

> [Imhotep] gave me information about the rise of the Nile and told me what men had written concerning it . . . . There is a town in the middle of the river from which the Nile makes its appearance, named Elephantine . . . . Here the Nile-god lives in the form of Khnum.

Content with the information Imhotep had brought to him, Djoser fell asleep. In a dream, Khnum appeared to him, saying

> I am Khnum, who fashioned you. . . . I know the Nile. I will make the Nile rise for you, and in no year shall it fail . . . and plants, herbs, and trees shall bend beneath [the weight of] their produce. . . . Starvation will end, and the emptiness of the granaries shall come to an end.

After this dream, Djoser decreed that lands and gifts be given to the temple of Khnum. He also ordered that every farmer, fisherman, hunter, and artisan (except those who crafted images of the gods) pay one-tenth of their income to the temple. He told his artisans to position a granite rock in the temple's sanctuary and to carve the words of the decree on it. Above the hieroglyphs, the artisans were to fashion a representation of Khnum and his companions. And it was to be made very clear that anyone who refused to obey the decree was to be punished.

Whether this decree refers to actual events is unknown, but it does prove the high regard later kingdoms and rulers had for Djoser. Scholars have used the passage that links Netjerykhet with Djoser as positive proof that both names refer to the same ruler. Another source, although not as reliable, also identifies the two as one person: Some 1,000 years after Djoser died, a tourist visited Netjerykhet's pyramid at Saqqara and scribbled the name "Djoser" on the steps.

FURTHER READING

Lehner, Mark. *The Complete Pyramids,* pp. 84–93. New York: Thames & Hudson, 1997.

Pace, Mildred Mastin. *Pyramid: Tombs for Eternity,* pp. 20–33, 34–41, 138–39. 1974. Reprint, New York: McGraw-Hill, 1981.

Imhotep

ROYAL ARCHITECT AND HEALER

Seal bearer of the King of Lower Egypt, First after the King of Upper Egypt, Administrator of the Great Palace, Hereditary Lord, High Priest of Heliopolis, Builder, Sculptor and Vase Maker in Chief—such were the titles King Djoser heaped on his most valued adviser, Imhotep. Proof of Djoser's confidence in Imhotep came when Egyptologists uncovered a partially ruined statue of Djoser. Carved in hieroglyphs on the base were all of Imhotep's titles. Succeeding generations of Egyptians, however, would honor Imhotep not for his building expertise but instead for his healing powers. They would even elevate him to the ranks of the divine and worship him as their god of medicine.

Yet, for a person so esteemed by contemporaries and descendants, little is known about Imhotep himself. Some scholars say he was the son of an architect from Upper Egypt named Ka-fer; others say he was a noble; still others maintain that he was a commoner whose intelligence and ability as an architect won Djoser's admiration. Records from ancient times show that Egyptian society was quite flexible and that commoners could easily rise from a lowly social status to a position of prominence.

To be sure, Imhotep was an exceptionally skilled person who cared deeply about his country and its people. The titles bestowed on Imhotep indicate that Djoser considered him his vizier and conferred with him on all matters of importance. As vizier, Imhotep was both Chief Treasurer and Chief Justice. Thus, he served as the official link between the central government and the various *nomes,* or districts, of Upper and Lower Egypt. He was also the High Priest. Imhotep's office was in the royal palace, where scribes kept records of every transaction—including tax accounts, contracts, and wills—throughout the Two Lands.

An inscription dating to around 200 B.C. names Imhotep as the person who advised King Djoser to end a seven-year drought by giving lands and gifts to the temple of Khnum, the god honored as the creator of the human race. The inscription tells how the annual flooding of the Nile had been below normal for seven years and starvation and death stalked the people. By following Imhotep's advice, Djoser pleased Khnum, and the normal flood levels returned, as did the plentiful harvests.

Although the priests of Khnum may have written the inscription to defend their claim to a certain parcel of land, the wording proves the high regard later generations had for Imhotep's wisdom. Djoser, too, valued Imhotep, and sought his advice on an important decision soon after he was named king.

most—Imhotep. Unfortunately, no architectural plans have survived, no purchase orders, no records of workers' hours—nothing that would give any indication of the processes involved in building the first great stone building in the world.

What has survived are sections of the pyramid and burial compound. By studying the stones and other artifacts uncovered during excavations and field work, Egyptologists have learned that Djoser's pyramid was built in several stages and that each is an enlargement of a prior stage. They also discovered that some of the outlying structures were "false" buildings. That is, their fronts were beautifully fashioned, but the interiors were filled with rubble. Because these buildings were meant to provide the setting for the eternal pageantry of the dead king's *ka*, the Egyptians focused on a well-designed and ornamented exterior and saw no need to recreate the interiors.

To organize a crew of workers, to find skilled artisans to fashion the radical new design, and to craft new tools required foresight, leadership skills, and a keen understanding of stone and other buildings materials. Imhotep had all three qualifications.

The basic layout of the burial complex was simple and followed tradition. Imhotep's job involved redesigning the tomb structure itself, and this is where he made radical changes. First, he did not use sun-dried mud bricks, because he realized that they could not support the weight and pressure of the enormous monument he planned to build. Because innovation requires

Following precedent, the new king Djoser began making plans for his tomb. He knew well the religious traditions governing royal tomb design: a burial chamber and surrounding rooms sunk deep into bedrock with a mud-brick superstructure covering them. Today, Egyptologists refer to these tomb structures as *mastabas*, from the Arabic word *mastaba*, meaning "bench"—and they do indeed have a benchlike shape. Djoser was also well acquainted with the colorful exteriors of these tombs, especially the mud-brick paneling, which was painted in bright colors to resemble the matting found outside Egyptian homes.

Djoser had no intention of changing the basic design. The burial vault was to be the same; so, too, were the accompanying rooms where everything that his *ka* needed for the afterlife could be stored. Nor did he intend to change the "false door" through which the deceased's *ka* (life force) could leave the tomb whenever it wished and reenter the world of the living. Djoser also approved the building of other small tombs, where those who would care for him throughout eternity would be buried. What Djoser wanted changed was the exterior.

To create such a complex, Djoser looked to the one person he trusted

Imhotep's tomb complex for Djoser, known today as the Step Pyramid, contains underground shafts, galleries, and a granite burial vault.

experimentation, Imhotep built Djoser's tomb in stages.

His selected site was a rocky plateau at Saqqara, an area just west of White Wall (later called Memphis), where the royal palace was located. The land was bedrock with no defects or crevices. It was also above the level of the Nile but close enough to the river for boats to bring building materials almost directly to the work site.

After choosing the exact spot, Imhotep ordered a vertical shaft dug straight down through the bedrock to a depth of approximately 95 feet. He designated the area at the bottom of the shaft as the royal burial chamber and ordered it lined with pink granite slabs.

Imhotep ordered an opening made in this "box" he had created so that, during the burial rituals, workers could place Djoser's mummified body in the chamber. As a permanent seal for this opening, Imhotep had a granite plug that weighed more than three tons specially made. This plug would act as a permanent seal.

With plans for the burial chamber complete, Imhotep turned to the tomb covering, that is, the *mastaba* itself. The dimensions of his design—approximately 27 feet high and 212 feet along each side—were too large for mud bricks to be used effectively. Therefore, he had workers make the *mastaba*'s inner core of rubble that was composed of desert

Imhotep

POSITION

Architect and physician

ACTIVE DATES

About 2700–2649 B.C.

ACCOMPLISHMENTS

Designed King Djoser's Step Pyramid, the first great stone building in the world; his reputation as a skilled physician led later Egyptians to worship him as the god of medicine

stone set into clay. Imhotep did not cover the *mastaba* with plaster, as was the tradition, but rather polished white limestone slabs from Tura (an area just to the east of present-day Cairo). The thickness of the limestone cover was to be approximately 10 feet. To provide a storage area for everything Djoser might need in the afterlife and to create burial chambers for family members, Imhotep followed custom and sank a series of shafts and passageways along the eastern, outside edge of the *mastaba*.

The result, as unique as it was, still seemed too small, and so a new plan was developed, one that called for extending each side of the tomb complex about 14 feet. But each extension was to be slightly lower than the original *mastaba*. Workers then applied a second facing of limestone to the "finished" structure.

Imhotep and Djoser were not satisfied with this tomb complex. Imhotep kept the step design that he had created with the two levels, but he also ordered a second extension, which was to be placed only on the east side. Approximately 28 feet long, this extension protected the shafts previously dug along the eastern perimeter of the *mastaba*. Because this addition was even lower than the previous one, the east side now had three steps. Still the design did not create an impressive effect. Set back as it was from the Saqqara ridge, Djoser's tomb did not dominate the skyline. Furthermore, anyone approaching the complex could not see the tomb because of the traditional enclosure wall that was being built around the entire compound.

At regular intervals along this massive wall were recessed and jutted areas—196 in all. The wall measured about 1,800 feet long, more than 900

feet wide, and about 33 feet high. To mark the boundaries of the wall, Imhotep used boundary *stelae* (pillar-like stone slabs) engraved with the name of Netjerykhet (Djoser's royal name) and the names of his daughters Hotpe-her-nebti and Intkawes. Imhotep liked the look of stone and the strength and durability it gave the structure, but he did not wish to abandon all traditional architectural forms. In small rectangular niches along the upper reaches of the wall, he had artisans carve stone slabs. These slabs were cut to resemble the wood beams used to strengthen the mud-brick walls found in buildings throughout Egypt.

Although the wall design had 14 apparent entrances, only the entrance in the southeastern corner was genuine. The other 13 were fake. Because this was not a building meant for everyday use and because large numbers of people would not be entering the complex, the doors, like the exteriors of the outlying buildings, were facades.

Just inside the one real entrance, and to the right, Imhotep positioned a narrow colonnade of 40 columns, each more than 22 feet high. Again Imhotep chose stone as his medium, and he gave orders that the columns be worked to resemble the reed bundles used to strengthen the walls and doorways of Egypt's traditional reed and wattle (interwoven twigs and sticks) buildings. Although columns of wood had recently replaced the reed bundles, Imhotep recognized wood as a temporary and weak building material.

Combining creativity and ingenuity, Imhotep faced the columns with limestone slabs that had been finely carved to imitate reeds. Instead of setting them as freestanding columns, he ordered them joined to the walls on either side of the entrance area with limestone blocks. In the centuries that followed, reed-imitating columns would become a standard design feature of Egyptian architecture.

For the columns in the Heb-Sed court just to the north of the colonnade, Imhotep based his design on natural features. He ordered workers to craft each capital (the top part of a column) in the form of lotus buds, papyrus flowers, and palm leaves. This, too, became a standard feature of Egyptian architecture.

The *mastaba* itself was a radical new design—a pyramidal structure with a series of steps, each narrower than the one below. Imhotep liked what he saw, but the size was still not right, and for the fourth time, he had workers enlarge the original design. The result was the so-called Step Pyramid, a four-tiered structure approximately 202 feet high. Imhotep used the east side of the four-step pyramid as his base, then extended the other three sides before creating a six-step pyramid. By design, the base of the pyramid was not a square. To ensure its stability, Imhotep had workers slant the rows of stone slabs, all of which had been cut from desert rock. He did so because he wanted the stones to act as internal wall supports.

Scholars estimate that workers used more than 850,000 tons of stone to create Imhotep's Step Pyramid. Some blocks weighed as much as 16 tons. For miles around, Egyptians must have been able to hear the noise of stones being quarried at Tura and pulled to the riverbank where they were loaded onto boats that ferried them across the Nile to Saqqara. There workers unloaded the stones, smoothed the sides to ensure a perfect fit, and hauled the heavy loads up earthen ramps to their final setting. To complete the project, Imhotep ordered each step of the tomb's exterior covered with finely polished white limestone slabs.

Though Djoser recognized Imhotep as a master craftsman whose originality and boldness in design made him the best of architects, later generations of Egyptians preferred to honor Imhotep as a great healer. No records exist of his medical activities, but uncovered hieroglyphs, written some 1,200 years after Imhotep's death, indicate that he held the position of court physician under Djoser. Because Imhotep was also a priest, he was thought to have magical powers.

By custom, the papyrus rolls on which scribes wrote information about diseases, cures, and prescriptions were kept in temples. Egyptians who wished to be cured of an illness or disease visited temples dedicated to deities with healing powers. Thus it followed that, some 2,000 years after Imhotep's death, Egyptians began to worship Imhotep as a god. They visited temples built in Imhotep's honor and followed a prescribed ritual while there: They prayed, then slept, hoping to dream of him. If Imhotep did appear to them in a dream, they believed that his healing powers would cure them.

Six annual festivals were held in Imhotep's honor, and many Egyptians made pilgrimages to Saqqara, where tradition said Imhotep was buried (his tomb has not yet been found). There they left offerings, either in thanksgiving for a cure or as a petition for a cure. Scholars believe that some of the thousands of mummified ibises found in the sacred animal cemetery near Djoser's tomb complex were such offerings. The ibis, a large, long-legged wading bird with a long, thin, curved bill, was associated both with Imhotep and with Thoth, the Egyptian god of wisdom, writing, and learning.

In time, the Egyptians began to fashion stylized statues of Imhotep, which showed him seated on a high, decorative chair. The back of the chair was fairly low, and Imhotep's feet rested on a low pillow-like block. On his lap lay an open scroll. According to tradition, Egyptian scribes honored Imhotep's great wisdom by sprinkling the area around them with a few drops of ink before they began to write.

FURTHER READING

Lehner, Mark. *The Complete Pyramids*, pp. 84–93. New York: Thames & Hudson, 1997.

Pace, Mildred Mastin. *Pyramid: Tombs for Eternity*, pp. 20–33. 1974. Reprint, New York: McGraw-Hill, 1981.

Snefru

THE BENEFICENT KING

Snefru wandered aimlessly about the palace; he was bored. It occurred to him that Djadja-emankh, a learned man who was the chief lector priest and the court magician, might help him. Snefru ordered several servants to ask him to come at once to the king's chambers.

When the chief priest arrived at the palace, Snefru explained his plight and waited for a recommendation. Djadja-emankh suggested that the king order a boat made ready for an excursion on a beautiful lake, whose shores were dotted with fields and gardens, and order 20 of the most beautiful ladies at the royal court to row it—not those regularly assigned to the task. The chief priest pointed out that Snefru's pleasure would be twofold: the rowers would entertain him, and he could enjoy the pretty lake.

Snefru liked the suggestion and ordered his servants to make the preparations. As they did so, the chief priest and Snefru made two more requests. The ladies were to wear clothes made of nets, and the paddles were to be inlaid with gold and silver.

When all was ready, Snefru gently stepped into the boat and sat down. As the maidens began rowing, his boredom vanished and he could feel himself relaxing. After a while the rowing stopped, to Snefru's surprise. An oar handle had become entangled in the long hair of one of the maidens, and as she tried to free herself, one of her hair ornaments had fallen into the lake. Upset by the loss, the maiden had stopped rowing. So, too, had her seatmates and all the other

With a whip in his left hand to guide his team of oxen, a farmer uses his right hand to sow grain seeds in the fertile lands along the Nile River. This tomb painting dates to the 4th dynasty and the reign of Snefru, a time of prosperity and relative peace.

At Saqqara, just north of Djoser's Step Pyramid, excavators uncovered this rose-granite statue of Metjen, a provincial magistrate under Snefru. The piece is about 18 inches high.

rowers. Snefru offered to buy her a new ornament or attempt to retrieve the lost one. When the maiden replied that she wanted the lost ornament, Snefru asked Djadja-emankh for help.

Djadja-emankh began reciting magic words and spells. As he did so, the waters of the lake parted, and the boat settled gently on the floor of the lake. Djadja-emankh stepped over the side of the boat and picked up the lost ornament. After returning it to the maiden, he again recited the magic words and spells, and slowly the waters returned to their normal levels. Pleased with the unique amusement Djadja-emankh had provided, Snefru thanked his adviser by giving him "all good things."

This story is inscribed on what is known today as the Westcar Papyrus, written probably during the 12th Dynasty—more than 500 years after Snefru's reign. Like many ancient Egyptian documents uncovered in modern times, it was named for one of its first owners, a Miss Westcar of Whitchurch, England.

Snefru was a son of the Egyptian king Huni, and his mother was probably a minor wife named Meresankh. Egyptian rulers often had several wives, one of whom was considered above the others and known as the Great Royal Wife. Through her, both the divine and human characteristics of the god-king's nature were passed to the heir to the throne. Snefru married Huni's daughter, Hetep-heres, probably because her royal blood would strengthen his claim to the throne of Egypt by linking him and their children with the deities. However, because the bloodline was not direct, later Egyptians did not consider Snefru a ruler in the same dynasty as his father. Instead, the Egyptian historian Manetho and at least two king lists (ancient lists of Egyptian rulers presented in chronological order) name Huni as the last king of the 3rd Dynasty and Snefru as the first king of

the 4th Dynasty. According to many scholars, the fourth was the most important of dynasties three through six, which are collectively known as the Old Kingdom.

Surviving records from the period indicate that Snefru was constantly involved in a major project, whether it was construction, organizing trade expeditions, or expanding Egypt's control over its neighbors. Certain inscriptions credit Snefru with several successful military expeditions. Details about these conquests were found carved on a stone known today as the Palermo Stone (the largest surviving fragment of which is housed in Palermo, Sicily). According to the hieroglyphs, which were carved during the 5th Dynasty and list the kings and major events of the preceding dynasties, Snefru's advance south into Nubia (modern Sudan) to crush a revolt yielded 7,000 prisoners (men and women) and 200,000 heads of cattle, sheep, and goats. The hieroglyphs also credit Snefru with similar results after a successful drive west into neighboring Libya.

Another rock carving, which survives on the Sinai Peninsula, also portrays Snefru as a victorious king. In one hand he holds an upraised war club, and in the other, the hair of a defeated enemy. Having forced the captive to his knees, Snefru prepares to strike him with the club. In the centuries that followed, artists frequently used this pose of a ruler smiting a defeated enemy in order to portray the power of Egypt's rulers.

Nubia, Libya, and Sinai were strategically and economically important. Egypt's rulers looked south to Nubia for gold to decorate their palaces and tombs. Nubia was also an important trade center, and through it passed central African goods such as ebony, ivory, incense, ostrich eggs, and animals.

Libya, however, posed a military threat. The barren desert areas along the country's western boundaries made Libya's tribal chiefs look east to prosperous Egypt. Determined to keep all Egypt under his control, Snefru kept a careful watch on Libyan activities and was prepared to stop any incursion into his land.

Since at least the 1st Dynasty, Egyptians had looked east to the Sinai for its supply of turquoise. By Snefru's time, Egypt was also importing malachite and copper ore from the region. Snefru recognized the importance of keeping the trade routes and the mines that produced these commodities open. He sent soldiers to subdue the local tribes and stationed Egyptian garrisons at key points in the Sinai to protect his nation's interests.

Snefru did not always rely on the battlefield to solve his problems. He promoted peaceful trading practices with Byblos in Phoenicia (modern Lebanon). The "cedars of Lebanon," a very strong wood with a distinctive sweet fragrance, came from Byblos. A contemporary account tells of 40 boats returning to Egypt laden with cedarwood. Other inscriptions note that Snefru commissioned the building of several ships, each approximately 175 feet long. These vessels transported more cedar to Egypt. Snefru liked to use wood as a decorative element in his palace, temples, and burial complexes. Egypt had some native lumber—pine, juniper, hardwoods, and ornamental woods such as cherry and plum—but those who could afford to do so preferred using the cedars of Lebanon.

Snefru began making plans for a tomb early in his reign. Delaying this task might cause problems. For the Egyptians, life, both here and in the afterworld, depended on the safe passage of their ruler from this existence to the next. A royal tomb provided a bridge between the two worlds and gave the ruler's ka (life force) a home.

Snefru followed the traditional design, but made several significant changes. He chose not to follow Djoser's plan of a walled-in tomb complex, which consisted of a tomb and buildings with decorated facades and fake, rubble-filled interiors. Snefru also had three (some say four) burial sites. The first was at Meidum, an area about 30 miles south of Saqqara. Graffiti scribbled by a visitor some 1,000 years after Snefru's reign claims that the tomb belonged to King Snefru, but archaeological finds seem to indicate that the Meidum tomb predates the two tombs he built at Dahshur. Some Egyptologists think that the Meidum structure originally belonged to Snefru's father and that Snefru completed it after his father's death. Whatever the case, the Meidum pyramid shows how the plan for the royal tomb evolved.

Begun as a step pyramid, it originally had seven outer levels or "steps." Later it was enlarged and became an eight-step pyramid. As with Djoser's, a casing of dressed stone covered the steps. The radical change came when Snefru's architects ordered workers to encase the entire structure a second time. This new casing was not to follow the step design but rather to form four straight sides that reached toward the sky at an incline. No longer was a ruler's burial structure just a series of steps leading to the heavens. It had also become a representation of the sun's rays shining down on earth.

The ancient Egyptian word for "pyramid" is mer, meaning "Place of Ascension." Our word "pyramid" is from the Greek noun pyramis, meaning "wheaten cake." When the Greeks began traveling in Egypt some 2,000 years after Snefru ruled, they called the structures pyramides because they looked like the Greeks' wheaten cakes.

The four smooth sides were not the only changes in the pyramid's design. The Heb-Sed court was gone, and the burial chamber was built into the superstructure rather than the substructure. Also, two new buildings had been

Snefru

POSITION

King of Egypt

ACTIVE DATES

About 2613–2589 B.C.

ACCOMPLISHMENTS

Led campaigns into Nubia and Libya; subdued local tribes in the Sinai Peninsula; supported trade with Byblos in Phoenicia; most likely responsible for finishing Huni's pyramid at Meidum—the first true pyramid; built the southern (Bent) and northern (Red) pyramids at Dahshur

Snefru, Great God, who is given satisfaction, stability, life, health, all joy forever.

—Inscription on the rock walls at Wadi Maghara in the Sinai Peninsula

added. Along the east face of the pyramid stood a mortuary temple, where offerings were left and rituals performed. A causeway linked this temple to the valley temple, which stood near the river. Snefru assigned a staff to the complex to perform the required rituals. Some made offerings on a regular basis. Others guarded the royal tomb complexes and their contents. To raise the money needed to support these people, Snefru granted tracts of farmland to the temple and decreed that the revenue from these estates would pay for the upkeep of the royal tomb site. An entry on the Palermo Stone credits Snefru with creating 35 estates and 122 cattle farms. In the valley temple of another of his tombs, the one at Dahshur, a relief shows a procession of peasant women. Each woman carries a tray of offerings, and written on her head is the name of the estate she represents.

Naturally, such tomb sites were tremendous undertakings and involved tens of thousands of workers and artisans as well as tremendous quantities of materials. That Snefru had the time and the means to complete more than one tomb proves that Egypt was, at the time, a unified, prosperous nation whose people firmly believed in the divinity of their king.

Recognizing this loyalty and devotion, Snefru considered it his duty to build monuments that reflected his dual role as king and god. However, before the Meidum pyramid was complete, Snefru ordered work on the site stopped. He wanted another tomb built, and this time he chose Dahshur as the site.

The design of this new tomb, called "gleaming pyramid of the south" by the ancient Egyptians, had several innovative elements. Of all the Old Kingdom pyramids, it alone had two entrances—the traditional north-face entrance and an east-face entrance. The roof above the burial chamber was corbelled, with each row of blocks, beginning at a certain height, set so that it projected inward until the two rows almost met. Since the tremendous weight of the pyramid structure might cause the stones to fall in on the burial chamber, the architects designed these chambers to distribute the weight of the superstructure. In addition, they reduced the possibility of a cave-in.

This southern pyramid has sides that extend upward from desert rock for approximately 165 feet at an angle of 54°31'. The incline of the sides then decreases to 43°21' for the next 175 or so feet. The pyramid's shape gave it the modern nickname "Bent Pyramid."

Snefru then built a second pyramid at Dahshur. This northern pyramid has the nickname "Red Pyramid" because the evening sun gives the stone a reddish cast. As proof that it was built by Snefru, archaeologists point to the *mastaba* tombs of several of Snefru's relatives and high-ranking officials that lie nearby. Archaeologists have also found Snefru's name written in red ink on casing blocks. (When archaeologists uncovered the corner blocks of stone of the southern pyramid, they found that quarry workers had carved Snefru's name into each.) Further proof is an inscription from a decree issued by Pepi I, who ruled approximately 350 years after Snefru's death. In it, Pepi exempted the priests who cared for the "Two Pyramids of Snefru" from paying taxes. Although no sarcophagus has yet been found, Egyptologists favor the Red Pyramid as Snefru's actual tomb.

Snefru must have felt a great sense of pride and accomplishment when he looked at his pyramids rising above the desert sands. His trading ventures had brought him cedar for the beams in the passageways between the chambers and elsewhere. The copper mines in the Sinai allowed his workers to use sharp copper cutting tools on the stone and other building materials. Artisans had used Nubian gold to fashion and decorate vases, personal items, and furniture that would be placed in the pyramid complex. In addition, Snefru's strong rule had ended Libyan raids and brought peace and stability to Egypt.

In the 29th year of his reign (some accounts say the 24th), Snefru died. Soon after, his reputation as a kind ruler with a pleasant personality won him the title of "the Beneficent King." Later Egyptian writers would refer to his reign as the Golden Age of Egypt, and for some 2,000 years Egyptians would continue to worship and honor him. Throughout Egyptian history, no other king or queen ever commanded the respect or honor given Snefru. In fact, to gain the trust and affection of the people, many later rulers compared themselves and their deeds to those of Snefru.

In recent times, archaeologists digging at Wadi Maghara in the Sinai uncovered an inscription that refers to Snefru as a god. At Dahshur, excavators found a small dish, dating to the Middle Kingdom—approximately 600 years after Snefru's time. It still held the charcoal offering an Egyptian had long ago dedicated to Snefru.

FURTHER READING

Lehner, Mark. *The Complete Pyramids*, pp. 97–106. New York: Thames & Hudson, 1997.

Pace, Mildred Mastin. *Pyramid: Tombs for Eternity*, pp. 70–88. 1974. Reprint, New York: McGraw-Hill, 1981.

Khufu

BUILDER OF THE GREAT PYRAMID

For years, Khufu's pyramid site at Giza echoed with the sounds of granite blocks being pulled, pushed, and expertly maneuvered into place. Indeed, the noise of copper chisels, stone pounders, papyrus-twine ropes, and wooden rollers could be heard everywhere. Almost 20 years had passed since the king had decided not to have his mortal remains buried at Saqqara, Meidum, or Dahshur—royal cemeteries that housed the great tomb complexes of his predecessors. As his final resting place, Khufu had chosen a site never before used for royal burials—Giza, a high rocky ridge just west of the Nile and approximately 15 miles north of the capital city of Memphis.

King Khufu, dressed in a loincloth, wears the red crown of Lower Egypt (a white crown represented Upper Egypt). His *horus* name, the first of an Egyptian ruler's five names, is carved beside the statuette's right leg.

The floor of the grand gallery at Khufu's Great Pyramid was so steep that excavators of Napoleon's expedition (1798-1801) had to crouch to climb it.

Following his accession to the throne after his father Snefru's death, Khufu had consulted with his architects about his own tomb. Although he believed that he, like his predecessors, was part divine, he knew his physical body would die. For Egyptians, the royal tomb provided the proper setting for a god-king to pass from this world to the next. It was an eternal home where the royal *ka* (life force) could continue to celebrate the same rituals the king had celebrated while on Earth. The Egyptians of the Old Kingdom looked to their god-king as an intermediary between themselves and the gods, both in this life and in the next. It was a king's duty to intercede for the security and prosperity of all Egyptians. Khufu accepted this responsibility just as his predecessors had, and he was determined to have his tomb complex reflect the majesty and might of his office.

However, unlike his father, Khufu devoted his energies to building only one great tomb complex for himself. So successful was his endeavor that the second-century B.C. Alexandrian scholar Philo of Byzantium labeled Khufu's tomb one of the seven wonders of the ancient world.

The Greek historian Herodotus wrote an account of Khufu's reign 300 years before Philo's time. In an effort to obtain accurate details, Herodotus traveled to Egypt and spoke with Egyptian priests and others. According to Herodotus's account, "Cheops [for thus did the Greeks call Khufu] closed the temples, and forbade all Egyptians to sacrifice, forcing them instead to labor, one and all, in his service. . . . One hundred thousand men worked constantly, and were relieved every three months by a new crew." For hundreds of years, Herodotus's representation of Khufu as a cruel, self-centered individual persisted. But much of Herodotus's

information was based on questionable stories that been passed down by word of mouth for almost 2,000 years. Only since the French scholar Jean François Champollion deciphered hieroglpyhs in the early 1800s have archaeologists gained a better understanding of this monarch.

Still, the facts are few. In 1903, an excavation team headed by the renowned English Egyptologist Sir Flinders Petrie uncovered a two-and-a-half-inch headless statue in the old temple of the god Osiris at Abydos. After a careful look at the hieroglyphs carved near the legs, he identified the statue as Khufu's. Because the neck break seemed fresh, Petrie ordered all work at the site stopped and had his crew sift through the rubble where the statue had been uncovered. After three weeks of sifting, they found a tiny head—approximately three-quarters of an inch in height—wearing the red crown of Lower Egypt. This beautifully carved ivory statue is believed to be the only surviving likeness of Khufu. The strong features of the face show a ruler who was self-assured, full of energy, and very determined.

Khufu must have needed such a personality to oversee the building of the world's greatest pyramid. Rising 481 feet (today it measures 451 feet) above the desert sands of Giza, it could be seen for miles around. The Egyptians called it Akhet-Khufu, or "the Horizon of Khufu." According to engineers' estimates, Khufu's workers used 2,300,000 stone blocks, averaging 2.5 tons each in weight, with the largest weighing 15 tons.

To attain such perfection in design, the workforce had to be well organized, with workers and supervisors knowing and understanding every task that was required of them. Khufu's chief advisor, Hemiunu, headed the team of architects and engineers. Khufu later showed

Khufu

POSITION
King of Egypt

ACTIVE DATES
About 2589–66 B.C.

ACCOMPLISHMENTS
Sent campaigns into Nubia; maintained control of the mines in the Sinai; kept Egypt a unified nation; his policies brought prosperity to Egypt; built the so-called Great Pyramid at Giza

All life and protection are with him [Khufu].

—Inscription on the rock walls of Wadi Maghara on the Sinai Peninsula

his respect for Hemiunu's expertise by allowing him to build his *mastaba* tomb close to the royal pyramid at Giza.

Following tradition, the official entrance to Khufu's pyramid was planned for the north face. From here, a descending corridor led to the burial chamber, a rectangular chamber cut out of solid bedrock. Khufu, Hemiunu, or some other architect decided later not to locate the burial chamber beneath the pyramid but rather inside the pyramid itself. Workers dug a new corridor, then a passageway from the corridor to a room that seems to have been the second choice for Khufu's sarcophagus; but it, too, was abandoned in favor of a chamber built even deeper into the pyramid structure itself.

As the work progressed, a third corridor was designed. Known today as the Grand Gallery, it was 153 feet long and 28 feet high. To disperse the tremendous weight of the stones resting on its ceiling, the architects designed the side walls so that each row of blocks would jut out three inches above the row below. At floor level, the corridor measured seven feet. It then gradually narrowed to 3 1/2 feet at ceiling level—truly, a masterpiece of design. At the end of the gallery was Khufu's burial chamber, lined completely with pink granite.

While Khufu's architects focused on how best to incorporate their innovative ideas into the master plan, the site was cleared, and the task of quarrying, hauling, smoothing, and fitting the heavy stone blocks began. Because this construction project would take years to complete, Khufu and his advisers approved a permanent "pyramid town" in the valley, with accommodations for as many as 4,000 skilled craftsmen. Provisions were also made for temporary quarters to house as many as 20,000 laborers during *Akhet,* the season from July to October when the Nile overflowed its banks and farming was impossible. During that period, able-bodied Egyptian men below the social rank of a scribe were called for this duty.

Khufu must have been pleased that the work on his pyramid was going so well. What he could not foresee were the robbers who, within centuries, would desecrate both his tomb and his body. To him, the three granite stones that workers would use to plug the entrances after his burial seemed sufficient to deter any thief. Each was five feet long and weighed approximately seven tons. Nevertheless, robbers twice avoided the plugs and dug their own entrances—once in ancient times and again in the ninth century A.D. Khufu, however, would be relieved to know that one of his statues survived. According to Egyptian belief, a person's *ka* needed a home to continue existing in the afterlife. For this reason, the Egyptians had adopted the practice of placing statues of the dead in their tombs. If someone or something destroyed the body, the statue, made in the exact likeness of the dead person, would provide a substitute home for the *ka.*

Another part of Khufu's burial site, however, remained untouched until 1954, when a public works crew began building a road near the pyramid. Onsite, at the time, was a young architect-archaeologist named Kamal el-Mallakh. As he watched workers clearing debris from the area, he noticed that the pyramid's southern boundary wall seemed closer to the baseline of the pyramid than the other three walls. Because the margin of error was small throughout the pyramid complex, el-Mallakh sought a reason for this discrepancy. He found one. Beneath a section of the wall lay an enormous pit covered by 41 limestone blocks—some weighing more than 15 tons.

An archaeological crew was sent immediately to the site, and the workers began removing the blocks. In the pit they found a 143-foot wooden boat, dismantled into 1,224 well-preserved pieces. Using the hieroglyphic symbols written on each piece as a guide to fitting the pieces together, workers slowly reassembled "Khufu's boat." Approximately 95 percent of the wood was cedar from Lebanon. Throughout history, the so-called cedars of Lebanon were prized for their durability. Ancient Egyptian texts noted that even the worm borers of the Nile left this type of cedar alone.

Archaeologists later uncovered a second boat pit on the south side of the pyramid. Using modern technological equipment to "see" inside the pit, scientists have learned that the chamber is no longer airtight—a beetle is scampering about in one of the photos.

Egyptologists hope the boats will reveal clues about their purpose. Some believe that the excavated boat was the one used for brief excursions on official state occasions; others think that it may have carried Khufu's body up the Nile to the Valley Temple. Still others believe that it was made and buried in the pit for Khufu to use in the next life.

Enormous resources would be needed to build such a tomb and to keep the country's economy prosperous, so Khufu sent campaigns south into Nubia to keep the trade routes open. He also continued to maintain garrisons in the mining districts of the Sinai Peninsula and sent campaigns against Libya.

Khufu, however, did not wish to spend all his time preparing for death or handling affairs of state. Like his father, he, too, sought a diversion from the daily routine. On one occasion, according to a passage in the Westcar Papyrus, which was written more than 500 years after Khufu's reign, Khufu's sons were taking turns entertaining their father with tales of the supernatural. After Khafre and Bauefre each told of magicians who lived in previous reigns, Hordedef stood up and said the following:

> My father, you have listened to deeds of magicians who are dead and gone. Hear my tale of a magician who still lives and whom you do not know. He is a man named Djedi. He lives at Djed Snefru and is 110 years old. He eats 500 loaves of bread and a side of beef. He drinks 100 jugs of beer unto this very day. This Djedi knows how to reattach a head to the body from which it has been cut off. He knows how to make a lion follow him while the rope with which he is tied drags behind him on the ground and he knows the number of the secret chambers of Thoth [the god of writing,

learning, magic, and the god credited with inventing hieroglyphs].

Khufu was intrigued. So he said to Hordedef, "My son, go and bring that magician to me."

When the ships were ready, Hordedef set sail. As he approached the shore near Djed Snefru, he disembarked and was carried the rest of the way in a sedan (chair) made of ebony wood and decorated with gold. He found Djedi lying on a mat near his home. One servant was holding his head and fanning him while another rubbed his feet. Hordedef greeted the magician and commented on his good health. He told Djedi that Khufu requested his presence at the palace. Djedi immediately made preparations to return with Hordedef, asking only that a second boat be made ready for his children and his books.

Hordedef did as instructed, and when they arrived Khufu asked Djedi, "Is it true, as they say, that you know how to rejoin a head to the body from which it has been cut off?"

Djedi replied, "Yes, my lord king."

"Then let a prisoner be brought to me so that his death sentence may be carried out."

But Djedi said, "Please, sir, not on a man. Let there be no command to do such to a human being."

Khufu agreed and ordered a goose brought to Djedi. After the animal's head was cut off, servants placed the body on the right side of the chamber and the head on the left side. Djedi recited certain magic phrases, and the body immediately rose up and waddled toward its head, and the head moved toward the body. When the two came close together, the head leaped onto the body, and the goose stood up on its legs and honked.

Djedi did the same with a second goose Khufu had brought to him, and a third time with an ox.

When Khufu asked Djedi about the chambers of Thoth, the magician replied that he did not know how many there were, only where they were—in a box of flint within a sandstone block in Heliopolis (the center of worship for the sun god Re). Before Khufu could speak, Djedi added that he was not the one who could provide the king with information, that the eldest of the three sons to be born to Reddedet was the person.

Puzzled, Khufu asked, "Who is Reddedet?" Djedi replied, "She is the wife of a priest of Re and is pregnant with the sons of Re." Djedi added that Re himself had told Reddedet that her sons would hold the highest office in the land.

At these words, Khufu became sad. "Why so sad, my lord? Is it because of the three children? Do not say so, for I say to you: your son . . . [will become king, then] . . . his son, and then one of hers."

This second part of Djedi's tale certainly could not have been entertaining for Khufu, since it predicted the end of his line. And, indeed, it happened as Djedi had said: After his sons Khafre and Menkaure ruled Egypt, a "son of Re" did ascend the throne. Thus, it seems reasonable to suggest that this tale was told by the next family of kings (the so-called 5th Dynasty) as a way of proving their right to the throne. And the 5th Dynasty kings were the first to call themselves Re's children.

Khufu, however, saw his sons as his successors. For this reason, he devoted himself and his country's resources to keeping Egypt the land favored by the gods. Believing that he was both human and divine, Khufu saw his life on Earth as a time when he could help guide a nation blessed by the gods. And as his name, Khufu-Khnum, suggests, he was "the one protected by Khnum," the god of creation.

FURTHER READING

Hart, George. *Pharaohs and Pyramids: A Guide Through Old Kingdom Egypt*, pp. 89–104. London: Herbert, 1991.

Jenkins, Nancy. *The Boat Beneath the Pyramid: King Cheops' Royal Ship*. New York: Holt, Rinehart & Winston, 1980.

Lehner, Mark. *The Complete Pyramids*, pp. 108–20. New York: Thames & Hudson, 1997.

Pace, Mildred Mastin. *Wrapped for Eternity: The Story of the Egyptian Mummy*, pp. 20–28, 58–61, 180–184. New York: McGraw-Hill, 1974.

Excavators uncovered this set of cone-shaped cups, long-necked containers, and a wand inscribed for Khufu in a Giza temple. They were used in the Opening of the Mouth ritual, a series of rites that, according to Egyptian religious beliefs, allowed the deceased person to come alive in the afterlife.

Ptahhotep

NO ARTIST IS
EVER PERFECT

O my sovereign lord! Old age has come. The limbs are painful and strength has given way to weariness. The eyes are weak and the ears are deaf. The mouth is silent and cannot speak. The mind is forgetful and cannot remember what happened yesterday. The bones are full of pain. The nose is blocked and does not breathe. Standing and sitting are equally difficult. All that was good is now bad. What old age does to people is evil in every respect.

Therefore, issue a command for this servant (that is, myself) to have a pupil on hand for old age. Let my son stand in my place in order that I may teach him the wisdom and thoughts of those who have gone before and have served the ancestors in times past. They then shall do the same for you so that all conflict may be gone from the people and the Two Riverbanks [all Egypt] may serve you.

The words were clear and to the point. The speaker was asking King Izezi of Egypt for permission to retire from public

Reliefs on tomb-chapel walls such as this one of a herdsman with his bulls in the chapel of the vizier Ptahhotep mirror everyday life in the 5th Dynasty.

Do not be arrogant because you are knowledgeable.

—Ptahhotep's *Instructions*

Ptahhotep

POSITION
Vizier and writer of maxims

ACTIVE DATES
About 2400 B.C.

ACCOMPLISHMENTS
Credited as the author of a set of 37 maxims, entitled *Instructions*; Egyptians used his maxims as a school text for hundreds of years

life. But was the plea really Ptahhotep's, as the Prisse Papyrus states? This document, the oldest surviving text that includes these words, dates to the Middle Kingdom (around 2040–1782 B.C.) and not to the Old Kingdom (2686–2181 B.C.), the period when Ptahhotep is believed to have lived. The text might be a revised edition. Or it may even be a document written during the Middle Kingdom and credited to the Old Kingdom in order to give its message more significance. Later Egyptians considered the Old Kingdom to be Egypt's Golden Age, a time when loyalty, honesty, and wisdom were highly valued traits.

Ptahhotep held the honored position of vizier, the highest public office in Egypt, and his authority was second only to the king's. The Prisse Papyrus lists Ptahhotep's honors and titles: hereditary noble and count, beloved of the God (a religious title that is most likely a reference to the king), the eldest son of the king (an honorary title considering that Izezi was not Ptahhotep's biological father), governor of the city (Memphis), and vizier. When Ptahhotep asked that his son be allowed to succeed him, the king had replied: "Instruct your son in the wisdom of the past. May he set an example to the children of the great and may obedience enter into him and good judgment also. Speak to him, for no one is born wise."

In his address, Ptahhotep does not mention war, nor does he praise warlike characteristics. He does not talk about finance or matters of state. Rather, he concentrates on the experience he has gained from living and working with people, and emphasizes that a person should try to be disciplined, moderate, kind, honest, unselfish, and compassionate. Such advice is what he considers the most important instruction he can give his son. He gives it in the form of 37 maxims, including the following.

8. If you are a trustworthy person, whom one great man sends to another, act rightly in the matters he sends you. Deliver his message as he said it. Do not lie with your words, for that might set one powerful person against another. Hold to the truth and do not exaggerate. Angry words spoken by anyone should not be repeated. Bad words should not be spoken against anyone, whatever his position. The *ka* [a person's life force] hates that.

11. Follow your heart as long as you live, and do no more than is ordered . . . for it offends the *ka* if its [the heart's] time is lessened. Do not use more daytime than is necessary to do your household chores. When riches come, follow your heart, for riches will do no good if work is abandoned.

21. When you are well-to-do and establish a household, love your wife at home as is fitting. Feed her well; clothe her back. Ointment is soothing to her body. Make her heart happy as long as you live.

24. If you are a wise man, and have a seat in the council chamber of the master, concentrate your mind on the proceedings in order to arrive at a wise decision. Be silent, for silence

These wood cases held a scribe's writing instruments, including reed pens, a palette with paints (usually black and red), and a container of water for mixing the paints.

Consult the unskilled person as well as the skilled person.

—Ptahhotep's *Instructions*

is better than talking too much. Speak when you know what arguments can be made to counter your words. To speak in the council chamber requires skill and experience. Speech is harder than any craft. The person who understands speaking makes it serve [his purpose].

30. If you have become great after coming from little, and have achieved wealth after having been poor in the city which you know, forget not how it was with you in the past. Trust not in your riches, which came to you as a gift from God.

Ptahhotep ends his delivery of the maxims with the following advice:

If you hear all this that I have spoken to you, all your affairs will be as good as the affairs of those who have gone before you. In their truth is nobility and value.

and a prayer:

May you reach me [in the next world] and be sound in body and the king satisfied with all that has been done. May you pass many years of life. It is not small what I have done on earth. I have had 110 years in life, as a gift of the king, and years surpassing those of the ancestors, because I acted rightly for the king until the blessed state [of old age].

It is finished from its beginning to its end, as that which was found in writing. [This is the traditional formal phrase used by ancient Egyptian scribes at the end of a text.]

The ancient Egyptians enjoyed works such as Ptahhotep's. For them, wise sayings were a teaching text and helped a person lead a successful life. Ptahhotep's advice was not just for his son but for every Egyptian. In a world controlled by the Nile River, the deities, and the king, Ptahhotep's maxims offered a set of instructions that reflected the Egyptian picture of the universe. And so it was only natural that his work, known as the *Instructions*, became a standard schoolroom text. Public officials believed that learning such precepts would teach young Egyptian boys about good manners and proper conduct. In fact, it became the mark of a well-educated person to be able to quote Ptahhotep. For more than 1,200 years, Egyptian philosophical texts and royal documents often quoted the sayings of the wise vizier, and in time, Ptahhotep's name became a synonym for wisdom.

FURTHER READING

Lichtheim, Miriam. *Ancient Egyptian Literature: A Book of Readings*, vol. 1, pp. 61–80. Berkeley: University of California Press, 1973.

Pritchard, James B., ed. *The Ancient Near East: An Anthology of Texts and Pictures*, pp. 234–237. Princeton, N.J.: Princeton University Press, 1958.

Weni

TRUSTED EMISSARY

"**I** was a child . . . under the majesty of Teti. My rank was that of overseer and I filled the office of inferior custodian of the king's estates."

Thus begins the inscription cut more than 4,000 years ago into the tomb walls of Weni, a highly respected official who served under Teti, Pepi I, and Mernere—the first three kings of the 6th Dynasty. Today, this text forms one of the longest narrative pieces to have survived from the period known as the Old Kingdom. The passages are historically significant because they prove that in Egyptian society a hardworking, honest official could advance up the political ladder and be appointed to one of the nation's highest-ranking positions.

Although nothing is known about Weni's parents, he seems to have proved quite quickly that he was a capable and loyal administrator. Teti's successor, Pepi I, certainly recognized Weni's abilities. Soon after his accession to the throne, Pepi promoted Weni to the rank of companion and

General Mesehti commissioned this set of 40 miniature wooden Egyptian soldiers holding spears and shields made of hides to accompany him in the afterlife.

Field workers prepare for the flood season in this temple mural from Weni's time. The ebb and flow of the Nile's waters dictated the three seasons in ancient Egypt: inundation, seed, and harvest.

deputy priest of the town that housed the artisans working on the royal pyramid complex. Some time later, Pepi granted Weni another promotion, this time to a judgeship. This position was a powerful one, because Weni, accompanied only by the chief judge and the vizier, would now hear every private case that involved the king, the royal queens, and the Six Great Houses (courts of justice).

For centuries, high-ranking public officials had built tomb complexes. Before Weni could begin work on his, he needed Pepi's approval to claim an area for himself. The Egyptians considered their king the earthly representative of Horus and, as such, the owner of all Egyptian land. Weni must have felt confident of his relationship with Pepi because he asked for permission not just to build at Abydos but also to order a

sarcophagus made of white limestone from the quarries at Tura. Egyptian artisans considered Tura limestone the best.

Pepi readily agreed to both requests, and he even ordered his keeper of the royal seal, assisted by a team of workmen, to accompany the barge bringing the sarcophagus from Tura to Abydos. When the group arrived in Abydos, they had more than just the sarcophagus. They also had a cover for the sarcophagus, slabs for the "false" door (a doorway painted on the wall of the burial chamber through which the deceased's *ka,* or life force, re-entered the tomb to obtain the provisions needed for survival), and a small table for offerings. Custom dictated that offerings be brought to the tomb to provide the *ka* with nourishment throughout eternity. According to Weni, nothing of the sort had ever

been done before for a king's servant.

Once the basic structure was completed, work began on the interior. Adopting a recent practice, Weni arranged for artisans to cover the walls of his tomb with hieroglyphs that recorded his many achievements. These inscriptions would keep "alive" his deeds, in much the same way Egyptians believed that statues of a dead person provided a "home" within the tomb for a person's *ka* and allowed the *ka* to continue living. Thus, surviving inscriptions provide a unique view of Egyptian life during this period. They also help Egyptologists better understand the sequence of political and historical events.

Whether Weni prepared the text himself is unknown. What is certain is that Weni had every one of his accomplishments recorded, beginning with his post as a low-ranking public official and ending with his acceptance of a position of the highest order. Weni also wanted the traditional phrases incorporated into the text, phrases that reflected the admiration and respect Pepi had for his deeds and his person. Repeated several times in the wall inscriptions were hieroglyphs that translate, respectively, as, "I was able and acceptable to the heart of his majesty," "his majesty praised me exceedingly," and "The heart of his majesty was satisfied with me."

Weni proved his loyalty to Pepi when a scandal threatened to disrupt palace life. Because the case concerned a royal wife who was involved either in a conspiracy or some other treasonous act, it had to be handled carefully and secretly. Many Egyptologists believe this wife most likely conspired with a prince or other member of the royal family against the king. No details have ever surfaced, but Weni did mention the

Weni
(also spelled Uni)

POSITION

Judge, general, governor, expedition leader

ACTIVE DATES

About 2300 B.C.

ACCOMPLISHMENTS

Served three kings (Teti, Pepi, Mernere) in important administrative positions; investigated a plot involving a royal wife; led successful military expeditions against Bedouins in the Sinai Peninsula; first Egyptian commander on record to lead expeditions into southern Palestine; led trading expeditions into Nubia; organized digging of five canals alongside First Cataract to transport stone for building pyramids

I was a person more perfect to the heart of his majesty than any official of his, than any noble of his, than any servant of his.

—Inscription in Weni's tomb

incident, noting that Pepi appointed him, along with another judge, to arbitrate the case. He also said that "never before had one like me heard a secret of the king's harem." Although he did not reveal the sentence passed, Egyptologists suppose it was the traditional penalty for treason—death. From the little that is known about the case, Pepi's actions definitely prove he had complete trust in Weni's judgment and integrity.

Unfortunately, Pepi had little time to relax after the scandal ended. Trouble was brewing to the east, and the situation needed his immediate attention. The Bedouins (nomadic desert tribes), or "sand dwellers" as the Egyptians called them, were revolting, and Pepi prepared to send an army against them.

The Sinai area was closely linked to Egypt's welfare, especially because it acted as a buffer between Egypt and the Middle East. To keep this policy in place, Pepi had to keep the Bedouins from invading his eastern lands. The Sinai's rich mines provided Egypt with turquoise, malachite, and copper—all of which were in short supply in Egypt. Because Egyptian craftsmen used the three materials regularly in their work, Pepi had to protect the trade routes between the two areas if he wished to preserve stability and prosperity throughout Egypt.

As a show of Egypt's military power, Pepi recruited tens of thousands of troops from Upper and Lower Egypt and from the land of Nubia to the south and ordered them into action against the Bedouins. He named his trusted official Weni to the post of general. Whereas other magistrates were responsible for individual regiments, it was Weni's job to devise and implement all military maneuvers. At this point in the narrative, Weni inserts the phrase, "but it was I who planned tactics for them, although my rank was only that of overseer of the royal estates." He continues, "No one quarreled with his neighbor, no one stole the food or sandals from any traveler, no one stole bread from any town, and no one stole a goat from any people."

Weni's discipline and strategies must have worked well, as he soon laid waste the land of the Bedouins and returned home victorious. His tomb walls told how "this army returned in peace, having thrown down the fortresses of the 'sand dwellers'; this army returned in peace, having cut down their fig-trees and vines; this army returned in peace, having thrown fire on all their large structures; this army returned in peace, having slain the soldiers there in many tens of thousands; this army returned in peace, bringing back with it vast numbers of fighting men as prisoners."

Pepi was so pleased with the manner in which Weni had conducted this military campaign that whenever the sand dwellers revolted he ordered Weni to raid their lands. Weni did this five times, and each time his expedition met with success.

The sand dwellers, however, were not Egypt's only foreign problem. Reports reached the royal palace of wild desert tribes to the north (believed to be a reference to southern Palestine and Syria) threatening Egypt's presence in the area. Again Weni was the general chosen to lead the punitive raid. After assembling his troops, he ordered them aboard large transport ships and set sail for the far end of the mountain range that lay north of the sand dwellers. Disembarking once he reached the chosen port, he advanced against the rebels on foot and killed every one. This is the first recorded account of an Egyptian attack against Palestine.

Pepi I died shortly after Weni's victory in the north. Pepi's son and successor, Mernere, appointed Weni to one of the nation's most powerful posts—the governorship of southern Egypt. Control of this area was critical to Egypt's economic prosperity because it was home to the trade route linking Nubia and Egypt. Weni's talents, however, were too valuable to keep him working only in this position. In search of specific supplies for his pyramid, Mernere asked Weni to sail to Ibhat at the Second Cataract on the Nile. There Weni was to find the items on Mernere's list, including stone for Pepi's burial complex, a sarcophagus, and the capstone for the pyramid known to the Egyptians as "Mernere shines and is beautiful" (thought to be the pyramid of one of Mernere's queens). Mernere also requested that Weni go to Elephantine (present-day Aswan) for additional pyramid-related supplies, including a stone table for offerings. After loading the requested items on six cargo boats, three barges, and three floats, Weni sailed north, accompanied by a warship for protection.

Mernere must have been pleased with Weni's efforts because, soon after, he sent him on another expedition—this time to Hatnub, a stone quarry site in Nubia. Weni was to bring back a great alabaster altar. To accommodate the altar on the return trip, Weni had his workers build a special barge of acacia wood that was approximately 100

feet long and 150 feet wide. In the third month of the third season (that is, November), Weni and his crew placed the altar on board and sailed north—a task that Weni prided himself on accomplishing in only 17 days. Weni also boasted that he had brought the altar safely to the pyramid even though the Nile was not in its flood stage, and there was no water on the riverbanks.

Pleased with the success of Weni's mission, Mernere was eager to send him on more expeditions to the south. Weni willingly complied with every one of Mernere's requests, but one problem persisted—the cataracts along the Nile. These rocky crags held up river traffic at six different places, forcing traders and travelers to leave their vessels and proceed overland around the cataracts.

To bypass these troublesome areas, Weni assigned workers to dig five canals. He also gave orders for three cargo boats and four barges to be made of acacia wood. Working with him jointly on this project were several Nubian chiefs who supplied the wood for his workshops. A year later, the task was complete and Weni was traveling through his canals on his return trip north to Egypt from Nubia. With him were vessels laden with huge slabs of stone for the royal pyramid.

Through the years, Weni had repeatedly proved himself a loyal and obedient servant of the king. Thus it seemed only fitting that he inscribe on his tomb's walls, "Whenever His Majesty gave an order for anything to be done, I carried it out thoroughly according to the order that His Majesty gave concerning it."

FURTHER READING

Lichtheim, Miriam. *Ancient Egyptian Literature: A Book of Readings,* vol. 1, pp. 18–23. Berkeley: University of California Press, 1973.

Pepi II

LONG-LIVED MONARCH

Cut into a rock on the Sinai Peninsula at Wadi Maghara were hieroglyphs that read "Neferkare, who lives forever, like Re." This was exactly what Egyptologists had been seeking—an ancient document linking Pepi II with the important copper and turquoise mines in the area. No carved image of Pepi accompanied the inscription on the rock, but that was not necessary. Neferkare was Pepi's "official name," the one he had assumed when he ascended the throne. It was also his "Son of Re" name, the name that reflected the Egyptian belief that every king was the earthly manifestation of the sun god Re. Pepi was actually his *nomen*, or birth name. Only 2,000 years later would the Greeks add numerals to differentiate between the father, Pepi I, and the son, Pepi II.

Before the find at Wadi Maghara, Egyptologists had already uncovered much about Pepi II and how he came to rule Egypt. The office of kingship was hereditary—usually the eldest son of a king's Great Royal Wife succeeded his

This alabaster statue depicts Pepi II as an adult wearing the royal headdress and sitting on his mother's lap. Pepi II had ascended the throne as a young child.

Nut [the sky goddess], make this Pepi a spirit-soul in you, let him not die.

—inscription on Old Kingdom pyramid wall

father on the throne. Sometimes, especially if the Great Royal Wife had no sons, the son of a senior wife might claim the title. (A senior wife was one whose family and bloodline ranked her above those of other royal wives.) Thus, the sons of senior wives customarily spent their youths preparing to rule. Circumstances, however, had allowed Pepi II little time to prepare.

Late in his reign, Pepi I had married two daughters of a noble from Abydos. Both women were called Ankhesenmerire, and each bore Pepi I a son. Mernere was the older of the two boys, and he succeeded Pepi I to the throne. The other son, who was named Pepi after his father, succeeded Mernere. According to most accounts, Pepi was only six years old at the time. For approximately 88 years he would wear the crown—the longest reign in Egyptian history.

At first, Pepi II was ruler in name only. His mother, Queen Ankhesenmerire II, acted as regent and her brother, Djau, assumed the post of vizier, the highest-ranking government official. Other close members of the royal family and experienced public magistrates also helped to maintain stability and unity throughout the Two Lands.

Hieroglyphs carved on the facade of the tomb belonging to Harkhuf, a caravan leader, tell of an incident that happened when Pepi was eight years old. Harkhuf had sent word to the palace about a pygmy he had found on an expedition. Pepi was so intrigued by the find that he gave detailed instructions about how Harkhuf and his men were to care for the pygmy. Pepi wanted the little person to reach the royal palace safely and in good condition.

Gradually Pepi II assumed more responsibility. His mother continued to

help him whenever necessary, and as mother of a god-king, she commanded the highest respect of the people. In fact, one of the most unusual statues to have survived from this period is a small (approximately 15 inches tall), beautifully carved alabaster figure of Ankhesenmerire holding Pepi in her lap. The expressions of mother and son are calm and regal with an overriding air of confidence. Pepi's face, however, is not one of a child, or even of a young boy, but that of a grown man. Crowning his head and symbolizing his position as king is the royal striped headdress known as the *nemes*.

Pepi proved himself an involved ruler. Following the example of his predecessors, he sent expeditions south into Nubia. Harkhuf was one of the men he assigned to lead these expeditions. Such trips must have involved a bit of adventure, especially when the Egyptians faced hostile natives, blinding sandstorms, and the unrelenting rapids of the cataracts along the Nile. To bypass the cataracts, expedition members had to carry vessels and goods overland until the river's waters became calmer and water travel was again possible. Traders usually traveled along the oases on the trip south, and down the Nile for the return home.

Records also indicate that Pepi sent traders down the Red Sea to the fabled land of Punt. Although the exact location of Punt is still a matter of debate, most historians believe it included the coastal areas of present-day Somalia and maybe parts of Ethiopia and Djibouti.

An account from Pepi II's reign also tells of an expedition organized to rescue the body of a nobleman who had been killed while building a ship for an expedition to Punt. Most expeditions, however, were trade related. And it was the rewards of these ventures that made everyone involved minimize the dangers. In Egypt, the royal family, nobles, and high-ranking officials eagerly awaited such prized items as incense, ivory, ebony, oil, leopard and cheetah skins, and gold. So, too, did the artisans who needed the imports to craft their exquisite works.

Because the Egyptians believed that everyone, not only the king, had a *ka*, family members regularly brought offerings to the tombs of their loved ones—in the hope that these offerings would sustain the deceased person's *ka* in the afterlife. While tomb offerings had no time limit, as the centuries passed and the number of tombs increased, the bringing of daily or even periodic offerings became burdensome, and a new practice developed. Kings began to set aside royal tracts of land and decreed that the revenue from these lands—that is, from harvests and other related products—would be used to provide offerings for their *ka* and to support the priests they charged with caring for the lands and performing the required tomb rituals. In time, kings also began granting tracts of land to nobles and then to high-ranking officials as rewards for loyal service. Because these lands were tax-exempt, none of the revenue derived from them returned to the nation's treasury.

By Pepi II's reign, the amount of land held by temples, nobles, and high-ranking officials was considerable. In addition, many of the *nomarchs* (governors of *nomes,* or districts) who held land had passed their right of ownership to their children.

What followed was a reduction in royal income and a gradual weakening of the king's power. The king's expenses, on the other hand, kept increasing, because he not only had to build his own tomb but also had to repair and care for the burial complexes of his predecessors and construct tombs for the royal family.

Pepi faced this problem as well as others. Egyptians who were responsible for a royal burial complex lived in a "pyramid-city" and were exempt from taxes. Very often they were also excused from "forced-labor" duty. This meant that they did not receive the annual royal summons requiring all Egyptians below the rank of scribe to work for a specific period of time on the king's pyramid.

With less money, less land, and fewer workers, the king's strength decreased. The power of the nobles, on the other hand, increased with each generation and with each new grant of land. The nobles were well aware of this change in the balance of power and wealth, and although they still paid homage to the king, they began attending more openly to their own concerns. They also began to think that nonroyals might enjoy a limited form of existence within the walls of their tombs. Thus, instead of hoping for a burial site near the royal pyramid, many officials now located their tombs closer to their *nome*.

An energetic and forceful ruler, Pepi must have sensed this eroding of the king's power. But he had too many responsibilities to rely solely on himself or on one vizier. To rule efficiently, he had to delegate power to others. Instead of having one vizier, Pepi divided the duties of the position between two viziers, one for Upper Egypt and one for Lower Egypt. He made each responsible for the collection of taxes, the tending of the land and livestock, the deeds for land ownership, and the enforcement of laws and royal decrees in his area. While this measure gave great

Pepi II

POSITION
King of Egypt

ACTIVE DATES
About 2278–2184 B.C.

ACCOMPLISHMENTS
Longest-ruling monarch in Egyptian history; sent trading expeditions into Nubia and farther south to Punt; expanded trade to both the south and the east; kept the economy stable and repressed revolts; had so-called Pyramid Texts carved into the walls of his tomb

powers to two rather than one person, it also contributed to the peace and stability experienced by those whom Pepi II ruled.

As his burial site, Pepi chose South Saqqara, a necropolis (ancient cemetery) used by several of his predecessors. Unfortunately, none of the treasures and artifacts buried with Pepi have survived. Ancient tomb robbers burrowed through the beautiful limestone exterior and cut through the interior construction, which was made of rubble held together with mortar made from Nile mud. These thieves were not the first people in Egyptian history to desecrate a tomb, nor were they the only ones to plunder Pepi's site. During the Middle Ages and later periods, architects and engineers reused tons of stone blocks and other materials from Pepi's pyramid in the construction of their buildings.

By the time French archaeologist Gustave Jéquier discovered Pepi's tomb in 1926, it was in ruins. As he cleared the debris, he found a large number of fragments inscribed with hieroglyphs. Realizing that they had once adorned the walls of the ancient royal tomb, he meticulously recorded each find. After months of work, Jéquier placed the fragments in their proper position along the walls of the inner chambers. Today they are known as the "Pyramid Texts," because similar texts have been found only on pyramid walls. They consist of spells or magic incantations designed to help the king enter the afterlife, where he would be welcomed as the equal of the gods. Some of the spells are meant to be spoken by the king; others by the priests. One tomb passage reads: "O Re, commend me to the ferryman of the Winding Waterway, so that he may bring me his ferryboat . . . in which he ferries the gods . . . to the eastern side of the sky."

The Pyramid Texts are the world's earliest known religious document. Pepi, however, was not the first to include them in a tomb. King Wenis, who ruled less than 100 years before Pepi, has that distinction. Such texts were also found on the walls in the pyramids of Pepi's three queens. This find suggests that, in Pepi's time, the Egyptians believed that a queen as well as a king would share a divine afterlife in the company of the gods.

To make sure that the inscribed hieroglyphs, artifacts, and scenes drawn on the tomb's inner walls would come to life and help the deceased in the afterlife, the Egyptians developed special rituals. These rites allowed inanimate objects within the tomb to come to life. They also activated the Pyramid Texts. Used at first only with kings, nonroyals adopted these practices for themselves in the decades following Pepi's rule. As part of the final burial ceremony within the tomb proper, the officiating priest sprinkled the mummy with water and perfumed it with incense. He then touched an adze to the face, hands, and feet both of the mummy and of the statues of the deceased. In later times, the designated son and heir performed the Opening of the Mouth ceremony.

A close look at the figures carved into Pepi's tomb walls shows that the Egyptians believed all within the tomb would come to life. To prevent any potentially harmful animal from coming to life and attacking the deceased king, artisans "cut" images of poisonous snakes in half with a line of plaster. They also smeared plaster across the rear parts of carved oxen, lions, and elephants to render them harmless.

After Pepi died, his priests performed the Opening of the Mouth ceremony on his mummy and prayed that peace would mark his transition from this life to the next. More concern, perhaps, should have been given to a peaceful transition in this world. In the last years of his long reign, Pepi might have grown too old to govern effectively, for he did not stop the foreign tribes invading Egypt's borders to the northeast. Nor did he stop the powerful governors of Upper Egypt from forming alliances or from fighting with their neighbors. In the years after his death, a period of chaos and instability descended upon the lands bordering the Nile.

Nut, grant you that this Pepi may be in you like an imperishable star.

——inscription on Old Kingdom pyramid wall

FURTHER READING

Lehner, Mark. *The Complete Pyramids,* pp. 161–63. New York: Thames & Hudson, 1997.

Harkhuf

INTREPID CARAVAN LEADER

"Count, Governor of the South, Bearer of the Royal Seal, Lord of Nekheb, Ritual Priest, Caravan Leader . . ." So read the newly carved inscription on the facade of Harkhuf's tomb. The hieroglyphs were clear and easy to read, and for centuries to come, anyone passing by the area would be able to read how Harkhuf had proved his loyalty to Egypt and to the king.

When choosing his tomb site, Harkhuf had followed a new practice among high-ranking government officials. He opted for a cemetery in the *nome* (district) where he had held his official posts, instead of in the royal necropolis. In accordance with Egyptian tradition, Harkhuf had artisans immortalize his accomplishments by writing them in hieroglyphs on the stone of his tomb site.

Harkhuf did not expect to share an afterlife with the gods—that privilege belonged only to the royals. But he did

The sailor to the right holds the heels of a crewmate who has fallen overboard during a fight with the crew from another boat. The inscription at the top of this stuccoed, limestone relief includes one sailor's frantic cry, "His back is broken." Not all expeditions along the Nile were friendly.

This tablet, found in a tomb at Giza and measuring only 1/2" by 3/4" by 3 5/8", lists the seven sacred oils used in the embalming process, and has an indentation to hold a drop of each. *Heknu-*oil, one of the goods Harkhuf brought back from a campaign, is second from the left.

not believe that death ended his existence. Rather, he envisioned his *ka* (life force) enjoying a limited existence in the afterlife, perhaps within the tomb itself. For this reason, custom said that the deceased's family and servants should perform certain rituals and bring food offerings to the tomb regularly. As a backup measure, in case the living could not bring their offerings at the appointed time or hold a proper ritual, the Egyptians carved on the tomb walls inscriptions and reliefs of whatever the deceased might need. During the funeral ceremony, the symbolic rituals would bring these representations to life, ready to meet the *ka*'s every need.

Thus, it was with great care that Harkhuf chose as his tomb site Qubbet el-Hawa (Arabic for "Dome of the Winds") near Yebu (modern Aswan). There, high above the west bank of the Nile River, he had workers cut his tomb into the rock. To make sure all who passed knew who was buried

within, Harkhuf had his titles carved above the entrance door. He also had them inscribe a few facts about his good deeds:

> I built a house, I set up the doors, I dug a lake, and I planted sycamore trees. The king praised me and my father made a will for me. . . . I was one whom everyone loved. . . . I gave the hungry man food, and clothes to the naked. . . . Anyone who shall enter this tomb improperly, I shall seize him like a bird, and he will be judged for his action by the Great God. . . . I was a person who spoke what was good. . . . I never spoke any evil word about anyone to another who was more powerful. . . . Nor did I ever judge two brothers in such a way that either one was robbed of his father's property.

Harkhuf's efforts and those of his workers brought the results he desired. Today, more than 4,000 years later, his name and deeds are still read and studied around the world. In fact,

Egyptologists and historians have used the information gathered from the inscriptions to gain a better understanding of the southern trade routes and of the products imported from the upper reaches of the Nile and beyond.

If the account is true and not just a series of flattering phrases, Harkhuf was a gentle, compassionate, determined, and honest man. But he did not consider these personal traits his most noteworthy accomplishment, even though he did want them recorded for all posterity. Rather, it was on the inscriptions flanking the sides of the doorway, at a level that was much easier to read, that Harkhuf preferred to focus the reader's attention. Here he had the artisans carve hieroglyphs detailing his four caravan expeditions to Nubia. Following the custom of the time, Harkhuf made no mention of any failures or personal defeats.

Harkhuf considered himself one of Egypt's best caravan leaders. His profession was a respected one, and a prestigious one as well. In recent decades, high-ranking officials and merchants in Upper Egypt, where Harkhuf lived, had become increasingly powerful. In fact, during Pepi II's reign, their authority in the area, and especially in their own *nome*, or district, closely rivaled that of the king's.

A major factor contributing to this increase in power was the profitable trade route linking Nubia and Egypt. Nubian stone was sought by those responsible for building the royal burial complexes, and Nubian gold was in great demand, both by jewelers and other artisans. Additional prized imports—including incense, ebony, oil, ivory, and ostrich feathers—came from the lands south of Nubia.

The officials who organized trading expeditions and regulated the trade routes naturally became leaders in the area. Imports played a dominant role in Egyptian life, and the king looked for people on whom he could rely to keep the imports coming on a regular basis, people who did not hesitate to find their way around the dangerous cataracts on the Nile. The king also wanted people who would not hesitate to be aggressive and take advantage of new trading opportunities. Harkhuf was such a man, and both Mernere and Pepi II readily employed his services.

Harkhuf had welcomed every order to lead an expedition and had faced all difficulties with courage and the will to succeed. Danger was his constant companion. Enemies might attack or desert storms strike on the route south. Water shortages could prove fatal. Organization was important, as were strong legs and hardy feet, because members of a caravan traveled on foot, accompanied by pack-carrying donkeys, and a trip lasted from seven to eight months.

Harkhuf's account of his first expedition reflects the pride he felt in a mission well done: "His Majesty Mernere sent me, together with my father, to Yam [the land south of the Second Cataract] in order to open up the road into this country. I made the journey in seven months. I brought back gifts of all kinds from that place . . . and there was very great praise to me for it."

With no pause in the inscription to indicate the end of an expedition, Harkhuf continued:

His Majesty sent me a second time by myself. I started on the Yebu road and returned from Arthet, Mekher, Terres, and Artheth in a period of eight months. I brought back very large

Harkhuf

POSITION

Caravan leader, explorer, trader, and local governor of a district in Upper Egypt

ACTIVE DATES

About 2275 B.C.

ACCOMPLISHMENTS

Led four trading expeditions into Nubia and lands farther south; successfully aided the Nubians in a battle against a neighboring enemy; brought back a pygmy from Punt quantities of offerings from this coun-try. Never before were such things brought to this land [Egypt]. . . . Never before had any companion or caravan-leader who went to Yam done this.

The third expedition Harkhuf un-dertook for Mernere was by far the most adventurous and the most profitable. Once again, the orders were to go to Yam. Harkhuf did so, but when he ar-rived in the region, he learned that the local ruler had recently advanced his troops against the neighboring Tjemeh. Determined that his expedition would be a success, Harkhuf immediately set out to find and aid the local ruler, even though this meant entering unknown and perhaps even hostile territory. Although the inscription does not provide a detailed explanation of Harkhuf's campaign, it does note that he was successful and returned to Egypt with 300 pack donkeys laden with in-cense, ebony, *heknu* oil, grain, panther skins, elephant tusks, throwing sticks, and other valuable trade items.

Egyptologists reading this account noted Harkhuf's reference to throwing sticks. It was not the first time they had read of throwing sticks in ancient texts. A few had been found in tombs, and uncovered wall reliefs show hunters holding curved sticks (mostly from later periods). Knowing exactly how they were used was the question. To settle the problem, several researchers devoted considerable time and energy to replicating these ancient weapons. Their findings indicate that throwing sticks acted as the perfect weapon to hunt waterfowl. If the stick failed to hit the bird, it returned to the thrower, somewhat like a boomerang.

Soon after Harkhuf's successful third expedition, messengers arrived in Upper Egypt with news of Mernere's death. Because his reputation as a fear-less explorer and intrepid caravan leader was well known at the royal palace, Harkhuf did not worry about losing his position. He had served Mernere well and looked forward to serving his successor, Pepi II.

About two years after Pepi II as-cended the throne, Harkhuf received a royal command to lead an expedition into Nubia and beyond. It was this trip that Harkhuf considered the highlight of his career and, for his work, he re-ceived a personal letter from the king himself. So pleased was Harkhuf with Pepi's response that he ordered his arti-sans to reproduce the letter on the wall flanking the entrance to his tomb.

Harkhuf reported regularly to the king about his activities. On this par-ticular trip, however, his news was not about objects or trade items but instead about a dancing pygmy. Pepi was about eight years old and Harkhuf was sure he would be delighted with his find. Pepi was pleased, and he wrote Harkhuf a letter that was far different in tone from the usual stern and heavy royal missives. Instead, this letter clearly reflects the young king's joy and excitement.

Year 2 [of Pepi's reign], third month of the first season [usually translated as 'autumn'], the 15th day. The Royal Decree to Harkhuf . . . leader of the caravan. I have understood the words of this letter which you made to the king in his chamber to inform him that you have returned in peace from Yam, together with the soldiers who were with you. . . . You say in your let-

I gave bread to the hungry, clothing to the naked, and one who had no boat, I ferried across the river.

—Inscription on the facade of Harkhuf's tomb

ter that you have brought back a pygmy who can dance the dance of the god.

Pepi, it seems, could barely contain his excitement. No caravan leader, general, or trader had brought such a treasure to the court since the seal-bearer Bauwerdjed brought a pygmy to Djedkare-Izezi (a ruler of the 5th Dynasty) about 100 years earlier. Pepi calms himself, however, and before continuing with his own commands, he shows the royal reserve when he acknowledges Harkhuf's staunch loyalty. In return for such devotion, Pepi promises to confer many honors on Harkhuf, honors that shall be hereditary and thus pass from Harkhuf to his son and grandson.

Pepi again seems unable to control his joy and his excitement. The tone of the letter quickly changes from the formal language of commands and praise to that of a young boy eager to receive a new toy:

Come down the river at once to the royal residence. Bring with you this pygmy whom you have brought from the land of the horizon-dwellers, alive, strong, and healthy, to dance the dance of the god, and to cheer and gratify the heart of King Neferkare [Pepi], who lives forever. When he comes down with you in the boat, appoint trustworthy people to be with him on both sides of the boat, to prevent him from falling into the water. When he is asleep at night, appoint trustworthy people to sleep by his side in his tent. See that he is checked ten times each night. My Majesty [Pepi] wishes to see this pygmy more than any offering from the countries of Sinai and Punt.

Fearing that something might happen to deprive him of such a wonderful gift, Pepi adds promises of additional rewards if Harkhuf brings the pygmy to the palace safe and in good health. He reminds Harkhuf of the great honors Djedkare-Izezi conferred on Bauwerdjed and says that those he has planned for Harkhuf are even greater. Harkhuf must have fulfilled Pepi's request and Pepi must have kept his promises—otherwise Harkhuf most likely would not have recorded the incident on his tomb wall. Thus, what the Egyptians believed about immortality is, to a certain extent, true. Inscribing one's achievements on a surface that endures will grant a person "immortality" for as long as there are people to read the inscription.

FURTHER READING

Lichtheim, Miriam. *Ancient Egyptian Literature: A Book of Readings*, vol. 1, pp. 23–27. Berkeley: University of California Press, 1973.

More Ancient Egyptians to Remember

Menes (active about 3050 B.C.) is the name most often used for the Egyptian ruler credited with uniting Lower and Upper Egypt into one kingdom around 3050 B.C. Some Egyptologists believe Narmer was the name of the king responsible for the unification. Many think that Narmer and Menes are the same person, hence the name Narmer-Menes that is sometimes used. The 5th-century B.C. Greek historian Herodotus wrote that Narmer-Menes banked up the Nile River at the junction of Lower and Upper Egypt just south of where he planned to build his future capital and royal residence. Narmer-Menes then ordered a new river channel dug for the Nile and

King Narmer grabs a kneeling enemy by the hair and prepares to strike him in this relief on one side of the Narmer Palette. The figure to the left is holding the king's sandals, and to the right six papyrus plants are growing out of a marshland. A falcon, the symbol of the god Horus and the king, sits on top of papyrus plants, representing Lower Egypt.

established his capital city on the reclaimed land. The site, which he called White Wall, later became Memphis, the capital of Egypt in the Old Kingdom.

Excavations at Nekhen (later known by its Greek name Hierakonpolis) have uncovered various artifacts that provide clues to this formative period in Egyptian history. Perhaps the most important is a slate palette (votive offering) with a relief carved along the top portion of each side of the palette, showing two human heads with cow's horns flanking the hieroglyphs representing the name *Narmer*. Because the predominant figure in the scenes is Narmer, the palette appears to be honoring his feat of uniting Egypt. One side represents Narmer as the ruler of southern Egypt. On his head is the *hedjet,* the tall white crown that later became the symbol of Upper Egypt. Narmer holds a defeated enemy by his scalp and prepares to kill him with his mace. To Narmer's right, the relief shows a falcon standing on marshes and leading a marsh dweller by the nose. The latter is most likely a reference to Lower Egypt and the marshy Delta region. Below Narmer are two corpses, believed to represent the towns he conquered. The reverse side shows Narmer wearing the *deshret,* the red crown that later became the symbol of Lower Egypt. Flag bearers, each carrying a standard with the insignia of a *nome,* precede Narmer as he inspects two rows of headless enemies on a battlefield. Below, a bull tears down a town wall and tramples on the enemy.

Hetep-heres (active about 2600 B.C.) was the wife of King Snefru and the mother of Snefru's successor, Khufu. Hetep-heres was also Snefru's half-sister—their father was Huni, the last king of the 3rd Dynasty. Because Hetep-heres's mother, not Snefru's, had been Huni's senior queen, it was Hetep-heres's blood, not Snefru's, that carried the true nobility. Little was known about this woman who played such an important role in the Old

Kingdom until February 9, 1925. On that day, a photographer who was helping the American Egyptologist George Reisner survey tombs near the Great Pyramid suddenly lurched forward when one of the legs of his tripod slipped into a hole. Workers slowly cleared limestone blocks from the hole—a shaft almost 100 feet in length. After a little more digging, they removed a block of wall filling and peered into a small room—Hetep-heres's burial chamber. The beautiful sealed alabaster sarcophagus was empty. Yet everything the queen might need in the afterlife was here for her use, including a bed, a carrying chair, and two armchairs. There was even a frame for a canopy bed, with gilded wooden rods topped with carved papyrus buds and wooden roofing-ties. Most likely, reed mats or light curtains would have swung from the rods to provide a cool breeze for the queen. Copper tools were also uncovered. Egyptologists think that tomb workers may have left them behind by mistake. Their presence offers a reason for Snefru's interest in protecting Egypt's claim to the Sinai copper mines. The furniture was simple yet elegant in design and fashioned of ebony wood with an overlay of gold. Restorers later followed the excavation team's meticulous notes and created exact replicas using new wood and the original gold leaf.

The chamber also contained many personal items, such as a manicure set made of gold, razors, a gold sewing needle, eight alabaster jars filled with oils and kohl eye makeup, and a box with 20 silver bracelets still hanging on two tapered wooden shafts. In a niche sealed with plaster and stone blocks, excavators found an alabaster box that had four compartments inside. One contained some decaying organic material. The other three contained a yellowish liquid. Under analysis, the mixture proved to be that of the remains of the queen's internal organs and a 3-percent solution of

During his excavations of Menkaure's pyramid complex at Giza, American Egyptologist George A. Reisner uncovered many sculptured pieces, including this finely detailed portrait head.

natron (a sodium carbonate) in water. This was the first such find of embalmed and mummified organs dating to the Old Kingdom.

Hemiunu (active about 2570 B.C.) held the important office of vizier under Khufu. In control of both administrative and judicial departments, Hemiunu was second in command and reported directly to Khufu. Most historians agree that Hemiunu was not the son of Khufu but rather a nephew—the son of Khufu's brother, Nefermaet. Like Nefermaet, who had held the position of master architect and had designed Huni's tomb, so Hemiunu held the post of the King's Master of Works and designed Khufu's tomb. Khufu was so pleased with Hemiunu's work that he granted Hemiunu the honor of building his tomb close to his own. As was the custom, Hemiunu constructed a *mastaba* for himself—in the 4th Dynasty only a god-king could, by right, have a pyramid tomb. When workers excavated Hemiunu's tomb, they found a seated statue of him carved of unpainted limestone. If we can judge that the sculptor accurately captured his subject's character traits, then Hemiunu was a resourceful man with a strong personality.

Khafre (active about 2558–32 B.C.) is best known as the son and successor of Khufu. But he was not his father's immediate successor. Djedefre, a younger half-brother by a lesser queen, had followed Khufu. After Khafre ascended the throne, he chose as his burial site an area southeast of his father's Great Pyramid. Because the ground here was higher, Khafre's pyramid appeared to be taller than his father's, although it was actually 10 feet shorter. As the polished white limestone of the two structures glistened in the sun, they must have seemed appropriate burial sites for rulers who called themselves the "son of Re." Djedefre had been the first ruler in

Egyptian history to adopt this title as one of his official royal names. Khafre did the same, and so did all succeeding rulers of ancient Egypt.

Following custom, Khafre wanted tomb statues carved in his exact likeness and had sculptors fashion as many as 23 seated statues of himself. All these he had placed in his Valley Temple (where priests performed the burial rites) in specially recessed areas. Workers then cut shafts through the stone of the temple so that the rays of the sun and the moon entered the temple and shone light on each statue. However, these statues were small in comparison with the one Khafre commissioned to stand just east of the Valley Temple. Here, out of the natural outcrop of limestone that had remained after quarrying the blocks for Khufu's pyramid, sculptors carved the crouching body of a lion with a human head. Many Egyptologists believe the face was shaped to resemble Khafre. Centuries after Khafre died, visiting Greeks called it a Sphinx. The word might come from the Egyptian phrase for "living image of the Atum (creator of the world)": *shesep ankh Atum*.

Menkaure (active about 2532–04 B.C.) inherited a stable kingdom from his father, Khafre. His pyramid, situated just southeast of Khafre's, was considerably smaller than those of his father or grandfather (Khufu)—only 228 feet in height. Menkaure and his architects, however, did make a few changes. They covered the lower courses of the pyramid with red granite from Aswan and the upper courses with gleaming white Tura limestone.

According to the 5th-century B.C. Greek historian Herodotus, Menkaure was a more compassionate ruler than either Khufu or Khafre. Herodotus also wrote about Menkaure's grief when his only child, a daughter, died. According to the story, Menkaure had artisans craft as her sarcophagus a hollow wooden cow in a reclining position, with its legs underneath its body. The exterior of the cow he ordered covered with gold.

Herodotus recounted a second tale about Menkaure that explained how the king outwitted the oracle of Buto who had said he had only six years left to live. Menkaure ordered that candles be kept burning every night. Thus, according to his reckoning, although he lived only the allotted six years, the "daylight" he enjoyed was equivalent to twelve years.

Pepi I (active about 2332–2283 B.C.) enjoyed one of the longest reigns in ancient Egypt—50 years, according to the Egyptian historian Manetho (35 to 40, according to modern Egyptologists). He sent military expeditions under the command of Weni against the Bedouins in the Sinai Peninsula and into southern Palestine. Surviving inscriptions found at quarries and carved into rocks in Nubia tell of Pepi's trading activity in the area. To lead these expeditions, Pepi again called on Weni.

As the site of his burial complex, Pepi chose South Saqqara. The name of his pyramid was Men-nefer-Pepi, which means "Pepi is established and beautiful." Little remains of the pyramid because succeeding generations of Egyptians used the stone facing blocks and the inner construction materials for their own building projects. Archaeologists have found wall fragments inscribed with passages, known today as Pyramid Texts from Men-nefer-Pepi.

As was the custom, Pepi had several wives. Two were sisters with the same name. Pepi's immediate successor, Mernere, was the son of Ankhesenmerire I, and Pepi II was the son of Ankhesenmerire II. A five-foot,

nine-and-a-half-inch-tall statue of the king, standing with a staff in hand and his feet in a walking position, was uncovered at Nekhen. It was fashioned by hammering sheets of copper onto a wooden form.

Pepinakht (active about 2220 B.C.), according to most historians, was Harkhuf's successor as governor of the south, the land beyond the First Cataract on the Nile River. Following the custom of the time, Pepinakht ordered that his tomb be cut into the rock cliffs at Qubbet el Hawa, near Yebu. He commissioned artisans to inscribe his deeds and victories on the inner walls. As an introduction, he had the artisans list the titles he held under Pepi II. These included "wearer of the royal seal, priest, caravan leader, governor of the pyramid-town, and judge."

What distinguishes Pepinakht from other officials is his elevation to the status of god, which came within decades of his death. The ancient Egyptians even dedicated a cult to him on the island of Elephantine, near the First Cataract. Members of the cult referred to Pepinakht by his nickname, Heqaib, meaning "He who is master of the heart." Many Egyptologists think that the Egyptians deified Pepinakht because of the daring expeditions he led against foreign tribes who were attacking Egypt's outlying districts. Pepinakht had the artisans record these deeds on his tomb wall: "I slew a great number there including the chiefs' children and commanders of the top units. . . . I brought a great many rebels to the royal palace as living prisoners." Pepinakht also had his artisans write of the campaign he led to Byblos. Pepi had ordered Pepinakht to retrieve the body of an Egyptian official who had been murdered there while overseeing the building of a boat for an expedition to Nubia.

The face of Pepi I wears a mysterious smile in this detail from a life-size statue made of hammered copper plates nailed to a wooden support. The eye sockets are inlaid with limestone and obsidian.

Only an eroded mass of mud brick remains of Amenemhet III's pyramid at Dahshur. Later generations of Egyptians took the original limestone casing blocks for their own building projects.

2 Disruption and Rebirth

(Middle Kingdom, about 2040–1782 B.C.)

Practices such as granting land to loyal followers and priests in charge of royal burial complexes slowly eroded the king's authority. As Pepi II grew older and less forceful, the *nomarchs* (governors of Egypt's *nomes*, or districts) assumed more power. The few records that survive from the period following Pepi II's reign tell of great turmoil throughout the land. One Egyptian who yearned for happier times wrote, "Laughter is dead and sorrow walks across the land."

Pepi's immediate successors, the rulers of the 7th, 8th, 9th, and 10th Dynasties, could not reverse the deteriorating situation. In Upper Egypt, several strong governors saw the problem as an opportunity to increase their own power bases. They sought ways to ally themselves with weaker neighbors and, in this way, gain control over a larger area. But their actions served only to intensify the divisions within Egypt. Egyptologists would later refer to these years of disunity and turmoil as the First Intermediate Period, because they considered them a bridge between two great eras in Egypt's early history—the Old Kingdom and the Middle Kingdom.

The Middle Kingdom technically begins with the reunification of the lands along the Nile under Nebhepetre Mentuhotep, an energetic and powerful *nomarch* from Upper Egypt (though some Egyptologists argue that Mentuhotep II deserves the credit for the reunification). The years of conflict and uncertainty, however, had left their mark on Egyptian society. The people's way of thinking had changed, especially concerning immortality, and they no longer wished to return to life as it had been under the early kings. Eternal life, they reasoned, was not just the prerogative of the king. Governors and other powerful figures could now look forward to the same privilege, and, in the years to come, all Egyptians would do the same.

Part 2 of *Ancient Egyptians* focuses on the Middle Kingdom and the individuals responsible for returning stability, unity, and prosperity to the lands of Upper and Lower Egypt.

Nebhepetre Mentuhotep I

UNITER OF
THE TWO LANDS

Mentuhotep, the powerful *nomarch* (governor) of Thebes in Upper Egypt, was well aware of the widespread turmoil that had followed Pepi II's death. Because Mentuhotep believed that Egypt could not progress as a nation until the present problems were addressed, he resolved to reunite the *nomes,* or districts, in Upper and Lower Egypt. His three predecessors, all of whom went by the name of Intef, had favored Thebes as Egypt's

When Egyptologist Howard Carter found this statue of Nebhepetre Mentuhotep I, it lay wrapped in fine linen in an unfinished room at the bottom of a shaft just in front of his mortuary temple.

capital city. The powerful magistrates in Lower Egypt, however, vehemently opposed this choice. They wanted their city of Heracleopolis, which lay closer to the area they ruled, to be the country's capital. Unable to resolve the conflict, the two sides moved their differences to the battlefield, and so the struggle for reunification had begun in earnest with the first Intef. Because the problem was a difficult one, it took many years to resolve.

When Mentuhotep succeeded the third Intef to the throne, he controlled only the area in Upper Egypt that stretched from the First Cataract to the tenth *nome* (there were 16 *nomes* in Upper Egypt). The northern *nomes* of Upper Egypt and those of Lower Egypt remained under the control of other *nomarchs* and nobles. In time, Mentuhotep extended his control over all the lands that bordered the Nile, defeating those who had made Heracleopolis Egypt's capital and officially establishing his own capital at Thebes.

When Mentuhotep learned that opponents to his rule had sought refuge at the Dakhla Oasis, an important trade center in the desert west of the Nile, he sent soldiers to capture them. He allowed those nobles and *nomarchs* who remained loyal to him to keep their posts, and he appointed locals to political positions in their own area. He believed that locals served their communities more effectively and efficiently than outsiders. In addition, their ties to the area would encourage loyalty and respect among their subjects and provide less reason for resentment or conflict. To other posts, especially key ones, Mentuhotep appointed trusted southerners. He also reinstated the powerful position of vizier, or chief minister. Surviving records from that time name Dagi and Ipi as two of Mentuhotep's viziers.

Although no records of Mentuhotep's progress toward reunification have yet been uncovered, references mark Year 14 as the turning point. In that year, he advanced his troops against Heracleopolis. Inscrip-tions also indicate that Mentuhotep felt his achievements merited recognition. Over the years, he assumed three official royal titles: "He Who Breathes Life into the Heart of the Two Lands," "Lord of the White Crown" (a reference to Upper Egypt, the land of his birth), and "Uniter of the Two Lands." Some sources note that he took the third title in Year 39—the year in which he considered the unification complete and deemed that he alone had the right to rule Egypt.

Unification, however, did not mean Mentuhotep could disband his army. The Two Lands were at peace, but leaders of tribes beyond the borders of Upper and Lower Egypt had taken advantage of the turmoil and launched raids into Egypt. To ensure the safety of his people and to alert outsiders to his intent, Mentuhotep marched his troops north and east against the Bedouins. Following the example set by his predecessors, he sent troops west against the Tjemehu and Tjehenu Libyans and welcomed reports of Egyptian victories.

Mentuhotep also sent soldiers south into Nubia, annexing Lower (northern) Nubia as far as the Second Cataract. The Nubian campaign proved beneficial to the economy, as the strong Egyptian presence in the area ensured safe passage for caravans traveling the trade routes to and from Egypt. As a result, trade relations with Nubia improved and imports increased. Egypt depended on the imports from Nubia's quarries and mines—especially the gold mines—for its building projects and royal burial complexes. Nubia was also a major African trade center, exporting to Egypt a wide variety of products from the interior of the continent.

Without question, Mentuhotep may be called one of Egypt's great "warrior kings." Succeeding generations

Behold, no one can take his possessions with him.

—Believed to have been carved in a mortuary chapel of an 11th-Dynasty king

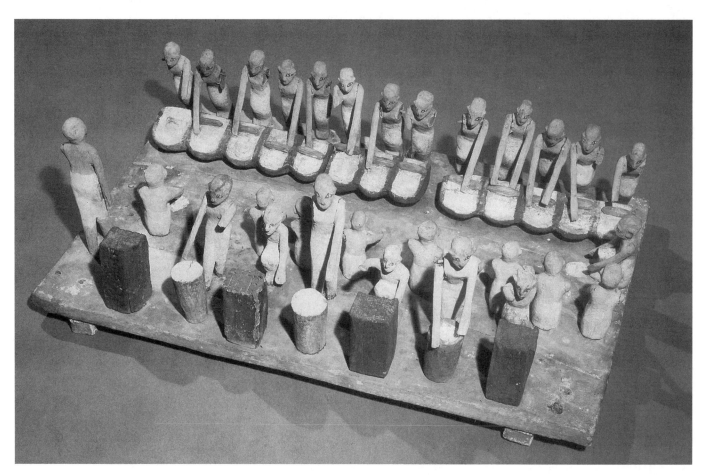

A painted-wood foreman oversees servant figures grinding grain, sifting flour, mixing dough, and stoking ovens. Model scenes such as this one found among the burial equipment of Mentuhotep I were commonly placed in tombs during the Middle Kingdom.

would recall the great deeds of Mentuhotep and praise him as the reunifier of the Two Lands. Still later, historians would look to Mentuhotep as the founder of the Middle Kingdom, the ruler whose forcefulness and determination ended the chaos and conflict of the period that followed Pepi II's reign.

In the 1920s, excavations near Mentuhotep's mortuary temple in Deir el Bahri, an area just across the Nile from Thebes, produced positive proof of his aggressiveness. Archaeologists uncovered a burial site containing the remains of 60 soldiers killed in battle—one of the world's first war cemeteries. Analysis of the remains, as well as the tomb's nearness to Mentuhotep's temple, suggests that these soldiers had been sent to fight the Nubians, that

they died in battle, and that their remains were brought back to Egypt for burial.

Once Mentuhotep had Egypt under his firm control, he began to focus attention on new building projects. After establishing his official residence at Thebes, he gave his architects orders to design a suitable royal palace. He then approved the restoration of many old temples. In el Kab, Gebelein, Deir el Ballas, Dendera, and Abydos, the hum at construction sites reflected a new era in Egypt. At el Tod, Mentuhotep ordered workers to prepare additional adornments for the sanctuary of his namesake, the god Montu, the Theban god of war. (Mentuhotep's name means "Montu is content.")

As the site for his burial complex, Mentuhotep did not choose one near

Nebhepetre Mentuhotep I

Behold, there was never anyone who, having died, was able to come back again.

—Believed to have been carved in a mortuary chapel of an 11th-Dynasty king

POSITION
King of Egypt

ACTIVE DATES
About 2060–10 B.C.

ACCOMPLISHMENTS
Reunified the lands of Upper and Lower Egypt; sent military expeditions into Nubia, the Sinai Peninsula, and Libya; annexed northern Nubia; opened the trade routes between Nubia and Egypt; promoted the arts and ordered the building and restoration of several temples; built a huge temple-tomb for himself at Deir el Bahri

the tombs of his predecessors, but instead opted for one farther south at Deir el Bahri. The location was a dramatic one, as it lay in an enclosed area at the foot of great rock cliffs. The design was also different from that of his predecessors' tombs. Unfortunately, much of the complex lies in ruins today. This is chiefly because, about 500 years after Mentuhotep's death, the 18th-Dynasty ruler Hatshepsut allowed her workers to use Mentuhotep's complex as a quarry for building materials.

While the basic layout of Mentuhotep's burial complex followed that established by the rulers of the Old Kingdom, the design did not. A causeway and ramp passing through a grove of trees led to a massive podium rising above the desert sands. On top of the podium stood a temple surrounded by square-cut pillars inscribed with Mentuhotep's name. Although positive evidence is lacking, some Egyptologists believe that a pyramid stood on a platform near the temple. Behind it, at the base of the cliffs, was a roofed structure supported by a row of columns. Here was a garden with tamarisks and large sycamore-fig trees positioned to provide shade for the stone statues of Mentuhotep.

In the early 1900s, directly in front of the temple, Egyptologist Howard Carter uncovered an entrance to a deep tunnel—now called Bab el Hosan, meaning "Gate of the Horseman." After some careful excavation work, Carter discovered a chamber beneath the temple. A finely painted and carved stone statue of Mentuhotep majestically sat there. It wore the red crown of Lower Egypt and the traditional white garment worn by rulers for the Heb-Sed ritual.

The statue's hands lay folded across the chest area in what Egyptologists refer to as the Osiris position. By Mentuhotep's time, Egyptians had turned increasingly to the worship of Osiris, the god of the dead and of fertility. According to legend, Osiris had once ruled the lands along the Nile, and it was he who had given the Egyptians the gifts of civilization and agriculture. After Osiris's brother Seth tore him apart in a jealous rage, Osiris's wife, Isis, lovingly gathered the scattered limbs and magically reunited her husband's body. For this reason, the Egyptians worshiped him as the god of the underworld and the dead, and began to believe that they, too, like Osiris, could continue to exist after death.

I shall not fear in my body for words and magic will overcome this evil for me.

—From Coffin Texts found in an 11th-Dynasty tomb

In the cliffs behind Mentuhotep's burial complex, archaeologists found a honeycomb of tombs that belonged to the king's nobles and high-ranking officials, including the tomb of Mentuhotep's vizier Dagi. Further digging revealed Dagi's limestone sarcophagus. The interior was covered with inscriptions, known today as "Coffin Texts." They are a later version of the Pyramid Texts that the kings of the Old Kingdom had carved into the walls of their tombs. According to the Egyptians, a person had to recite magic spells and prayers to make the journey from this world to the next less strenuous. If a dead person forgot the words or the proper order of the words, that person might not be able to share in an afterlife. To prevent such a terrible fate, the Egyptians adopted the practice of writing the spells and prayers on the interior and exterior of their coffins. They also inscribed a map of the underworld to help guide the deceased along the correct path. As an additional safety measure, the Egyptians began to paint a pair of eyes on the left side of the coffin. With these eyes, the deceased could "look" to the outside of the coffin and read the texts. The eyes could also see and take in the food offerings the priests and relatives had left for them, as well as the food offerings depicted on the walls of the tomb.

But the Coffin Texts did not provide everything that was needed for an Egyptian to do exactly what he had done in this life. So the Egyptians placed in the tomb small, often wooden, statues of workers performing a variety of tasks, from plowing to breadmaking, to fishing, to brewing beer. The Egyptians believed that if they recited magic spells and prayers, these "people" would come alive and do whatever the deceased asked them to do.

Some of the best servant models ever uncovered were found in a secret chamber in the tomb of Mentuhotep's chancellor and chief steward, Meketre. All the figures were dutifully working at their special tasks, just as they had been for thousands of years.

During the Middle Kingdom, some years after Mentuhotep, the belief in an afterlife kingdom ruled by Osiris became increasingly widespread, and a new type of servant figure, the *ushebti*, appeared. According to some etymologists (people who study words), *ushebti* comes from the Egyptian verb *usheb*, meaning "to answer" or "to respond." Found in the tombs of wealthy Egyptians, the *ushebti* are mummiform figures often inscribed with their owner's name. The Egyptians believed that should Osiris himself summon helpers to prepare his Field of Reeds in the underworld, a dead person could send the appropriate *ushebti* to do the work.

FURTHER READING

Lehner, Mark. *The Complete Pyramids*, pp. 166–67. New York: Thames & Hudson, 1997.

Amenemhet I

RETURN TO TRADITION AND UNITY

hen shall come a king from the South. Ameni, the triumphant, will be his name. He will take the white crown [of Upper Egypt], and wear the red crown [of Lower Egypt]. He shall unite the Two Powerful Ones [the vulture goddess Nekhbet of Upper Egypt and the cobra goddess Wadjet of Lower Egypt] and delight the Two Lords [the gods Horus and Seth] with what they love.

So reads the prophecy of a fictional ancient Egyptian priest named Neferti. Since the name Ameni is a shortened form of Amenemhet, it is believed that the author used Ameni to indicate that Neferti was referring to Amenemhet I. In fact, many Egyptologists believe that Amenemhet himself most likely commissioned the author to write the tale. Thus, it is not the prophecy but the tale itself that intrigues Egyptologists.

More than 20 copies of the prophecy survive, but all date to the 18th Dynasty, approximately 500 years after Amenemhet ruled Egypt. Passages from the prophecy have

The Sacred Lake at Karnak. Every Egyptian temple had a sacred lake where, several times a day, the temple priests bathed and washed the implements they used for rituals.

Archaeologists uncovered this painted detail of Amenemhet I's head carved on a block over the doorway into his mortuary temple at Lisht.

also been uncovered on two writing boards and on various pieces of clay. These also date to the 18th Dynasty. But according to the text, Neferti lived during the reign of Snefru, a 4th Dynasty ruler who preceded Amenemhet by approximately 600 years.

In the tale, Sneferu asks Neferti to speak of "what is going to happen" and prepares to write the priest's words on a scroll of papyrus paper. Neferti foresees a time when people will know no happiness, a time when the land will live in an uproar and there will be no grain. The future ruler, Ameni, will bring order and justice to this world. Neferti says he will be born in Upper Egypt and that his mother is from the land to the south, the land of Nubia. (Actually, nothing is known about Amenemhet's mother. As for his father, an inscription at Karnak notes that he was a

commoner named Senwosret.) Neferti asks the people of Ameni's time to rejoice because their king is one who will make his name known for all eternity.

This wording has led Egyptologists to believe that the prophecy was written to establish Amenemhet's right to the throne of Egypt. Records indicate that Amenemhet did not inherit the throne, but rather succeeded to it by some unofficial means. To justify his actions, Amenemhet had to align himself with a ruler and a time period that all Egyptians respected and honored. The natural choice was Snefru, because Egyptians considered his reign a Golden Age and referred to Snefru by the honorary title of "Beneficent King."

The details of how Amenemhet came to power are sketchy. Nebhepetre Mentuhotep I had united the lands bordering the Nile, but his successors—Mentuhotep II and Mentuhotep III—lacked his strength and drive. Because the situation would only worsen, Amenemhet had decided to act. A powerful *nomarch*, or governor, in Upper Egypt, he knew well the workings of Egypt's government. Under Mentuhotep III, he had held the post of vizier. An inscription uncovered at Wadi Hammamat, an area east of Thebes, describes what was probably Amenemhet's last official assignment as Mentuhotep's vizier.

The king was planning his burial complex and had ordered Amenemhet to travel to the stone quarries at Wadi Hammamat to find a stone block for the lid of his royal sarcophagus. To help Amenemhet complete the task, Mentuhotep placed an army of 1,000 soldiers under his command. According to the inscription, a pregnant gazelle appeared before Amenemhet and led him to an enormous rock. Recognizing the excellent quality of the stone, Amenemhet ordered his men to cut a huge block from the rock and arranged for it to be taken to Mentuhotep at Thebes. Soon after, Amenemhet, with the support of his soldiers, claimed the throne for himself. (Neither the lid, nor the sarcophagus, nor Mentuhotep's tomb has yet been discovered.)

To consolidate his power, Amenemhet sailed a fleet of ships up and down the Nile and successfully defeated those *nomarchs* who opposed his rule. Because good government depended on cooperation at all levels, Amenemhet revived some of the ancient titles and awarded them to deserving officials. To curb the influence of the *nomarchs*, he redistributed the *nomes* by assigning a different set of cities to most of the *nomarchs*. Amenemhet also established new rules regarding registration of land and land ownership. His aim was to reduce the possibility of conflict between the *nomarchs* and the king.

Amenemhet took as his Horus name Wehem-mesut ("He who repeats births"), which clearly meant that he considered himself the first of a new royal line. Egyptologists now recognize Amenemhet as the first king of the 12th Dynasty. As his capital city, he chose a site about 20 miles south of the old capital of Memphis and named it Amenemhet-itj-tawy, which translates, "It is Amenemhet who has conquered the Two Lands." In time, the name was abbreviated to Itj-tawy. The exact site has not been found, but archaeologists believe that it was located somewhere near present-day el Lisht.

Uniting the "two Egypts" politically and militarily was important, but it

was not enough. Amenemhet also had to protect Egypt's commercial interests in the turquoise and copper mines on the Sinai Peninsula. Like his predecessors, Amenemhet was well aware that Egypt's architects and artisans depended on the steady import of raw materials not found in the lands along the Nile. The sand dwellers, or desert tribes living on the Sinai Peninsula, saw caravans moving along the trade routes as easy prey. To prevent attacks, Amenemhet ordered a line of fortresses built in the Wadi Tumilat, a fertile area along the eastern edge of the Delta. This Wadi led to the Bitter Lakes, which, in turn, led to the Red Sea, a key maritime trade route for the ancient Egyptians. History often refers to Amenemhet's defense system as the "Walls of the Prince." Archaeologists have uncovered no trace of these fortresses, probably because they were built of mud bricks.

Amenemhet also turned his attention south to the lands beyond the First Cataract. Here lay Nubia, rich in gold and other natural resources. Nubia was also the gateway to the interior of the African continent and its great variety of products.

Not all Egyptians, however, acknowledged Amenemhet as the new leader of the Two Lands. Segerseni refused to do so and sought the title for himself. To eliminate this potentially serious rival, Amenemhet sent a fleet of 20 ships, under the command of a loyal *nomarch* named Khnumhotep, against Segerseni. The expedition was successful, and Amenemhet rewarded Khnumhotep with increased political responsibilities. To protect himself and Egypt against further rebellion, Amenemhet reinstated compulsory military

Amenemhet I

POSITION

King of Egypt

ACTIVE DATES

About 1991–62 B.C.

ACCOMPLISHMENTS

Reunited Upper and Lower Egypt; built defensive wall of fortresses (Walls of the Prince) along the eastern edge of the Delta; sent two military expeditions into Nubia and extended Egyptian control as far as the Second Cataract; established a new capital at Itj-tawy; refurbished and built several temples; established the worship of Amun throughout Egypt service. This meant that, in any emergency, he would have a corps of soldiers trained and ready for action.

As peace and prosperity gradually returned to the lands along the Nile, Amenemhet directed a variety of building projects. These included a granite altar dedicated to Osiris, the god of the underworld, at Abydos; a granite gateway consecrated to Hathor, the goddess of the sky, at Dendera; and a temple built in honor of Ptah, the god of creation, at Memphis. In honoring the many deities of Egypt, Amenemhet followed a precedent set by a number of his predecessors. Yet he differed from them in his worship of the god Amun. For centuries, the chief god worshiped in Upper Egypt had been Montu, the god of war. Osiris and the sun god Re had been the principal deities in both Upper and Lower Egypt. Amenemhet, however, felt a special devotion for Amun, who was worshiped mainly in Thebes. Even Amenemhet's name, which means "Amun is in the lead," reflected his close relationship with Amun.

Amenemhet commissioned architects to adorn a temple to Amun at Thebes. He also ordered that a shrine to Amun be constructed on the east bank of the Nile at Ipet-isut, "the most select of all places." (Ipet-isut is known today as Karnak, a name taken from that of a neighboring modern village.) In time, Amun would become the principal god of the Egyptian nation, and Karnak would become the religious center of all Egypt.

Amenemhet then turned to a more personal construction project—his burial complex—and chose a site near his new capital. In an attempt to recall the glories of past generations, he chose the pyramid style for his own tomb.

Though his would not be as grandiose as that of Khufu or other Old Kingdom rulers, it would have a *temenos*, or enclosure wall, surrounding the pyramid area, a mortuary temple, and over 100 *mastaba* tombs for high-ranking officials. And, just as in the past, these *mastaba* tombs would be located close to the royal pyramid.

To construct the inner core of the pyramid, Amenemhet's architects had workers take limestone blocks from the royal burial complexes at Giza and Abusir. To face the pyramid's exterior, workers used white limestone brought from the quarries at Tura. Today these blocks are gone because later builders did exactly what Amenemhet's workers had done—they removed and reused the limestone for their construction projects.

Having provided for his afterlife, Amenemhet looked to the future of Egypt and began to make provisions for a successor. Because he believed that unity depended on a smooth transition of power from one ruler to the next, in Year 20 (of his rule), he named his eldest son, Senwosret, as his co-regent. This meant that the two would rule together until Amenemhet's death. No Egyptian monarch had ever had a co-ruler, but Amenemhet's new policy set a precedent that all rulers of the 12th Dynasty would follow.

For Amenemhet, the position of co-regent was not an honorary one. He saw it as an opportunity to provide Senwosret with on-the-job training and experience. Therefore, he named Senwosret his chief assistant and, more important, gave him command of the army. Amenemhet even drew up a detailed list of duties and responsibilities for his son. Records show that three years after his appointment, Senwosret led a military campaign south into Nubia and extended Egyptian rule beyond the First Cataract. The following year, the Egyptian army defeated Bedouin tribes in the Sinai and reaffirmed Egyptian dominance in the area. At the same time, Amenemhet and Senwosret renegotiated trade treaties with Byblos and other trade ports in the eastern Mediterranean Sea. Shipments of cedars of Lebanon (a hard, strong wood that was especially good for boatbuilding), wine, vegetable oil, and textiles were traded for such Egyptian exports as ivory, precious stones, and ostrich shells.

In Year 29 of Amenemhet's rule, Senwosret led a second campaign into Nubia and extended Egyptian rule farther south. To mark Egyptian presence, he established a fort at Semna at the southern end of the Second Cataract. The following year, Senwosret led a campaign west across the desert sands against the Libyans. Again he met success, but his joy soon turned to sorrow and anger when reports reached him that his father had been assassinated.

Exactly what happened is not clear, but several surviving documents include details of the plot. Because each of these writings dates to some 500 or more years after Amenemhet died, they must be viewed with reservation. Nevertheless, close analysis of the passages proves that the ancient Egyptians knew of the conspiracy. In fact, schoolmasters used the account entitled *The Instruction of Amenemhet* as a writing exercise and as a textbook on rules for leaders.

Amenemhet is the narrator of *The Instruction* and speaks in the first person to his son Senwosret. At first, Egyptologists thought that Amenemhet wrote the document after surviving an

Harden yourself against all subordinates. Do not approach them alone.

—The Instruction of Amenemhet

assassination attempt. Now it seems more probable that Senwosret ordered a scribe to compose the text after his father's murder. The purpose was twofold: to reveal the conspiracy and to establish a written record of Amenemhet's advice to his son on the duties and responsibilities of a king.

As the text begins, Amenemhet tells Senwosret to trust no one—not even a brother or a friend because such relationships profit a ruler nothing. After more comments about the wickedness of people and the corruption of society, Amenemhet tells of his good deeds: "I gave to the beggar, I nourished the orphan." He adds, "He who ate my food raised opposition against me. The one in whom I placed my trust used it to plot."

Amenmehet actually describes his murder, although briefly:

It was after the evening meal, night had come. I had taken an hour of rest and laid myself on my bed. . . . Weapons that were for my protection were turned against me. . . . I awoke to fight, utterly alone . . . one cannot fight alone and success cannot come to me without you.

From this passage it seems clear that the conspirators achieved their goal. Yet, in the next passage, Amenemhet says that the assassination

attempt happened before the officials had heard he was handing his power over to Senwosret. As a result, some historians feel this statement refers to an earlier assassination attempt that failed.

The text does not end with more details about the plot but instead with Amenemhet's own list of accomplishments: "I sent to Elephantine [a town on the boundary between Egypt and Nubia], I reached the delta, I stood at the borders of the land, I inspected its interior. . . . I was the one who cultivated grain. . . . The Nile honored me on every field, no one went hungry while I was king, no one was thirsty."

Amenemhet even includes a description of his palace at Itj-tawy. "I made a palace adorned with gold. Its ceilings are of lapis lazuli [a semiprecious blue stone], the walls within of silver . . . the doors of copper, and the door-bolts of bronze. This house is built for endless time and prepared for eternity." *The Instruction . . .* ends with a look to the future, as Amenemhet wishes his son "life, prosperity, and health."

FURTHER READING

Parkinson, R. B. *Voices from Ancient Egypt: An Anthology of Middle Kingdom Writings,* pp. 48–52. Norman: University of Oklahoma Press, 1991.

Senwosret I

AN EFFICIENT LEADER

"I t was he who subdued the foreign lands while his father was within the palace. . . . He is a champion who acts with his own mighty arm, a fighter without equal."

With these words Sinuhe praised Senwosret I, the reigning king of Egypt. It had been many years since Sinuhe lived in Egypt, but as old age crept into his bones, he felt the need to return home. He wanted to be buried in Egyptian soil and needed time to prepare his tomb. For Sinuhe, only a proper burial in Egypt, with all the attendant rites and customs, could offer him true peace and happiness in the next life. Yet it had been Sinuhe's choice to leave Egypt and live in Palestine.

Years earlier, as a high-ranking official in the court of Senwosret's father, Amenemhet I, Sinuhe had been assigned to care for Amenemhet's daughter, the princess Neferu. Because Amenemhet saw his descendants as his successors, he followed custom and arranged a marriage between Neferu and his son, Senwosret. Later, Amenemhet had also named Senwosret his co-regent and placed him in charge of the army. For 10 years father and son ruled the lands along the Nile together, with Amenemhet attending to domestic issues and Senwosret to foreign matters.

Of concern to both were the trade routes leading south into Nubia. To ensure the continued dominance of Egypt and Egyptian traders in the region, Senwosret sent an army into Nubia and took control of several important areas, including a quarry at Wadi Tushka. In Year 4 of his co-regency, Senwosret led an expedition against the sand dwellers, the ancients' name for the Asiatics, nomadic tribes who lived on the Sinai Peninsula.

Six years later, Senwosret led his army west against the Libyans. Victory was swift, and Senwosret soon gave the order to return to Egypt. With him on this campaign was Sinuhe. When a messenger reported to Senwosret that his father had been murdered, Sinuhe was close enough to hear the message. Sinuhe also heard Senwosret swear his loyal attendants to secrecy about the murder before he set out for the palace. Not knowing any of the details, Senwosret consolidated his position first before taking control of Upper and Lower Egypt and prosecuting those responsible for his father's death.

Sinuhe panicked and fled to the Sinai Peninsula. Scholars suspect he may have feared that Senwosret would think him one of the conspirators and arrest him on charges of treason. Sinuhe migrated to Palestine, where he married a chieftain's daughter and soon became a respected leader in the area.

As the years passed, Sinuhe's thoughts turned increasingly to Egypt. Unhappy with the prospect of his body being buried in foreign soil, he wrote to Senwosret, begging the king's pardon and requesting permission to return. Senwosret gladly granted Sinuhe's request and replied: "What have you done, that anyone should act against you? . . . This plan of yours [to live in exile] carried away your heart; I had nothing against you. . . . Come back to Egypt. . . . You shall not die in a foreign land and Asiatics will not be the escorts at your burial. You shall not be placed in a sheep-skin and earth mounded over you. . . . Consider your dead body and return."

Rejoicing at the warmth of Senwosret's answer, Sinuhe settled his affairs in Palestine and returned home. Senwosret gave him a house and had meals sent to him every day from the palace kitchen. Senwosret even ordered a pyramid tomb built for Sinuhe and assigned his best engineers to design it. Senwosret also instructed his artisans to fashion a statue of Sinuhe and to overlay the body with gold leaf and the kilt with fine gold. In surviving accounts, Sinuhe noted that Senwosret treated no other commoner in this manner.

For Egyptologists, Sinuhe's tale reveals much about the life and customs of Senwosret's time. But its author is never mentioned, and no reason for the text's existence is ever given. Generations of Egyptians enjoyed reading it, and many schoolmasters used it as a text. Certainly, the message was one that Egyptians wished their children to know and appreciate: The political foundations of Egypt were sound and worthy of praise and respect. So, too, were the nation's rulers. The tale also contained a subtler message: It clearly identified how Egypt surpassed—at least, to the Egyptian way of thinking—

other lands in customs, refinement, and civility. Other texts, such as *The Prophecy of Neferty* and *The Instruction of Amenemhet* also told of Egypt's greatness under Senwosret and his father.

When Amenemhet died, Senwosret became the sole ruler. His plan was to follow up on the campaigns he had led as co-regent. For centuries, Egypt had had a fortress at Elephantine (modern-day Aswan), just north of the First Cataract on the Nile River. Egyptian influence was strong here, as merchants regularly led trading expeditions into Nubia as far as Kerma, which lay south of the Third Cataract. By Year 5 of Senwosret's reign, a large Egyptian fort, measuring about 504 feet by 464 feet, had been established at Buhen at the Second Cataract. Senwosret now pushed Egypt's boundary line even farther south beyond the Second Cataract. To establish Egyptian presence and as a sign of his control of Lower Nubia, Senwosret had his commanders build additional forts and fortify several towns in the areas he conquered.

In the west, Senwosret took measures to prevent Libyan raids onto Egyptian land. Even more important to him, however, was establishing Egyptian control of the five oases in the desert sands between the Nile and the border with Libya. These oases were fertile regions where Egyptians raised cattle and harvested such crops as grapes and dates. And although their proximity to the border with Libya made them natural military outposts, they were also great trading centers. Because Senwosret considered Kharga, the oasis farthest west, key to Egypt's military supremacy in the area, he took special care to maintain close links with its officials.

An energetic king, Senwosret kept himself well informed about developments throughout his kingdom.

This finely detailed wooden statue of Senwosret I, holding a crook-topped staff called a *hekat* and wearing the white crown of Upper Egypt, measures 23 inches high. This and a similar statue, with the king wearing the red crown of Lower Egypt, were found in a high priest's tomb just east of Senwosret's pyramid.

This piece of an inscription found on the walls of Senwosret I's chapel at Karnak records the names of Egypt's *nomes* or districts (top row), deity of the *nome* (second row), number of cattle in the *nome* (third row), and length of the *nome* along the Nile (bottom section).

Because the nation's economic welfare also depended on laborers doing their job in areas to the east of the Nile, he monitored all work at the gold mines in Coptos and at the quarries in Wadi Hammamat and in Hatnub.

Following the precedent set by his father, Senwosret had military contingents carefully maintain the garrisons in this area east of the Nile. Copper and turquoise imports from the Sinai played an important role in the

nation's economy, and Senwosret intended to keep Egypt the dominant power in the area. To promote international trade prospects, Senwosret encouraged peaceful relations with Syria and Palestine. If the political references in Sinuhe's tale are true, Senwosret wanted to maintain diplomatic relations with Asian countries and had no plans to send troops beyond the Sinai.

Like his father and so many of his predecessors, Senwosret saw construction projects as a mirror of the country's strength. In Year 3, he ordered the rebuilding of a temple at Heliopolis, an ancient religious center dedicated principally to the worship of the sun god Re. An inscription from this temple, which was written on a roll of leather, named Senwosret I as the individual responsible for building the temple and praised him as a king who performed many good works. It listed the various procedures involved in planning such a structure.

Senwosret also had his laborers and artisans adorn more than 25 sites along the Nile River between Nubia and the Mediterranean Sea, including the religious complex dedicated to the sun god at Karnak. Only a few of Senwosret's building efforts have survived. One, Senwosret's processional temple, is considered an excellent example of the architecture of the Middle Kingdom even though the building, as it stands today, is a reconstruction. Archaeologists who were working on a *pylon* (grand gateway leading to an Egyptian temple or religious building) at Karnak realized that the limestone blocks used as fillers had actually been taken from another site. After carefully removing and measuring each block, the archaeologists recreated the original temple—using the same blocks. Within the temple, four pillars flank the stone pedestal that once served as a resting station for the sacred boat that held the god Amun's statue. During major festivals, priests would walk in the procession, carrying the boat and statue. The carved reliefs and inscriptions on the temple pillars indicate that the structure was designed for Senwosret's Heb-Sed jubilee.

A ruler rarely lived until the 30th year of his reign to celebrate the first Heb-Sed in this world—that is, unless he altered the rules, and some did. Therefore, kings who did celebrate it considered the festival one of the most important events of their reign. To commemorate such a significant event in his reign, Senwosret erected other structures as well. In front of the temple to Re that he had refurbished years earlier at Heliopolis, he now had engineers erect two 66-foot-high red granite obelisks. Each was a solid block of stone and weighed 121 tons. Only one has survived, and it is the oldest obelisk still standing in Egypt.

Obelisks are large upright stone columns with four sides. The top section resembles a pyramid with its sides tapering to a point. Used as religious symbols, they were associated with the worship of the sun god—hence Senwosret's decision to erect obelisks at Heliopolis. The Egyptians called them *tekhenu*. Many centuries later, Greek visitors to Egypt referred to them as obelisks, from their word *obeliskos,* meaning "a small spit." The Romans adopted the Greek term, and so, too, did the English language.

Following the example of his father, Senwosret named his son Amenemhet (later Amenemhet II) co-regent. For the next 150 or so years, the descendants of the first Amenemhet would continue the practice of naming their sons co-regents in the final years of their reign.

As the site of his burial complex, Senwosret chose el Lisht. Unfortunately, years of water seepage have completely flooded the internal chambers of the pyramid and made it impossible for

Senwosret I

POSITION

King of Egypt

ACTIVE DATES

About 1971–28 B.C.

ACCOMPLISHMENTS

Extended Egyptian control of Nubia to the Second Cataract and established forts to protect Egypt's interests in the area; secured access to the copper and turquoise mines on the Sinai Peninsula; extended his authority over the five oases in the western desert areas; stopped Libyan incursions into Egypt; promoted trade with Syria and Palestine; oversaw a massive building program

The land is mine; I am its lord.

—Inscription on a wall in Re's temple at Heliopolis

excavators to gain access to the interior. Study of the complex, however, reveals that it followed the traditional design used for royal tomb complexes—a pyramid with a mortuary temple nearby. In fact, it was almost identical to the one built by Pepi II more than 200 years earlier.

Inside the pyramid, excavators found several limestone statues of Senwosret. Ten of them had carved into their sides a relief that historians believe reflects the union of Lower and Upper Egypt. In the center is a pole with horizontal lines that represent both the word *lungs* and the verb *to unite*. The hieroglyphs in the oval disk "sitting" atop the "lung-pole" represent one of Senwosret's royal names. To the left of the pole is a relief of the god Horus and a clump of papyrus—the symbols of Lower Egypt. To the right of the pole is a relief of the god Seth and a clump of reeds—the symbols of Upper Egypt. To symbolize the union of the Two Lands and the unity kings such as Senwosret promoted, Horus and Seth tie a knot about the pole.

Excavators at the site also found the remains of nine small pyramids that had been built for ladies of the royal household. As was fitting, the pyramid of Queen Neferu, the Great Royal Wife, was slightly larger than the others.

In the nearby tomb of Imhotep, the High Priest of Heliopolis, archaeologists uncovered two 23-inch wooden statues of Senwosret, one wearing the red crown of Lower Egypt and the other wearing the white crown of Upper Egypt. Both depict the king in a standing position, with one foot placed ahead of the other. However, the best representation of Senwosret to have survived was uncovered by the French archaeologists J. E. Gauthier and Gustave Jéquier in 1894. Although in poor condition, the black granite torso appears quite realistic in its detail. The broad face and firm lips seem to reflect a determined man who understood authority and how and when to use it.

FURTHER READING

Lichtheim, Miriam. *Ancient Egyptian Literature: A Book of Readings*, vol. 1, pp. 115–18. Berkeley: University of California Press, 1973.

Senwosret III

STRONG AND DETERMINED

ifteen hundred years after Senwosret III's death, the Egyptian historian Manetho described him as an outstanding warrior who stood more than seven feet tall. Manetho may have just been quoting long-accepted details, but Senwosret's bravery and his height were legendary, and both attributes must have worked to his advantage as he set about restructuring the government and advancing new military policies. Whether Senwosret served as official coregent with his father Senwosret II is not stated explicitly in the records, but he did have the same goals as his father: He wanted to rule the Two Lands as one nation, and he intended to protect the country's international trade interests.

Nubia, the land to the south of Egypt, claimed his attention first. For years, the Egyptians had controlled several Nubian mines and had set up fortresses to guard their interests in the region. Still, the skirmishes had continued, with Nubian troops attacking Egyptians both in Nubia and in Egypt itself. Senwosret's great-grandfather, Senwosret I, had successfully curbed the rebellious activities of the Nubians and built fortresses to establish Egyptian presence and power. Senwosret's grandfather and father had reinforced these defense measures.

Sculpted from black granite, this head lacks identifying inscriptions, but its features are clearly Senwosret III's.

He is like a dike that keeps back the river's floodwaters.

—Third Hymn to Senwosret III

Senwosret III resolved to strengthen Egypt's position and ordered a string of fortresses built south of the Second Cataract. To make sure these forts were provisioned properly, Senwosret focused on the cataracts (especially the First Cataract) because they forced troops and merchants to abandon river travel and proceed around the area by land. This meant a loss of time and money; it also exposed troops and goods to attacks from hostile tribes.

Centuries earlier, Egyptian rulers had ordered canals cut around the First Cataract at Yebu (present-day Aswan), and Senwosret decided to follow suit. He sent workers to widen and deepen the ancient channels. Sometime later, when reports reached him that river traffic through the canals had slowed, Senwosret again sent workers to remedy the situation.

For Senwosret, however, the First Cataract was not an appropriate southern boundary. To ensure safe travel routes for Egyptian merchants and their caravans, he wanted full control of the mine-rich areas farther south. For this reason, Senwosret considered the Second Cataract a better boundary. In Year 8, he ordered a stele (stone column or pillar) set up at Semna, a town just south of the Second Cataract. He had artisans inscribe on the stele a decree that named Semna as Egypt's southern boundary. The inscription also made clear Senwosret's order forbidding any Nubian from "crossing [the boundary], by water or by land, with a ship, or with any herds, except a Nubian who shall come to trade in Iken [a fortress site at Mirgissa at the Second Cataract] or with an official message."

Senwosret also sent a military expedition with orders to set up forts south of the Second Cataract. According to ancient accounts, there were 13, and all were made of mud bricks. The largest was L-shaped and measured approximately 426 feet square. When the Great High Dam was built at Aswan in the 1960s, many of these mud-brick fortresses were drowned by the newly created Lake Nasser. Prior to the dam's construction, archaeologists were granted time to record information about sites that would be submerged.

The Nubians did not accept foreign domination without a struggle, and on several occasions, Senwosret had to send military expeditions to quell unrest. Finally, in Year 15, his troops overwhelmingly defeated the Nubians. To commemorate this decisive victory, he erected a red granite stele at Semna and a duplicate stele at the newly built fortress on the neighboring island of Uronarti. The hieroglyphs carved into the stelae clearly express Senwosret's feelings:

> I have made my boundary beyond that of my father's. I have increased that which was left to me. I am a king who speaks and acts; that which my heart conceives is that which comes to pass by my hand. . . . I have carried off their [that is, Nubian] subjects. . . . I have taken their grain and set fire to it. . . . As my father lives in me [the words used when taking an oath] I speak the truth, without a lie coming out of my mouth.

Senwosret also had a stern warning engraved on the stelae:

> As for every son of mine who shall maintain this boundary, which my majesty has made, he is my son. . . . As for him who shall neglect the boundary, and shall not fight for it, he is not my son.

In 1844, German Egyptologist Karl Lepsius found the Semna stele, damaged and in two pieces. After recording the find, he carefully wrapped each piece in paper and prepared to ship them back to Berlin, Germany. By mistake, Lepsius's workers left one piece on the riverbank at Semna, where it lay forgotten until another archaeologist discovered it approximately 50 years later—wrapped just as Lepsius had left it. The "lost" piece was shipped to Germany and remains there today, in the Egyptian collection at the Staatliche Museen in Berlin.

The power of the *nomarchs* had become an increasing concern for Egypt's kings. Over the centuries, *nomarchs* had gradually come to treat their positions as hereditary and had even been granted the right to maintain their own military troops and fleets of unarmed ships. Some 100 years earlier, several *nomarchs* had usurped the king's power and brought disunity to the lands along the Nile. Furthermore, the legitimacy of Senwosret's dynasty was questionable: its founder, Nebhepetre Mentuhotep I, had himself been a *nomarch* who extended his control over Upper and Lower Egypt. Because succeeding kings had been careful not to offend the *nomarchs*, the power of these provincial governors had continually increased. Realizing the potential danger to his rule, Senwosret ended many *nomarch* privileges, including the practice of building lavish tombs.

To further strengthen the kingship, Senwosret revamped the administration of the provinces, dividing the country into three *warets*, or districts: Upper Egypt, Lower Egypt, and Elephantine and Lower Nubia. In charge of each *waret* was a high-ranking official who reported to the vizier. Each of

Senwosret III

> *How great is the lord of his city: he is like a mountain that shuts out the storm's blast when the sky rages.*
>
> *—Third Hymn* to Senwosret III

POSITION

King of Egypt

ACTIVE DATES

About 1878–41 B.C.

ACCOMPLISHMENTS

Sent several military expeditions into Nubia; ordered a string of fortresses built south of the Second Cataract; had a canal re-dug around the First Cataract; revamped the central government; divided Egypt into three districts, each headed by a vizier; decreased the power of the *nomarchs*

the three officials had his own assistant and a council of senior magistrates who reported on the economic, agricultural, and military matters that affected the *waret* under his control. Senwosret opened the newly created positions to artisans, farmers, merchants, and traders. The result was an increase in the power of the middle class.

Senwosret's policies also had an effect on religious thinking. For generations now, the middle class had questioned the Egyptian belief that only kings and nobles could enjoy an afterlife. Some had even begun to look forward to an afterlife for themselves. This thinking accelerated under Senwosret, and soon all Egyptians would consider the afterlife a real possibility.

Accompanying these changes was an increasing devotion to Osiris, the god of the dead and the underworld. According to Egyptian beliefs, Abydos was the site of Osiris's tomb, and the belief had developed that direct contact with Abydos would enhance a dead person's chances of spending eternity in Osiris's kingdom, the "Field of Reeds." Therefore, considering the role Osiris and other deities played in the afterlife, it seemed only proper that, as the riches from the trade with Nubia swelled the state treasury, Senwosret should use this wealth to build new temples and rebuild old ones. Excavations at Abydos have unearthed a stele erected by Ikhernofret, Senwosret's chief treasurer. On it, artisans had carved an inscription that told how Senwosret had commissioned

Ikhernofret to go upriver to Abydos. There he was to build monuments for Osiris and to adorn Osiris's burial place with Nubian gold.

To learn more about Senwosret's personal life and traits, historians have spent much time analyzing the six life-size statues Senwosret had artisans sculpt of himself dressed in the *neme.* Senwosret had these statues set up on the lower terrace of Nebhepetre Mentuhotep I's temple in Deir el Bahri. Compared to the statues of Egypt's early kings, those of Senwosret (as well as those of his immediate predecessors) were much more realistic. This change in treatment, that is, this preference for realism, was also affecting how Egyptians regarded their king. No longer was he considered a god-king. He was but an ordinary human, a human whom the gods had chosen to rule their beloved nation.

Thus it seemed only fitting that Senwosret's face and stance should reflect strength and determination. A closer look at the statues, however, reveals a feeling of weariness, a weariness that seems to say this king assumed the burden of ruling because he cared deeply about the land and its people.

As the years passed, Senwosret followed the custom of his predecessors and named his son Amenemhet coregent. After his death, succeeding generations of Egyptians honored Senwosret's memory and achievements. By the fifth century B.C., he had become a legendary figure and was known to the ancient Greeks as Sesostris, the king

A match between an Egyptian wrestler and a Nubian wrestler is the theme of this carefully drawn scene, which decorated the wall of a *nomarch's* tomb around the time of Senwosret III. The sport of wrestling dates back to very ancient times.

Aggressiveness is the sign of bravery. Retreat is the sign of cowardice.

—From a boundary stele of Senwosret III, Year 16

who "conquered every people who fell in his way."

For his burial complex, Senwosret followed his father's example and chose Dahshur. Senwosret also followed his father when he ordered a pyramid built for his final resting place and had builders incorporate a natural outcrop of rock into the design. The architects set stone retaining walls on the rock and used mud bricks to fill in the empty areas. As a covering for the entire pyramid, Senwosret had his builders use a layer of fine Tura limestone.

In 1894, French archaeologist Jacques de Morgan excavated Senwosret III's tomb complex. While de Morgan did not find Senwosret's mummy or treasures, he did uncover the tombs of Mereret, Senwosret's queen, and of the princess Sit-Hathor, Senwosret's sister. Ancient robbers had long since entered these rooms, but in their haste to escape undetected, they missed jewelry that had been wrapped and placed in an area apart from the mummies.

De Morgan likewise acted in haste and did not take time to record exactly where and how he found the items, nor did he note the details of their appearance. When the finds arrived at the Cairo Museum, conservators could not fit the pieces together. Only when archaeologists found the remains of similar jewelry in nearby tombs and carefully recorded each find were conservators able to reconstruct more accurately the jewelry that had once belonged to Senwosret's royal ladies. The pieces are considered among the finest ever found in ancient Egypt and reflect the high quality of craftsmanship during Senwosret's reign.

De Morgan moved beyond the enclosure walls of Senwosret's pyramid complex to see if he might locate the original subterranean entrance to the pyramid. There he found six full-size wooden boat burials and a wooden sledge that the ancients had used to drag the boats from the water's edge to the burial site. Because the boats were found near Senwosret's complex, it is believed that they were part of his funerary equipment or were used to carry the equipment from the east to the west bank of the river. Buried in sand pits dug expressly for this purpose, the boats rested on mud bricks and had their steering oars ready on deck. Approximately 32 feet in length, the boats provide a unique glimpse of boatbuilding procedures in ancient Egypt. To date, the whereabouts of only four of Senwosret's boats is known. Two are in the Egyptian Museum in Cairo, Egypt; a third is at the Carnegie Museum of Natural History in Pittsburgh, Pennsylvania; and the fourth is in the Field Museum of Natural History in Chicago, Illinois.

FURTHER READING

Lichtheim, Miriam. *Ancient Egyptian Literature: A Book of Readings*, vol. 1, pp. 118–20. Berkeley: University of California Press, 1973.

Parkinson, R. B. *Voices from Ancient Egypt: An Anthology of Middle Kingdom Writings*, pp. 43–47. Norman: University of Oklahoma Press, 1991.

Amenemhet III

DEVELOPER OF
THE FAIYUM

Amenemhet III was determined to foil any thieves who might try to break into his tomb. As the site for his pyramid, Amenemhet chose Dahshur, just as his father, Senwosret III, had. With great care, workers followed the custom of the time and used mud bricks to build the inner core of the pyramid and faced the exterior with limestone blocks. The structure was enormous, with the base of each side measuring approximately 342 feet. Instead of the traditional entrance on the side facing north, Amenemhet's architects designed his pyramid with an east-face entrance.

Amenemhet, however, chose not to have his mummified remains buried at Dahshur. In checking the Dahshur site, archaeologists found that some areas of the foundation are lower than others, and they reason that Amenemhet may have considered the tomb structurally unsound. Or Amenemhet may have simply been following the ancient custom of building two tombs: one for his mummy and one a cenotaph, or empty tomb, built in his honor. Egyptologists theorize that this practice of two tombs may have begun during the Old Kingdom to indicate a king's authority over

This head and the colossal granite statue of Amenemhet III to which it belonged probably stood originally at Memphis. Centuries later it was taken to the Delta region, where it was found.

Made of semiprecious stones in reds, blues, and tans, and with an outline in gold, this pectoral (an ornament worn on the chest) blazes with color. The two standing figures represent Amenemhet III holding the kneeling enemy by the hair. Above is the vulture goddess Nekhbet, the guardian deity of Upper Egypt. She holds an ankh, the Egyptian symbol of life, in each of her talons.

both Upper and Lower Egypt. Today the limestone casing of the Dahshur pyramid is gone, not because of tomb robbers, but because later generations used the outer blocks to construct their own buildings. Only the huge interior survives, and this crumbling mass has been nicknamed the "Black Pyramid" because of its dark color.

As the site for his second pyramid, Amenemhet chose Hawara, to the south of Dahshur. For the basic design, his architects followed precedent—but not when they came to the inner chambers and passageways. Here, again, were "tricks" to foil robbers. Even the English Egyptologist Sir Flinders Petrie, who excavated the tomb in the 1880s, found the task exasperating. There had to be a "correct" corridor leading to the burial chamber, but only after spending much time carefully examining the floors and walls of every corridor did Petrie notice a ceiling area that appeared slightly different. Upon closer investigation, Petrie discovered that Amenemhet's workers had used a stone

weighing more than 22 tons to conceal the opening that led to an upper corridor. After sliding the stone sideways, in just the way ancient builders had designed it to work, Petrie climbed up and through another passageway. This, too, he found had been built to foil robbers because it led nowhere. Searching the ceiling area again, he found another hidden passageway, a door that led to a third corridor, another sliding stone block, still another fake passageway, and another sliding stone block.

For the clever robber who might manage to reach this area of the complex, Amenemhet had his engineers design a few more surprises. Workers cut two vertical shafts that reached from the floor straight down into the pyramid. They filled both with rubble and sealed them, but did not conceal them. Amenemhet and his architects wanted robbers to concentrate their efforts on finding a burial chamber at the bottom of one of the shafts. Petrie did exactly that and found nothing.

The actual burial vault was an enormous piece of quartzite weighing more than 100 tons and measuring approximately 22 feet long and 8 feet wide. Here, again, Amenemhet seems to have broken with tradition. Instead of having his royal pyramid house only his mummy, he appears to have made plans to have this huge burial chamber hold both his sarcophagus and that of his favorite daughter, the princess Neferuptah. Excavators did find two sarcophagi in the chamber—one large and one small, but Egyptologists question whether the princess was, in fact, buried with Amenemhet.

Despite all Amenemhet's precautions, robbers did find his burial chamber and his mummy. Petrie and his crew, on the other hand, found no bodies and no treasure, but they did uncover bits of charred remains.

Amenemhet III

POSITION

King of Egypt

ACTIVE DATES

About 1842–1797 B.C.

ACCOMPLISHMENTS

Regulated the flow of floodwaters into the Faiyum and reclaimed much agricultural land in the area; promoted the use of nilometers to determine the height of flooding for a given year; built two pyramids, one at Dahshur and one at Hawara; built an enormous mortuary temple, later known as the "Labyrinth"; extended Egypt's southern boundary to the Third Cataract; brought stability and security to Egypt with a minimum of military force; protected Egypt's interest in the turquoise mines on the Sinai Peninsula

Worship the king Nimaatre [Amenemhet III], living forever, with your bodies. Enthrone his majesty in your hearts.

—Inscription on the stele of Sehetepibre, Amenemhet III's chief treasurer

In the chamber excavators also found two quartzite chests for holding canopic jars. Before beginning the mummification process, an incision was made along the right side of a dead person's body, and the liver, lungs, stomach, and intestines were removed. These inner organs were cleaned and treated with natron, a substance that acts as a drying agent, then placed in four special containers (the canopic jars) made of stone or clay. The stoppers sealing these jars resembled human heads. Beginning with the 18th Dynasty, the stoppers were in the shape of four different heads, each representing a son of Horus: human, ape, jackal, and hawk. Canopic chests were specially designed to hold the four jars.

Amenemhet's pyramid at Hawara was enormous, but his mortuary temple just south of the pyramid was even larger. In fact, the fifth-century B.C. Greek historian Herodotus referred to the temple as a labyrinth, and he wrote that it

> surpasses the pyramids. It has twelve courts, all with roofs, and with gates set exactly opposite to each other, six face north and six face south. A single wall encircles the labyrinth, which has 3,000 rooms. Fifteen hundred rooms are under ground and the other 1,500 are above ground. The latter are constructed on top of the former. . . . I saw the upper chambers with my own eyes. . . . Everywhere the roofs and the walls were of stone. In addition, the walls were covered with reliefs of various figures . . . [and] each courtyard was faced with white marble and surrounded by a colonnade.

From Herodotus's account, it seems likely that Amenemhet considered this gigantic complex as more than a mortuary temple. It likely was also an administrative office building and living area for construction workers and artisans.

Amenemhet, however, did not just concern himself with burial complexes. He took great interest in an area that lay less than six miles northwest of his burial complex. Known as the Faiyum, it was a lush fertile area in the midst of desert sands. Growing and harvesting enough food to feed his people was critical to Amenemhet's maintaining stability and peace throughout the Two Lands. He had officials keep accurate counts of the grain supply, especially of the amount stored in the country's granaries. Should the floodwaters of the Nile be lower than usual and the harvests poor, Amenemhet wanted to be sure his people would not go hungry. Surplus food was also good for economic reasons. Egyptian merchants could trade the extra food for resources Egypt lacked and for additional revenue.

Several other fertile areas, or oases, lay west of the Nile River, but none were as large as the Faiyum. Every year, during the inundation period, the floodwaters of the Nile overflowed the river's banks. Some of these waters ran along the Bahr Yosuf River, a tributary that links the Nile River with the Faiyum, and spread across the Faiyum. Over time, the floodwaters had formed a body of water known as Lake Moeris. (Moeris is the Greek form of the ancient Egyptian name Mi-wer, meaning "Great Channel.") Because the area is a natural depression, the waters did not recede in the months that followed the flood season. Rather, they remained in the lake and provided the inhabitants with a water source not available to other regions.

To provide more arable land in the Faiyum for farmers to sow and harvest, Amenemhet had workers drain marshlands and dig irrigation canals that would carry the water to outlying districts. Egyptologists estimate that Amenemhet may have reclaimed as much as 150,000 acres or more of land in the area. The result was greater economic prosperity and a greater sense of security throughout Egypt, but especially in the north, where low floodwaters meant smaller harvests.

Amenemhet had a temple built in the Faiyum to honor Sobek, the crocodile god. He also ordered two huge statues of himself erected at Biahmu, just north of Hawara. Petrie found traces of sandstone and of limestone that led him to believe that each statue was at least 35 feet high and depicted Amenemhet in a sitting position. As each statue probably rested on a base that stood at least 21 feet high, they must have looked awesome to anyone approaching the Faiyum.

Amenemhet had many other statues of himself erected throughout Egypt. One, at Hawara, depicts him in the early years of his reign, and its features are youthful, serene, and almost smiling. Another, uncovered in Medinet el Faiyum, portrays him as a priest with a heavy ritual headdress and necklace and a leopard-skin cloak. The serious and stern features of this statue reflect the forceful and determined ruler he must have been. Amenemhet,

however, did not spend all his time on construction projects. The stability and prosperity of his nation also depended on secure boundaries and free access to trade routes.

The mines in Nubia and on the Sinai Peninsula provided Amenemhet with hard stone and gold for his many building projects. Amenemhet recognized the importance of the forts his father had established beyond the Second Cataract, and he kept them well maintained. However, he thought Egypt's boundary should be extended even farther south and ordered his troops to move the boundary line to the Third Cataract. Despite such action, relations between the Nubians and the Egyptians remained fairly quiet during Amenemhet's reign. But on several occasions, Anemenhet did find it necessary to send punitive raids against the Nubians.

Amenemhet had another reason for protecting Egypt's interests as far south as the Third Cataract. He was very interested in the nilometers (unit of measure) marked off at various sites beyond the First Cataract. On stone slabs, engineers noted the rise in the Nile's waters at the beginning of every flood season. By comparing the various "rises" over the years, they could calculate how high the waters would rise each year and warn the towns and cities of Upper and Lower Egypt if flooding was to be expected.

Like Nubia, the Sinai was also strategically and economically important to Egypt. It formed the nation's eastern boundary and was rich in turquoise-producing mines. Because turquoise was used both for jewelry and in religious and burial ceremonies, Amenemhet considered it his duty to protect Egypt's rights to the turquoise mines and the people who worked them. For this reason, he

favored establishing towns with good water supplies (mainly from wells) for those who worked in the mines and ordered garrisons built to protect the miners against Bedouin attacks.

Having worked hard to increase Egypt's prosperity, Amenemhet now looked to the future. Following the example set by his great-great-great-grandfather, Amenemhet I, he, too, made his son a co-regent. Exactly how long the two ruled together is not known. Some evidence suggests that Amenemhet IV was quite young when he died and that a queen named Sobeknefru took command of the Two Lands. As king, Amenemhet III had proved himself the worthy bearer of a name that meant "Justice belongs to Re." Later

generations would recognize his 45-year rule as one of the great periods in Egyptian history and agree with the words Sehetepibre, Amenemhet's chief treasurer, had inscribed on his stele:

He [Amenemhet] illuminates the Two Lands more than the sun-disk.

He makes the Two Lands green more than a great Nile.

He has filled the Two Lands with strength.

FURTHER READING

Lehner, Mark. *The Complete Pyramids*, pp. 181–83. New York: Thames & Hudson, 1997.

This pyramidion (the small stone pyramid that topped a pyramid) once crowned Amenemhet III's pyramid at Dahshur. Carved in black granite, the design represents Amenemhet III himself, with his eyes looking toward the sun god. It is about four feet, three inches high.

More Ancient Egyptians to Remember

Meketre (active about 2030 B.C.) served as Mentuhotep I's chancellor and chief steward. Like so many of his contemporaries who held important administrative posts, Meketre had workers cut his tomb into the rocky cliff that rose above Mentuhotep's temple and tomb at Deir el Bahri. In antiquity, robbers stripped the tomb of all the valuables, but they missed a small chamber. In 1919–20, excavators found in this room 24 (some say 25) models of the type that Egyptians gave as gifts to *nomarchs* and high-ranking officials. Crafted of wood, they represent, in minute detail, scenes from daily life, including a two-story butcher shop with workers preparing cattle for slaughter, a carpenter's shop, and a bakery. Here also were two beautifully crafted models of Meketre's house, with its walled garden and copper-lined pool bordered by leafy trees.

Egyptian fishermen prepare to haul in their catch. They and other servant figures found remarkably well preserved in Meketre's tomb are housed at the Egyptian Museum in Cairo.

Heqanakht (active about 2030 B.C.) was a farmer and prosperous land-holder under Mentuhotep I. A chance find of some of his letters and business accounts in a pack of crumpled papyri in the cliff tombs overlooking Deir el Bahri have provided a unique glimpse into Heqanakht's life. Most of the papyri appear to be palimpsests, that is, papyrus paper that has been used and then washed clean for reuse. The letters addressed to his eldest son make it clear that Heqanakht wanted the workers on their land to work hard for their wages and to take pride in their tasks. His attitude to his younger son, Snefru, is different. Heqanakht wrote to his eldest son, "If Snefru wants to look after bulls, then let him look after bulls. . . . Whatever he wants, you should let him enjoy it."

In another letter, Heqanakht reviews the payment of rent on his lands and then complains about receiving old grain. From the text, it appears that Heqanakht's land holdings were near Thebes and that his income came from the lands he farmed for himself and his family and from plots of lands that he rented to others. Heqanakht appears to have been a cautious businessman who watched expenditures closely and kept careful track of every transaction.

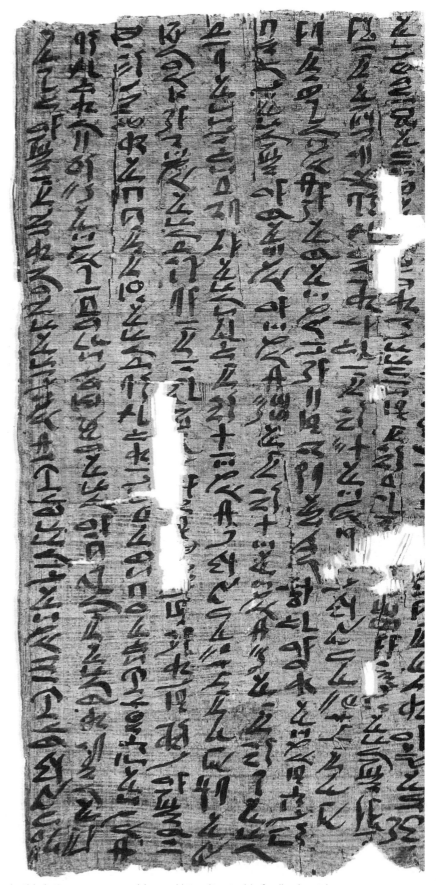

In this letter on papyrus, Heqanakht writes to his family about home and farm matters. Only a few pieces are missing from this section.

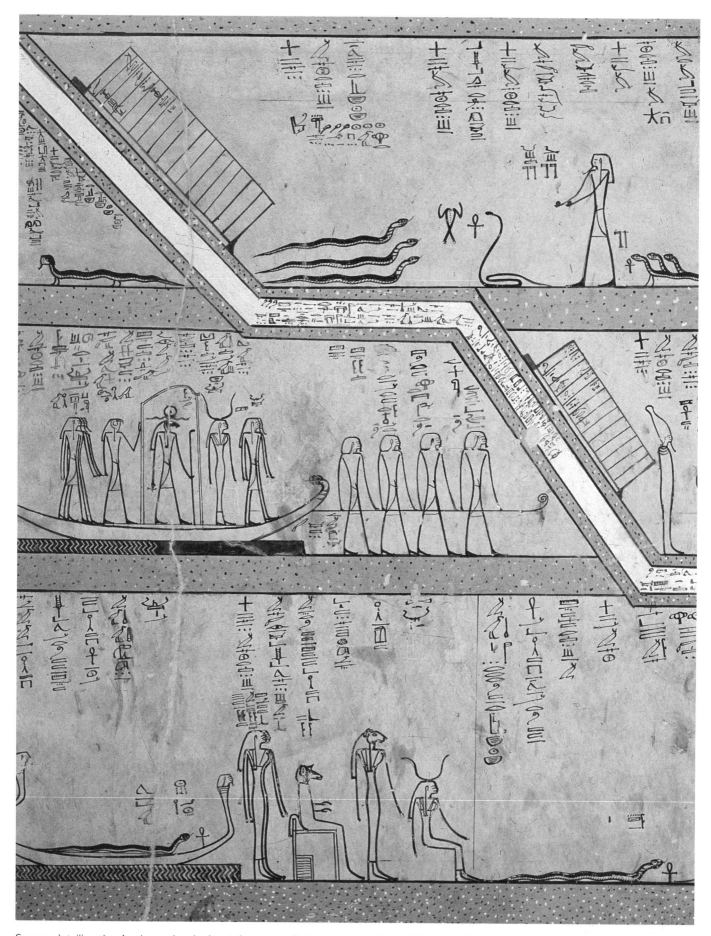

Scenes detailing the *Amduat,* a book about the sun god's journey through the 12 hours of the underworld, decorated the walls of Thutmose III's burial chamber. This section depicts the fourth hour. Also represented is the descent of the sarcophagus into the tomb.

3

Growth and Expansion (New Kingdom, about 1570–1440 B.C.)

Under Senwosret III and Amenemhet III, peace and prosperity had spread across the Two Lands bordering the Nile. The Nubians to the south and the Bedouins to the east had been subdued, and trade was booming. The Faiyum had become a rich agricultural region, and being self-sufficient added to the people's sense of security. The arts and architecture flourished. But just as the country had experienced disruption and decline after the long reign of Pepi II some 200 years earlier, now, only a few years after the death of Amenemhet III, turmoil and uncertainty spread again across the Two Lands. Even the ancients referred to these two periods as a time of misery and chaos, although such descriptions seemed to have been encouraged by later rulers who wished to confirm their right to sit on the throne. Egyptologists have labeled the years after Pepi II the First Intermediate Period and the years after Amenemhet III Second Intermediate Period.

A series of weak rulers gradually led to a decentralization of power. This, in turn, led to the viziers assuming more power. Still, the *nomarchs* of the 13th Dynasty who had their capital at Thebes managed to keep Upper Egypt relatively calm and stable. In the Delta region to the north, however, several leaders refused to pledge their allegiance to the rulers in Thebes. Instead, they established their own rule. The Egyptian historian Manetho called these kings (he listed 70 of them) the 14th Dynasty.

In the midst of this uncertainty, Egypt came under foreign rule. A people known as the Hyksos crossed into Egypt from the east and gained control of Lower Egypt. They also claimed control of Upper Egypt—not directly, but through Egyptian overlords responsible to them. The name Hyksos is a Greek variation of the name the Egyptians used for these people—and for other foreigners as well—*hekau-khasut*, meaning "chiefs of foreign lands." Although Manetho says that the Hyksos conquered Egypt without warning, most Egyptologists believe that the "takeover" happened gradually. Ongoing excavations at Avaris, the site of the Hyksos capital, have uncovered important information that Egyptologists are using to learn more about this period.

Through the years, the number of Asiatics and other foreigners entering Egypt from the east had been increasing steadily. Some were prisoners of war, whereas others were immigrant workers looking for jobs in a prosperous land. Inscriptions and historical records dating to Amenemhet III's reign confirm this fact. Yet surviving accounts and uncovered artifacts suggest that the Hyksos rulers did not impose their customs on the Egyptians. Rather, they preferred to adapt their ways to the traditions of the Egyptians. Nevertheless, the Hyksos did introduce new ideas and objects to the Egyptians. These included bronze weaponry, the war horse and chariot, advanced building practices, the vertical loom, and the lyre. Still, their influence was confined chiefly to the Delta region of Lower Egypt. Manetho credits the Hyksos with a rule that lasted approximately 100 years, and he grouped their kings into two dynasties, the 15th and the 16th. The Egyptians, however, refused to accept foreign rule for long.

Part 3 of *Ancient Egyptians* profiles the individuals who restored control of the Two Lands to the Egyptians and established a new line of kings that would extend Egypt's influence and power far beyond the Nile and the confining borders of the desert sands. And it is with these kings that the Egyptian words *per wer* ("Great House") refer no longer to the royal palace but to the king— the "pharaoh"—himself.

Ahmose, Son of Ebana

FEARLESS WARRIOR

"**A**hmose, son of Ebana [and] captain of a crew of sailors, says: 'I will tell you . . . of the favors conferred on me. Seven times was I given gold in the presence of the whole land, and likewise slaves, both male and female. . . . Gifts of many fields to be held by me forever were also made to me.'" So begins the long autobiographical inscription that Ahmose had his workers carve into the walls of his tomb at Nekheb (present-day el Kab), an ancient town on the eastern shores of the Nile River. Ahmose took pride in his accomplishments and in the recognition and grand rewards he received from the rulers he served.

As a preface to the main text of the inscription, Ahmose explains that he grew up in the city of Nekheb and that his father, Baba, was an officer in the army of the Theban ruler Seqenenre Tao II. Like his father, Ahmose joined the military and later served as an officer on a ship named the *Wild Bull*. After Seqenenre died, Ahmose pledged his allegiance to Kamose, Seqenenre's son and successor.

Both Seqenenre Tao and Kamose were native Egyptian rulers, but neither one could claim control of Lower Egypt. At the time, a people known to history as the Hyksos ruled the Delta area. These foreigners had gradually gained con-

At the time of Ahmose, son of Ebana, the king's war chariot most likely resembled this two-wheeled, two-horse chariot, which is missing the front and sides of the section in which the driver and passenger stood.

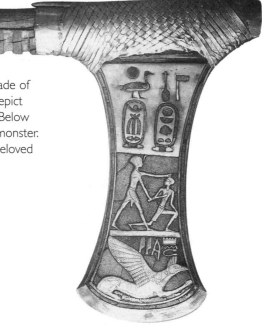

The relief figures decorating the blade of Ahmose I's ceremonial axe head depict the king smiting an Asiatic captive. Below is the figure of a griffin, a mythical monster. The inscription above translates, "Beloved of [the war god] Montu."

When the king learned of the son of Ebana's dedication and military prowess, he assigned him to the northern fleet. This was an honor, because only the best troops, both in the army and in the navy, were sent to fight the Hyksos. Ahmose also made sure that his artisans recorded his great pride in this promotion, which had been granted because of his bravery and loyalty. Ahmose even had the artisans carve on the tomb walls his pledge to follow the king on foot whenever he made a journey in his war chariot. This passage is the first mention of Egyptians using the chariot and horse, both of which the Hyksos had introduced into Egypt, in battle.

Ahmose, son of Ebana, first proved his bravery against the Hyksos during the difficult siege of Avaris, the chief city of the Hyksos. Stressing that he acted on his two feet, Ahmose, son of Ebana, told how he performed a remarkably brave deed in the presence of his king. While no further details accompany this statement, the tomb hieroglyphs mention that King Ahmose was so pleased with the loyal son of Ebana that he commissioned him to serve on the ship, the *Shining in Memphis.*

Avaris, however, did not fall easily or swiftly. A second assault had to be ordered and Ahmose, son of Ebana, again took his place on the front line—this time in a canal called Pa-Djedku. Fighting in hand-to-hand combat, Ahmose valiantly overwhelmed a Hyksos warrior and "brought away a hand." Following the accepted custom, Ahmose had taken the hand of the enemy he had killed in battle as proof of his valor. This deed, too, was reported to the royal herald, who announced it to the king. As his reward, Ahmose, son

trol in the region and were looking to expand their power farther south. At first, there had been little resistance to the Hyksos, and Egypt's kings had even made treaties with them to avoid conflicts. As the years passed, a few powerful Egyptian families began expanding the area under their control. Seqenenre had been one of the first to oppose the Hyksos militarily, and his son Kamose continued the drive north, extending his rule into Middle Egypt.

When Kamose died less than three years after his father, his brother Ahmose (not Ahmose, son of Ebana) ascended to the throne. Because the new king was still quite young, his mother ruled as regent, and the war against the Hyksos was downgraded to a matter of lesser importance. Once Ahmose I became old enough to rule, he gave orders to continue the war against the "foreign intruders." As a loyal Egyptian and as a military officer, Ahmose, son of Ebana, eagerly awaited the chance to prove his valor on the battlefield.

of Ebana, received the "Gold of Valor" (or Flies of Valor), a gold pendant shaped like flies or lions.

Avaris, however, remained under Hyksos control, and so a third battle followed. Once again Ahmose eagerly entered hand-to-hand combat with the enemy. Again, he killed his foe and cut off his hand—and again he received a Gold of Valor.

The hieroglyphs that follow tell of more fighting, this time to the south of Avaris. Whether Ahmose meant the land lying just to the south of Avaris, or whether the phrase refers to a revolt or problem that occurred closer to home in Upper Egypt, is unclear. What was important to Ahmose were the details of the expedition and the difficulties involved. The fight had taken him to the other side of a river or stream, where he managed to capture an enemy alive, made him his prisoner, and carried him across the water to the main encampment. When the royal herald reported the incident to the king, Ahmose I honored the son of Ebana with two more Gold of Valor awards.

This last campaign seems to have ended the problems in the South, because Ahmose I (Kamose's brother and succesor) now turned his attention to conquering Avaris. Ahmose, son of Ebana, tells us that in the final battle he captured four enemies alive— one man and three women. As a reward, the king gave him the captives as slaves.

Finally, the long struggle against the Hyksos was over, and the Two Lands once again belonged to the people who lived along the Nile. Yet Ahmose I was not content with his victory on Egyptian soil. Determined to squash Hyksos power, he pursued them to the town of Sharuhen in Palestine, where

they had regrouped. According to the inscription on the son of Ebana's tomb, the struggle lasted three years. Many Egyptologists believe this mention of three years refers not to a period of time but to three separate battles.

In Palestine, just as in Egypt, Ahmose, son of Ebana, proved himself a valiant warrior and received more gold for his actions. He also accepted, as personal slaves, two women he had taken as prisoners.

With peace now to the north and the east, Ahmose I sailed south with his army to Khent-hen-nefer in Nubia. Victory followed victory, with the son of Ebana eagerly joining every battle. For his efforts, he received more "Gold of Valor" awards and more slaves.

The unrest in Nubia erupted into rebellion when a Nubian leader named Aata led his people against the Egyptians. Ahmose, son of Ebana, seized two of the enemy from Aata's ship. In return for his bravery, Ahmose received the customary rewards, as well as tracts of land in his city of Nekheb. In his tomb inscription, Ahmose took care to have his artisans note on his tomb walls that he was not the only one who received such gifts, but that the king had granted the entire crew of his vessel the same rewards for their bravery.

By now the son of Ebana was a very wealthy person. He must also have been a well-known military figure, considering the number of battles in which he had served honorably and well. Thus, it was only natural that the son of Ebana would be summoned to serve under Ahmose I's successor, Amenhotep I.

When reports of Nubian unrest reached the royal palace, Amenhotep I followed the example of his predecessors and prepared to march south. Ahmose, son of Ebana, joined him. In the

Ahmose, Son of Ebana

POSITION
Navy Captain

ACTIVE DATES
About 1535 B.C.

ACCOMPLISHMENTS
Fought under Ahmose I in campaigns aimed at expelling the Hyksos from Egypt; fought under Amenhotep I and Thutmose I in Nubia and in Syria; won many "Gold of Valor" awards and tracts of land for his bravery; recorded his exploits on his tomb walls

The name of a man brave and bold in his achievements shall not perish in this land forever.

—Inscription in Ahmose, son of Ebana's tomb

battles against the Nubians, Ahmose seems to have distinguished himself more than ever. His inscription boasts, "I fought incredibly and the king saw my bravery. I took two hands and gave them to his majesty." Amenhotep I awarded Ahmose for his valor with the special title of "Warrior of the Crown."

At this point details of his service under Amenhotep I end, and the focus of the text shifts to his bravery under Amenhotep I's successor, Thutmose I. By this time, Ahmose must certainly have been one of the older officers, especially considering that Amenhotep I ruled for approximately 25 years.

When news of unrest in Nubia reached Thutmose I, he quickly sailed with a fleet up the Nile to Khent-hennefre. Ahmose helped guide the Egyptian vessels around the cataracts. For this service, Thutmose appointed Ahmose "Chief of the Sailors."

Yet even after Thutmose finally subdued the rebellious Nubians and punished their leaders, he allowed no time for peace. Instead, he readied his troops for a march into Retinu (the Syria-Palestine area). With him was Ahmose, who, despite his age, still fought bravely and honorably, winning two more "Gold of Valor" awards for his seizure of a chariot, its horses, and the charioteer.

With the passing years, Ahmose found that his body could no longer endure the rigors of military life. The awards and honors, however, continued—at least according to the inscription on his tomb's walls. Nevertheless, for Ahmose, the concerns of this life were over, and he looked to prepare himself for the next life. In this, too, he proved successful, because the "autobiography" he had carved on his walls brought him enduring fame and immortality.

FURTHER READING

Lichtheim, Miriam. *Ancient Egyptian Literature: A Book of Readings*, vol. 2, pp. 12–15. Berkeley: University of California Press, 1976.

Hatshepsut

THE QUEEN WHO BECAME KING

A series of unexpected circumstances brought Hatshepsut to the throne of Egypt, but she readily wielded the power entrusted to her. She did not concern herself with the fact that she was a woman and that only men had ruled Egypt. Like her father, Thutmose I, she was strong-willed. He had not been in direct line for the throne either but had claimed the right to rule through his wife Ahmose, who was the daughter of Ahmose I and his Great Royal Wife, Ahmose Nefertari. In the official king lists of the Egyptian historian Manetho, Ahmose I founded the 18th Dynasty.

Many of Hatshepsut's statues bear marks of intentional destruction, but a few small, kneeling figures such as this escaped relatively untouched; even the traditional royal beard is still in place.

Egypt was made to work with bowed head for her, the excellent seed of the god, who came forth from him.

—Inscription in the tomb of Ineni, an official, recording the joint ascension of Hatshepsut and Thutmose III to the throne

Thutmose I had proved himself a strong leader, and to provide for a smooth transition of power, he groomed his two sons by Queen Ahmose, Wadjmose and Amenmose, as his successors. To ensure a supply of royal heirs in case anything should happen to those next in line, he married his daughter Hatshepsut to her half-brother, Thutmose—a son he had fathered with one of his minor queens. For generations, kings had arranged such marriages.

Events soon proved that Thutmose I had acted wisely. Both Wadjmose and Amenmose predeceased their father, and Thutmose I died after a brief reign of approximately six years. No one, however, considered Hatshepsut an heir. In the past, queens had acted as regents and, on occasion, had even governed the land for short periods of time, but no woman had ever inherited the throne of Egypt. Nor had any queen ever assumed the title of "king." Because the Egyptians considered their ruler the son and representative of the great god Amun-Re and of the god Horus, how could a female be king? Thus, it followed that Hatshepsut's husband succeeded her father as Thutmose II.

Records suggest that Thutmose II had some physical problems, and although he gave orders to continue military campaigns into Nubia, his participation in them was minimal.

Meanwhile, the strong-willed Hatshepsut had begun to consolidate her power and win followers. She also looked to the future. She and Thutmose II had only one child, a daughter named Neferure, but Thutmose also had a son by Isis, a girl in his harem. Therefore, to ensure the continuation of the family line, Hatshepsut and Thutmose II did just as their father had done—at least according to most Egyptologists: they married Neferure to her half-brother (Isis's son), who was also named Thutmose.

Then came the unexpected. Thutmose II died in his early 30s. Thutmose III succeeded his father, but because he was too young to rule in his own right, Hatshepsut assumed the role of regent. No one objected. The precedent had been set centuries earlier when several queen mothers had done the same. What no queen had done, however, was keep the power for herself. Yet no documents prove that Hatshepsut had intended to do so when she first became regent.

Resourceful and intelligent, Hatshepsut quickly adapted herself to her new role. Several of her father's advisers, confident of her ability to rule, continued in their posts. One was Hapuseneb, who held the office of High Priest of Amun, one of the most powerful positions in Egypt. Hapuseneb also served as Hatshepsut's vizier. There were new advisers as well, people whom Hatshepsut had learned to trust. Chief among these was Senenmut, a commoner who had proved his loyalty and to whom Hatshepsut entrusted the education of her daughter, Neferure. Senenmut was also Hatshepsut's chief architect and in charge of all royal construction projects.

Hatshepsut had no plans to rival her father's exploits on the battlefield;

nor did she wish to consider military matters a top priority. She preferred to devote her energies to projects that reflected Egypt's greatness. Her close connections with government officials, first as princess and then as wife of Thutmose II, had taught her the importance of maintaining a strong Egyptian presence in Nubia and in the Sinai Peninsula. The imports traveling along the trade routes leading to and from these areas provided Egypt's artisans and builders with the necessary raw materials for their projects. In addition, the revenue from this trade helped sustain the high standard of living the Egyptians were enjoying.

By all accounts it was Hatshepsut's choice not to extend Egypt's boundaries beyond those she had inherited. But surviving records written by two soldiers seem to prove that Hatshepsut did not avoid the battlefield. These soldiers told of her leading them into battle against Nubia and taking several chiefs as prisoners.

As the months passed, Hatshepsut saw herself, not her stepson Thutmose, as heir to the throne and proclaimed herself "king" of Egypt. Yet Hatshepsut realized that naming herself "king" and assuming the title was not enough. She had to prove that she had the right to sit on the throne, and there was only one way to do this—Hatshepsut had to establish a divine connection between herself and the all-powerful Amun-Re. Surviving inscriptions and reliefs on Hatshepsut's funerary temple at Deir el Bahri, an area that lies to the west of the Nile and directly across from Thebes, clearly show how she handled the situation.

Carved onto the walls are scenes depicting the story of Hatshepsut's birth. The god Amun is seated on a throne, and he is announcing to an assembly of the gods that he intends to give Egypt a new king. Thoth, the god of learning and wisdom, recommends to Amun that he choose Ahmose, the wife of Thutmose I, to be the mother of this new ruler. The next scene shows Amun and Ahmose seated on the heavens and facing each other.

Carved onto the wall next to Amun's relief are the words: "Amun-Re . . . made his form like the majesty of the husband Thutmose I. He [Amun] then found her [Ahmose] as she slept in the beauty of her palace. She awoke at the fragrance of the god, which she smelled in the presence of his majesty."

The relief continues with Amun telling Ahmose that "Khnemet-Amun-Hatshepsut shall be the name of this my daughter, whom I have placed in your body. . . . She shall exercise great kingship in this whole land. My soul is hers . . . my crown is hers, that she may rule the Two Lands." It is significant that the text uses the masculine word "king" when referring to the official position but uses the feminine forms for the adjectives and pronouns when referring to the person who is to become king.

Amun summons Khnum, the god of creation and childbirth, and asks him to use his potter's wheel to create his new daughter and a double to serve as her *ka* (life force). After completing the assignment, Khnum says: "I have formed you of these limbs of Amun, patron of Karnak. . . . I have given to you all health, all lands; I have given to you all countries, all people . . . while you shine as King of Upper and Lower Egypt, of North and South, according as your father who loves you has commanded."

Hatshepsut could not have stated her right to rule more clearly, especially considering that the artisans had used

Hatshepsut

POSITION

King of Egypt

REIGN

About 1498–83 B.C.

ACCOMPLISHMENTS

Claimed the hereditary right to rule Egypt as king; had her tomb built in the Valley of the Kings; restored direct maritime trade with Punt; ordered the construction of a magnificent mortuary temple at Deir el Bahri; ordered many new temples built and old ones restored; had four giant obelisks erected at Karnak the feminine form of the hieroglyphic sign for "you"—a direct reference to Hatshepsut, the female "king."

Still, associating herself with Amun and calling herself "Daughter of the God" did not seem enough. Hatshepsut had the artisans follow the birth reliefs with scenes depicting her coronation. In this series Amun presents Hatshepsut to the other gods and she is crowned in the presence of her father. The Egyptians revered the dead Thutmose I and considered him one of their great rulers. Thus, in a sense, the relief would be an official proclamation of her father's desire that she was his rightful successor. In the accompanying inscription, Thutmose says, "This is my daughter Khnemet-Amun-Hatshepsut . . . she is my successor on my throne. . . . She it is who shall lead you. You shall proclaim her word; you shall be united at her command."

To associate herself even more closely with her father, Hatshepsut had a sarcophagus fashioned for her father's mummy and made plans to place it in the tomb that she had built for herself. Because ancient priests later reburied the royal mummies from this period in a joint tomb to protect them from tomb robbers, it is impossible to know whether Hatshepsut actually did have her father's mummy transferred from its original tomb to hers.

Hatshepsut gave orders that two obelisks be set up in the temple of the great god Amun, her divine father. Hatshepsut's trusted and loyal advisor Senenmut oversaw this tremendous undertaking. Again the reliefs at Deir el Bahri provide the details of the task.

At the quarries at Aswan, Senenmut supervised the workers who carefully cut and fashioned two solid columns out of red granite, each approximately 95 feet high. As was the custom, the top of the obelisk was shaped to resemble a pyramid. Sculptors carved the

figure of Amun with his arm around Hatshepsut onto each of the four flat triangular surfaces of the *pyramidion* (the term for the top section of an obelisk). Reliefs of Hatshepsut with her stepson Thutmose ran up the sides of the obelisks. When both were in position at Karnak, the workers coated the obelisks with electrum, a light-yellow alloy of gold and silver. For years after, the sight of these columns catching the rays of the sun god Amun-Re and reflecting them about the temple area must have been awe-inspiring.

In Year 15, Hatshepsut ordered another pair of obelisks. These, too, were to stand at Karnak and honor Amun. In charge of this project was an official named Amenhotep, who, according to surviving records, accomplished the daunting assignment in only seven months! (One of this second pair of obelisks still stands at Karnak and is the largest obelisk to have survived in Egypt—approximately 97 feet high.)

Determined as Hatshepsut was to rule, she had no intention of radically changing Egyptian customs. Rather, she labelled herself a king and had sculptors carve her statues in the same way as they did for kings, but with her female face. Surviving statues clearly bear witness to this fact. In New York's Metropolitan Museum of Art, a carved stone sphinx (a mythical creature with the body of a lion and the head of a man, ram, or hawk) stares out at the world from a female face, supposedly fashioned to resemble that of Hatshepsut. A similar sphinx reclines in a room in the Cairo Museum in Egypt.

To further identify herself with the kingship, Hatshepsut assumed all the emblems and insignia associated with the office, including a royal Horus name—this name told all that she, as "king," was the earthly representative of the male sky-god Horus. Her statues show her in the short royal kilt and

crowned with the striped royal *nemes*.
Attached to her chin is the rectangular
beard that was traditionally included on
statues of kings.

Yet making herself a king was not
Hatshepsut's chief concern. Instead she
focused her energy on governing Egypt
and on adorning the lands along the
Nile with buildings that reflected the
country's greatness, including new temples and other religious structures.

Hatshepsut also made plans to construct a tomb that reflected her new position. As "king," Hatshepsut considered it only proper that she be buried in
ta set aat ("the Great Place")—which is
known today as the Valley of the Kings.
Years earlier, when she was the wife and
queen of Thutmose II, she had had
workers cut a tomb into the rock cliff of
a secluded valley to the west of *ta set
aat*. It was no longer appropriate, so she
had a second tomb cut into the cliffs at
the eastern end of *ta set aat*. However,
because the valley was such a narrow
and confined area, the traditional design of a mortuary temple connected to
the burial structure did not work.

Hatshepsut's father had faced the
same problem. Records indicate that
Thutmose I was the first king to choose
ta set aat as his burial site. In doing so,
he set a precedent that Egypt's rulers
would follow for approximately 500
years. Thutmose's architects had cut his
tomb into the rock in *ta set aat*, and located his mortuary temple on the flat
plain just to the east of the valley's rock
cliffs. Although separated by the cliffs,
both the tomb and the temple lay to
the west of the Nile, that is, on the side
of the Nile that for centuries Egyptians
had associated with the setting sun and
the afterlife.

To design and oversee the construction of the mortuary temple, Hatshepsut chose Senenmut. The plan was simple, yet grand, and perfectly comple-
mented its backdrop—the salmon-red

rock cliff. The two lower terraces, each
lined with a row of columns, served as a
base for the third terrace, whose
columns were fronted with statues of
Hatshepsut. Standing guard along the
avenue that led to the temple was a row
of sandstone sphinxes. Even today, approaching visitors feel compelled to
stop, at least for a moment, just to gaze
at this architectural wonder, this masterpiece of Egyptian design. Hatshepsut

The four figures carved into the top of
this stele (a rock slab erected as a
memorial) found near a temple to the
sky goddess Hathor all look human. But
only two represent humans: Hatshepsut
(second from left) and Thutmose III
(second from right). To the far left is
Amun-Re and to the far right is the
Egyptian city of Thebes as a person.

named the temple Djeser-djeseru, which means "Holiest of Holy Places." In the seventh century A.D., Arabic-speaking Egyptian Christians built a monastery on the temple's ruins and called the site Deir el Bahri.

For Hatshepsut, the temple was more than a funeral monument; it was a testament to her right to rule and to her accomplishments. Besides the reliefs depicting her birth, her coronation, and the fashioning of the obelisks, additional scenes told of other major events. Chief among them were those detailing an expedition to the resource-rich land of Punt that took place late in Year 8 of Hatshepsut's reign.

By design, the scenes were a travelogue in themselves: The sections that refer specifically to action taking place in Punt are located at the south end of the relief. The bows of the vessels setting sail for Punt point south, while the bows of the vessels returning to Egypt from Punt point north. Each vessel is carved with every piece of equipment in its proper place. The detail proves that the Egyptians built their vessels for use on the Nile, not for open waters or high seas.

The captain's command, "Steer to port," carved above the stern of the last of five vessels leaving a port on the Red Sea for Punt, gives the scene a personal touch. The action quickens as the expedition leader advances to meet Perehu —the tall and thin Puntite king. Pictured, too, are Perehu's two sons, daughter, and wife Eti, a fat woman with a deep curve in her lower back and very heavy legs. In the background is a village with its houses built, as was the custom, on stilts—the oldest surviving image of African tribal life.

The scenes that follow bustle with activity. A group of Puntite villagers eagerly ask, "Why have you come here to this land, which the people of Egypt do not know? Did you come down upon the ways of the heavens, or did you sail upon the waters, the sea of God's land." The Egyptian leaders stand near their tents, ready to start trading. In the background are the Egyptian ships, laden with trade items that have already been brought aboard. Walking along the planks leading from the port to the vessels are several men, who carry a variety of goods, including live myrrh trees with their roots carefully wrapped in sacks. Hatshepsut planned to use them to decorate her monuments and the colonnaded terraces of her temple at *ta set aat*. One Egyptian, who is afraid that he might loose his footing or his tree, says to another, "Watch out for your feet! Watch out now, the load is very heavy!"

The scene then shifts to Egypt, where scribes are shown making a record of every import item. Proud Hatshepsut welcomes the returning expedition and gives thanks to Amun for its success. An inscription near the image of Amun has the god saying, "My dear daughter, Hatshepsut, my favorite, king of Upper and Lower Egypt . . . I have given to you all Punt."

In the sections that follow, Hatshepsut takes full responsibility for ordering the expedition, announces that it was a tremendous success, and publicly exhibits the goods imported from Punt. Hatshepsut ends her speech saying that she has done as Amun, her father, commanded her. That is, she has established a Punt for him in Egypt by planting the prized myrrh trees in a garden beside his temple.

What is especially interesting about this Punt relief is the figure of young Thutmose III offering fresh myrrh to the sacred boat of Amun that is being carried by the god's priests. Why Thutmose's figure was included in the relief is not known. Thutmose was still king in name, but even as he grew older, Hatshepsut chose not to grant him any royal power. She did recognize his leadership qualities on the battlefield, though, and entrusted him with command of the army.

Hatshepsut, however, could not control fate. When she died (some Egyptologists believe she may have ruled for as many as 20 years), Thutmose immediately assumed sole control of the Two Lands. That no records list the cause of her death has led some to believe that Thutmose decided that he, not she, should be king and took measures to place himself on the throne. No proof, however, has ever surfaced to support this argument.

Some years after her death Thutmose ordered Hatshepsut's monuments torn down and her name erased from all records throughout Egypt, including the king lists. Centuries later, others would recognize her achievements, reinstate her name on the monuments, and restore what had been destroyed. The hieroglyphs on Hatshepsut's obelisk at Karnak seem to have foreshadowed her role in history: "I shall be unto eternity like an 'Imperishable.'"

FURTHER READING

Roberts, Russell. *Rulers of Ancient Egypt*, chap. 2. San Diego, Calif.: Lucent, 1999.

Tyldesley, Joyce A. *Hatchepsut: The Female Pharaoh*. New York: Penguin, 1998.

Senenmut

FOREMAN OF
THE FOREMEN

ho was this man named Senenmut who became the close confidant and adviser of Hatshepsut, one of ancient Egypt's most powerful rulers? How did he rise to such a position of power and influence? And why did he suddenly lose favor with the royals?

Surviving records suggest that Senenmut's parents were commoners, with no titles, and that they lived in Armant, a city to the south of Thebes. Senenmut may have joined the Egyptian army under Amenhotep I (Hatshepsut's uncle). His superiors most likely made his achievements and abilities known to Thutmose II (Hatshepsut's husband), who appointed him as steward to Hatshepsut. (In ancient Egypt, stewards were in charge of areas of a royal household or financial matters connected with the household.) The relationship was undoubtedly an agreeable one, for Senenmut was soon promoted to chief steward, one of the most powerful positions in Egypt. Hatshepsut must have trusted him completely, as she named him the tutor of her daughter Neferure, whom she considered her heir and successor. Further proof of the close relationship between these three are the statues archaeologists have uncovered of Senenmut holding the young Neferure on his lap.

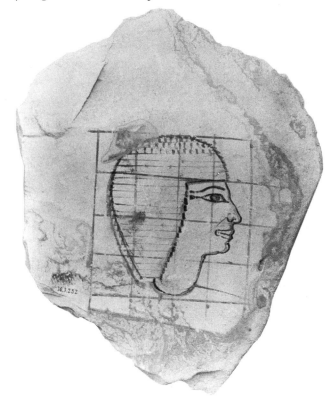

Scholars suggest that the face on this *ostracon* (a piece of limestone used as a sketchpad by an Egyptian artist) found in Senenmut's tomb is Senenmut himself.

Hatshepsut's magnificent mortuary temple is terraced into the base of the cliffs at Deir el Bahri. At the far left are the remains of Mentuhotep I's temple. On the other side of the cliff is the Valley of the Kings.

Hatshepsut also recognized Senenmut's ability as a capable engineer and architect and placed him in charge of several building projects soon after she claimed the title of king. One of his first official duties as "superintendent of the buildings dedicated to the god Amun" (a position also known as "steward of Amun") was a trip upstream to the granite quarries at Elephantine (present-day Aswan). There he was to oversee the cutting of two gigantic obelisks that were to adorn the great temple dedicated to the god Amun at Karnak.

Senenmut's position was one of great honor, but the task proved difficult and stressful. An obelisk had to be fashioned from a single solid column of stone, and the only way to cut such a column was to find a huge block of stone with no imperfections—even a slight fault in the stone might cause it

to split as it was being cut or shaped. With orders to erect two obelisks (custom dictated that obelisks be raised in pairs), Senenmut needed to find two sites, each with rock solid enough to produce a column measuring approximately 95 feet tall. Before any worker began cutting into stone, Senenmut must have searched the bed of the quarry very carefully, talking to all who had worked the site previously. Finally, he chose two spots. Both proved to be good, and workers soon had the columns cut, maneuvered onto the sledges, and pulled to the barges that waited to transport them downstream to Karnak. Carved onto the walls of Hatshepsut's mortuary temple at Deir el Bahri are scenes of Egyptian laborers ferrying the giant obelisks down the Nile to Karnak.

Senenmut also had workers carve a record of his success on the rocks near

the quarry site. The inscriptions accompanying the figures of Senenmut and Hatshepsut state that Senenmut came to the area as the "hereditary prince . . . who pleases the Mistress of the Two Lands by his command . . . to inspect the work of two great obelisks. . . . It took place according to that which was commanded . . . [and] because of the fame of her majesty."

Senenmut's job, however, was not finished. Although the obelisks were at Karnak and their upper sections had been sheathed in electrum, a light-yellow alloy of gold and silver, as was the custom at the time, they still had to be raised and set in position in the eastern part of Amun's temple. Making Senenmut's task a little easier was the fact that years of temple building had created a pool of skilled laborers. Time, however, has not been kind to Senenmut's obelisks, and only their

Senenmut

POSITION

Adviser to Hatshepsut, chief steward, architect, tutor

ACTIVE DATES

About 1495 B.C.

ACCOMPLISHMENTS

Rose from commoner to chief steward under Hatshepsut; believed to be responsible for the design and construction of Hatshepsut's mortuary temple at Deir el Bahri; oversaw the obelisk project—two enormous obelisks quarried at Aswan and erected at Karnak; oversaw many construction projects throughout Egypt, including at Karnak and Armant; involved in overseeing the distribution of trade items imported from Punt

I was the greatest of the great in the whole land.

—Inscription on a statue of Senenmut commissioned by Hatshepsut

bases stand today amid the ruins of the temple.

Hatshepsut also chose Senenmut to design and build her mortuary temple at Deir el Bahri. The site was a dramatic one, with great salmon-red rock cliffs rising up from the dry and dusty desert sands. Senenmut would have spent hours surveying the area, focusing special attention on the funerary complex King Nebhepetre Mentuhotep I had built on the same site some 500 years earlier. Once the overall plan of the temple was complete, Senenmut had his workers use Mentuhotep's complex as a quarry.

Using excellent judgment and a keen sense of place, Senenmut had the temple complement, not compete with, the lofty, natural backdrop of the cliff. He saw the temple as one with the cliff—not freestanding, but built directly into the cliff. He did not include any pyramid-shaped buildings or single columns because the rock cliff would only dwarf such structures. Rather, he stressed horizontal lines, and thus set one terrace upon another, much in the same way that the cliff itself was composed of rock layer upon rock layer. A wide ramp, probably lined with trees, led to the first terrace. A second ramp led to the next terrace. Along the front of each terrace was a colonnade (a series of columns) that gave a sense of openness, as well as a feeling of oneness

with the cliff behind. Although the colonnade was horizontal in design, its columns served to pull in a vertical direction the gaze of anyone approaching the temple or proceeding up the ramps from one level to the next.

Senenmut also incorporated into the design several chapels, including one in honor of Anubis, the guide in the afterlife, and another in honor of Hathor, the protectress of women and of the cemeteries along the Nile. The most sacred area in the temple was the section where three chapels had been cut directly into the rock cliff. The most important was the chapel that held the sacred barque (a small sailing ship) of the sun god Amun-Re. On festival occasions, priests placed the image of Amun-Re in the boat's cabin and, in solemn procession, carried the barque and the image on poles laid across their shoulders. To associate Hatshepsut more closely with her divine "father," Senenmut placed statues of Hatshepsut in niches cut into the rock that flanked the chapels.

Senenmut and Hatshepsut took advantage of the extensive wall space to record the events they considered deserved special attention. These included a scene that showed Amun-Re announcing himself as Hatshepsut's divine father and another that depicted Thutmose I acknowledging Hatshepsut as his rightful heir. Other reliefs focused on the successful expeditions in which Senenmut played a major role—such as the obelisk project and the great trade expedition to the resource-rich land of Punt. As the overseer of the storehouse of Amun-Re, Senenmut had been directly involved in the distribution of the trade items.

While these images of both religious and political events confirm Hatshepsut's confidence in Senenmut's advice, it is the personal images of

Wearer of the royal seal, companion, great in love, chief steward, Senenmut.

—Inscription Senenmut had carved on rock at the quarry site for Hatsheput's obelisks

Senenmut that reveal the close relationship between the two. Archaeologists have discovered numerous reliefs of Senenmut that artisans carved into the walls of temple niches and doorjambs. Although these locations made them difficult to see, that they were even included in the building design is surprising. Hatshepsut must have approved their placement, for it is difficult to believe that Senenmut would have done so without consulting her first. Certainly, no other adviser, no other nonroyal, had ever been so honored.

Archaeologists have also uncovered more than 20 statues of Senenmut in other buildings whose construction he oversaw. Such discoveries have led Egyptologists to believe that Senenmut was Hatshepsut's closest adviser and confidant. On one statue that Hatshepsut commissioned and had carved in Senenmut's likeness, she had the artisans list a few of the more than 80 titles she conferred on Senenmut. She also had the artisans inscribe her praises of him: "He was so excellent for the royal heart . . . strong-hearted, not lax concerning the monuments of the lord of the gods . . . master of all people, chief of the whole land, steward of Amun, Senenmut . . . revered by the great god."

Like all Egyptians, Senenmut took time to prepare for the afterlife. He chose a site where many nobles of the period had their tombs. Today the area is called Sheikh Abd el Qurna. As his own power and prestige increased, Senenmut decided that his eternal resting place should be closer to Hatshepsut's and chose a tomb site just north of her temple at Deir el Bahri. He planned to locate his burial chamber directly under the outer court of Hatshepsut's mortuary temple. This was actually quite close to Hatshepsut's intended burial chamber beneath he temple. The rock cliff, however,

prevented workers from completing the tunnel that would have connected Hatshepsut's tomb site and mortuary temple. Thus, although Senenmut's burial chamber was completed as planned, Hatshepsut's was not.

Architecture and advising Hatshepsut were not Senenmut's only interests. Archaeologists have uncovered artifacts in both of his tombs that suggest he was a cultured person who enjoyed literature. Several texts, including *The Instruction of Amenemhet* and the *Tale of Sinuhe*, were found in the Sheikh Abd el Qurna tomb. The planetarium-like designs on the ceiling of his tomb at Deir el Bahri point to an interest in the stars and the workings of the universe.

After Senenmut has reached the pinnacle of power—a position second only to Hatshepsut's—his name suddenly disappears from the record. The reason remains a mystery; he may have assumed too much power, or, after the untimely death of Neferure, made an alliance with Thutmose III.

Approximately three years later, Hatshepsut herself disappears from the scene, again for unknown reasons. However, late in the reign of Thutmose III, orders were issued throughout the Two Lands to destroy everything related to Hatshepsut. Because Senenmut had allied himself so closely with Hatshepsut, Thutmose also ordered that Senenmut's name be deleted, erased, and forgotten as well. Creative talent, however, is not easily suppressed, and Senenmut's buildings have "lived" to immortalize him.

FURTHER READING

James, T. G. H. *Pharaoh's People: Scenes from Life in Imperial Egypt*, pp. 31–37. Chicago: University of Chicago Press, 1984.

Thutmose III

WORLD CONQUEROR

atshepsut was dead, and for Thutmose III, the long years of waiting were over. The throne of Egypt was finally his alone. It was true that, since his father's death some 21 years earlier, he had shared the throne with Hatshepsut, his stepmother, but he had not been allowed to really share the royal power. Now he intended to prove that he was worthy of the office and that he, like his grandfather Thutmose I, would make Egypt "the superior of every land" (taken from an inscription that recorded the works of Thutmose I). Soon after Hatshepsut's death, Thutmose had his chance.

A column of text on the back of this white marble statue identifies it as Thutmose III. Measuring about 11 inches high, it shows the king making a ritual offering of two round vessels. He wears the traditional royal pleated kilt and the royal striped headdress, called a *nemes*, and cobra-shaped *uraeus*.

In Syria and Palestine, the kingdoms subdued by Thutmose I had stopped paying the tribute required of them by treaty and were making plans to retake their own lands. Farther to the east, in the land between the Tigris and Euphrates valleys, a powerful people known as the Mitanni were also looking to extend their influence. They even sent envoys to kings in Syria and Palestine with offers of soldiers and equipment. Egyptian officials in these areas began sending Thutmose III reports of enemy troop mobilization, of former allies uniting against Egypt, and of enemy alliances being made with the Mitanni. Then came news that the prince of Kadesh, a city on the Orontes River in Syria, was leading his troops south into Palestine. Because indecision would further weaken Egypt's position, Thutmose immediately called his troops into action.

His goal was the conquest of Kadesh. But Kadesh was too far north, too entrenched in enemy territory. It made more sense to march east across the Sinai Peninsula and attack Megiddo, in Palestine, and other major cities to the south of Megiddo that had turned against Egypt. If Thutmose were victorious, Egyptian troops would have allies, not enemies, to their rear as they marched north.

Confident in his mission, Thutmose began the first of 17 military campaigns against Syria-Palestine. Thutmose had his private secretary inscribe the events of each campaign on leather rolls. He later had these accounts transcribed onto the walls of the temple dedicated to the great god Amun-Re at Karnak. To record dates, Thutmose had his scribe use the traditional format, which meant labeling a year according to how long the ruling king had been on the throne. Thus, Thutmose's first military campaign took place in Year 22. Even though the campaign took

place shortly after he became the sole ruler, Thutmose counted his regnal years (his time spent as king) from the moment he technically succeeded to the throne after his father's death.

Authors and years, however, are not as important as the records themselves, and those detailing Thutmose III's first campaign are the most complete and the most exciting. Within 10 days of the start of the march, Thutmose III had crossed the Sinai and reached the city of Gaza. An uncovered papyrus manuscript tells how, after Gaza fell to Egyptian forces, the king commissioned a general named Djehuty to lay siege to Joppa (present-day Jaffa) while he marched northward. Djehuty did as he was commanded, but he could not take the city. According to the manuscript, Djehuty ordered 200 large baskets made and brought to him as quickly as possible. After choosing 200 soldiers, he told each to step into a basket and carefully sealed all 200 lids. Djehuty commanded other soldiers to carry the baskets to the gates of Joppa. There they were to say that they were carrying the spoils of war captured by the prince of Joppa. When the gates opened, the basket carriers were to calmly walk within the gates. That night, under cover of darkness, they were to cut open the basket seals so that the soldiers inside them could leap up and open the gates of the city for Djehuty and his troops. The plan worked perfectly, and the next day Thutmose's clever general claimed control of Joppa.

Thutmose, meanwhile, had marched to the city of Yehem, where he called a meeting of his troops about how best to approach Megiddo. Of the three possible routes, two went along level ground and a third cut through a narrow pass in the hills. The officers spoke almost in unison against the third pass: "How is it that [we] should

go upon this [third] road, which threatens to be narrow? . . . Let our victorious commander proceed on the road he wishes; but cause us not to go by the difficult path."

Thutmose listened, but refused to be swayed by the officers' arguments. Why should he fear any road? "Let those of you who wish to follow the [easier] paths do so and let those who wish to take the narrow path follow me."

The soldiers shouted their approval—"We will follow your majesty wherever you go." Thutmose marched forward on foot and entered the narrow pass at the head of the troops. Such bravery gave strength to the troops who immediately followed his example.

Thutmose's strategy worked, and the enemy found themselves unable to counter the attack. Panicking, they turned in retreat, abandoning both their horses and chariots. The people within the walls of Megiddo, seeing

their army in complete confusion, barred all entrances to the city. They hauled their own retreating soldiers over the walls, "pulling them by their clothing."

Complete victory seemed certain, until the glint of gold and other spoils left by the retreating enemy distracted the Egyptian soldiers. Instead of pursuing the enemy to the walls and forcing open the gates, they pillaged the abandoned enemy campsites. Thutmose's scribe wrote in his journal, "If only the soldiers of his majesty had not given their heart to plundering the spoils of the enemy, they would have taken Megiddo . . . [rather, they] captured horses, chariots of gold and silver."

Thutmose saw no cause for rejoicing. The chance to defeat those who had conspired against him was lost because a desire for profit clouded the minds of his soldiers. After scolding them for their unprofessional actions, he ordered them to lay siege to the city.

Three Syrians bear gifts from their homeland for their Egyptian king. As Thutmose III extended Egyptian control north and east into the Syria-Palestine area, the tribute flowing into Egypt increased.

His majesty [Thutmose III] rejoiced exceedingly when he saw the great wonders that his father [Amun] had performed for him.

—Inscription on a large granite stele in the great temple to Amun-Re at Karnak

For seven months, those within and without the city's walls waited until finally the people of Megiddo could resist no longer.

The terms of surrender were quite lenient. Thutmose demanded tribute from Megiddo's citizens and placed an Egyptian governor in charge of the area. The spoils were considerable and included "340 living prisoners, 83 hands [by custom, the Egyptians cut off a hand from every dead enemy], 2,041 mares, 191 foals, 6 stallions, a chariot adorned with gold that had belonged to the ruler of Kadesh, a beautiful suit of bronze armor that belonged to the chief magistrate of Megiddo, 200 suits of armor belonging to his wretched army, 502 bows, 7 wooden poles adorned with silver that belonged to a tent of the enemy, 1,929 large cattle, and 20,500 white small cattle."

This first campaign was relatively brief—approximately 175 days from the time Thutmose marched into the Sinai to the time he returned to the royal palace at Thebes. Yet the tactics he used set the standard for all subsequent campaigns, and "lightning-speed" marches and sudden attacks became the trademark of his military style.

After returning to Thebes, Thutmose ordered a five-day victory feast, during which he had great quantities of food and beer distributed among the people. He also presented those whom he considered worthy of special honors with a variety of gifts. Yet, the most sig-nificant event for Thutmose seems to have been his purification in the temple of Amun-Re. Thutmose had brought with him on the campaign a small portable shrine of Amun-Re, but it was not the same as a temple service. With the help of the priests who sprinkled him with holy water and burned incense, Thutmose prepared to enter the innermost section of the temple, the area known to the Egyptians as the "Holy of Holies." To purify his mouth and make it worthy of uttering the proper prayers, Thutmose chewed a pellet of natron (a salt substance found along the banks of the Nile). With the darkness of the temple brightened only by the light from oil lamps, Thutmose opened the wooden door of Amun-Re's shrine. He looked upon the divine face of his "father" and performed the special ritual reserved only for Egypt's kings. At the end of the service, Thutmose closed the doors, sealed them shut with a clay seal, and swept the floor behind him with a broom to eliminate all trace of footsteps within the divine precinct.

Thutmose's scribe did not provide as much detail for the other 16 campaigns, but the record shows that Kadesh and its leaders continued to oppose Egyptian control. The goal of the sixth campaign was the conquest of Kadesh, because Thutmose believed that control of Syria and Palestine depended on his crushing Kadesh's opposition.

Having won control of the region to the south of Kadesh and of neighboring coastal areas, Thutmose could now transport his troops by boat from northern Egypt east along the coastline and up to the port city near Kadesh. After disembarking his army, he quickly led them overland and attacked Kadesh. This time, victory was his, and according to his scribe, "the children of the chiefs and their brothers were brought to be strongholds [that is, hostages] in Egypt. When any one of the chiefs died, his majesty [Thutmose] would return the son [who has been kept as a hostage in Egypt] to stand in his place."

This policy of using royal hostages to keep peace worked well for Thutmose and for his successors. Foreign rulers took the terms of the alliance treaty they had signed with Egypt very seriously, as their sons' lives depended on their allegiance to Thutmose and Egypt. And keeping foreign princes in Egypt had a second advantage. These princes learned the ways of the Egyptians and even adopted many Egyptian customs as their own. When they inherited the throne in their own kingdoms, they naturally felt affection for the country where they had spent their youth.

Whenever possible, Thutmose allowed the royal families in conquered territories to remain in power—as long as they agreed to maintain peace, pay an annual tribute, and cooperate fully with the Egyptian official assigned to oversee the lands in the area. This administrative policy won Thutmose the loyalty of leaders in lands that were militarily and economically important to Egypt. Centuries later, the Romans would follow this same policy as they set about organizing their vast empire.

Thumose, however, still faced opposition, especially in Kadesh and Mitanni. Therefore, he once again marched his troops to the coast, boarded them on seafaring vessels, and set out for the eastern coast of the

Mediterranean. Sailing from harbor to harbor, he forced city after city to submit to his rule, gathered what supplies (especially wheat and fruit) he needed for his garrisons, and stored provisions in granaries for future operations.

Thutmose then decided to conquer the Mitannians and other peoples who supplied and supported Egypt's enemies to the east. Unfortunately, his scribe wrote very little about this eighth campaign, but it was the most extensive. From Egypt, he sailed his troops along the eastern Mediterranean coast to Byblos, and then took them across the mountains of Lebanon and through the Orontes valley. With him were oxen pulling carts laden with the boats that would ferry his troops across the Euphrates River. Thutmose defeated the Mitannians with little difficulty and took several hundred soldiers as captives. In honor of his victory, he set up a commemorative marker near the one his grandfather Thutmose I had erected years earlier.

Accepting the Euphrates as the eastern boundary of his power, Thutmose III turned west. Surviving records tell of a near disaster. Only the quick thinking of an officer named Amenemhab saved Thutmose from being skewered on the tusks of a charging elephant. Amenemhab had leaped between the animal and the king and cut off the elephant's trunk. The account notes that Amenemhab had also saved the king's life in the battle for Kadesh. When the prince of Kadesh let a mare loose along the front lines to distract the stallions pulling the Egyptians' chariots, Amenemhab had bolted forward and chased the mare until he killed her. He brought her tail to Thutmose.

Despite Thutmose's military successes, the unrest continued and so, too, did the campaigns. To patrol the areas he conquered and to prevent insurrections, Thutmose ordered garrisons built on the coast, on hills, and at

other key sites. Even after he quashed opposition to his rule in most areas, Thutmose still organized campaigns—not as military expeditions, but as inspection and intimidation tours. Accounts of these later campaigns focus chiefly on the tremendous amounts of tribute and gifts that were pouring into Egypt, including hardwoods, copper ore, incense, sweet oils, bronze spears, and grains.

In Year 50, to keep the trade routes in and out of Nubia safe and accessible to Egyptian caravans and merchants, Thutmose led a campaign south into Nubia. When he reached the First Cataract, he was unable to use the canal dug by Senwosret III's workers because it had filled with sand, silt, and debris. Thutmose immediately ordered the canal cleared, and to prevent blockage in the future, he made cleaning the canal the yearly responsibility of the local fishermen. In Nubia, Thutmose met success everywhere and extended Egypt's southern border to Gebel Barkal, at the Fourth Cataract. He set up a boundary marker similar to the one he had left at the Euphrates.

Although much of his time was spent extending and fortifying Egypt's borders, Thutmose also focused attention on construction projects. Following his orders, architects, engineers, artisans, and laborers restored old temples and built new ones. Special attention was given to Amun-Re's temple at Karnak. Karnak had served as Egypt's major religious center for approximately 500 years, and Thutmose had an official king list inscribed on the walls with 62 names, each accompanied by an image of the king. Thutmose did not, however, have the kings listed in chronological order.

Thutmose also chose Karnak as the site for a special black granite stele about six feet in height. On it, he had his artisans carve his "Hymn of Victory" (25 lines that celebrate the victories and conquests of his reign).

Thutmose III

POSITION

King of Egypt

REIGN

About 1504–1450 B.C.

ACCOMPLISHMENTS

Led 17 military campaigns into the Syria-Palestine area and brought the area under Egyptian control; extended the boundaries of Egyptian rule to the Euphrates; defeated the Mitannians; established the foundation of the Egyptian Empire; led a military campaign against Nubia and extended Egyptian control as far as the Fourth Cataract; cleared the canal that bypassed the First Cataract; rebuilt and restored many temples and buildings; refurbished the Karnak temple of Amun and commissioned many new buildings erected there; brought peace to Egypt and the lands under its control; encouraged trade expeditions; filled Egypt's treasury with tributes and gifts from conquered lands and allies

Thutmose's successors followed his example and encouraged this new style of poetic literature.

To design the extensive changes he envisioned at Karnak, Thutmose chose a master architect named Ineni, who had worked there years earlier. Because Thutmose III wished to disassociate himself from Hatshepsut, Ineni designed a sandstone covering to hide all but the tips of the two giant obelisks Hatshepsut had set up near the entrance to the temple area. This "cover-up" proved a boon for archaeologists because it preserved the inscriptions on the obelisks. Thutmose then had another pair of obelisks set up at Karnak. Today one stands in Istanbul, Turkey, and the other in Rome, Italy. The obelisk in New York City's Central Park dates to Thutmose's reign as well, but it was commissioned to adorn Amun's temple at Heliopolis.

Thutmose also had Ineni design and construct a great Festival Hall. Here, Thutmose planned to celebrate the traditional Heb-Sed, a festival that proved a king's fitness to rule and commemorated the unification of Lower and Upper Egypt. What made Thutmose's Festival Hall unique was the design of the central columns. Each was shaped like a tent pole and was positioned so that the thickest part of the column was at the top. Behind the Festival Hall, in a small room known as the "botanical garden," Thutmose had his artists display flowers and animals he had seen while on campaign in the East. One animal that particularly fascinated Thutmose was "a bird that lays an egg every day" (thought today to be a chicken).

Thutmose also chose Karnak as the place to dedicate a special copper plate. Once, to prove his ability as a marksman, Thutmose had ordered his chariot driver to ride by targets made of copper plates (according to the records, a plate measured about four fingers in width). Each plate was on a pole, and as the chariot raced by, Thutmose shot an arrow at a plate. His strength was such that the arrow flew across the field, pierced the copper plate, and stopped only after it poked out the other side.

Sometime late in his reign, Thutmose issued orders to erase Hatshepsut's name from all monuments and records. Excavators have found countless markers, inscriptions, and monuments with the section that once gave praise to Hatshepsut neatly cut out.

As his burial complex, Thutmose chose a site halfway up a rock cliff in the Valley of the Kings. Its design followed the traditional pattern for royal tombs of the period, with an entrance stairway and a corridor leading down to a well shaft. Along the walls artisans painted the *kheker* frieze (a stylized motif that resembled a protective type of fence). The ceiling was painted with stars to simulate the sky. Adorning the walls of the antechamber, the room that preceded the burial chamber, were stick-figure representations of the gods and goddesses found in the *Amduat* ("The Book of the Secret Chamber" or "The Book of What Is in the Underworld"). Following the practice that had developed in recent decades, a short flight of stone steps carved into the rock cliff led from the antechamber down to the burial chamber itself. Recorded on the two columns standing in the middle of the chamber was the hymn to the sun god, known as the "Litany of Re."

Here, too, were scenes representing the hours as described in the *Book of the Secret Chamber*. According to the Egyptians, every night the sun god traveled through the 12 divisions of the underworld, and this journey, in turn, corresponded to the 12 hours of night. To represent this concept graphically, the Egyptians pictured various deities as the representatives of each hour. Thus, in Thutmose's tomb, a series of squatting baboons, each accompanied by text designed to help and instruct the deceased, represents the first hour. The complete text of *The Book of the Secret Chamber* has been found only in the tomb of Thutmose III and of his successor Amenhotep II.

About 400 years after Thutmose's death, the priests in charge of the royal tombs in the Valley of the Kings took drastic steps to foil robbers who were plundering the site. They entered the tombs and gathered the mummies, including Thutmose's. They reburied them in a new site at Deir el Bahri, where they remained until the late 1800s.

Thutmose was in his mid to late 60s when he died. His 18-year-old son and co-regent, Amenhotep, succeeded him. Modern analysis of Thutmose's remains show that this fearless warrior, hunter, and ruler was fairly short by modern standards—no more than five feet, three inches tall.

Soon after Thutmose's death his deeds became legendary, and a cult developed that honored his memory. Thus, the words he had the god Amun-Re speak in the "Hymn of Victory" seem most appropriate:

> Thutmose, living forever, who has done for me all that my *ka* desired . . . [y]our monuments are greater than those of any king who has been.

FURTHER READING

Lichtheim, Miriam. *Ancient Egyptian Literature: A Book of Readings*, vol. 2, pp. 29–39. Berkeley: University of California Press, 1976.

Pritchard, James B., ed. *The Ancient Near East: An Anthology of Texts and Pictures*, pp. 175–182. Princeton, N.J.: Princeton University Press, 1958.

Rekhmire

SECOND ONLY
TO THE KING

As Rekhmire approached the gate to the royal palace, the chief official cleared the way before him, and the courtiers bowed low as a sign of their respect. All knew the pharaoh, Thutmose III, had summoned Rekhmire to his audience chamber so that he could officially name him vizier of Egypt. Soon all Egypt would know Rekhmire's name, as the office of vizier brought with it authority that was second only to the king's. Dressed in his finest white linen garment to match the solemnity of the occasion, Rekhmire stood firm and resolute as he listened to Thutmose's instructions:

> Be watchful over all that is done [within the vizier's room]. That is the foundation block of the whole land . . . as for the office of vizier, it is definitely not pleasant. Indeed, it is as bitter as gall. See to it that you do everything in accordance with the stipulations of the law and with what is right . . . consider the person whom you do not know the same as a person you know. The official who acts in this manner shall

Fine detail and a sense of calm characterize this delicate drawing of a girl playing the harp. It was just one of many scenes adorning the walls of Rekhmire's tomb at Sheikh Abd el Qurna.

Being vizier is definitely not pleasant . . . it is as bitter as gall.

—Inscription on the wall of Rekhmire's tomb

In this detail from a wall painting in Rehkmire's tomb, two workmen at the lower left and upper right use ropes and poles to balance heavy loads of stone building blocks on their shoulders. The figures to the left and above are making mud bricks.

succeed greatly. . . . Do not be angry at a person unjustly, but be angry concerning those matters about which you should be angry. . . . A just official is one who truly inspires respect.

Rekhmire knew well the advice that Thutmose was giving him. Years earlier, Thutmose had addressed the same words to Rekhmire's uncle Woser after naming him vizier. Neither Woser nor Rekhmire was a member of the royal family. After the 4th Dynasty, about 1,000 years earlier, rulers had abandoned the practice of only naming members of the royal family to key government positions. In the intervening centuries, the appointment of competent people regardless of their social status had become the procedure. As a result, throughout Egypt, many nonroyals held powerful posts. These officials encouraged their children and even their other relatives to prepare themselves

to inherit the positions. Rekhmire's succeeding his uncle as vizier was just one example.

Rekhmire did an admirable job. Nowhere in surviving texts is there any hint of scandal; nowhere is there any mention of his dismissal or replacement by a more capable person. Thutmose recognized Rekhmire's loyalty and gave him permission to build a magnificent tomb for himself. As the site, Rekhmire chose the limestone hills on the west bank of the Nile at Sheikh Abd el Qurna—a favored burial site with nobles and high-ranking officials.

Rekhmire had no desire to be innovative in the overall plan for his tomb. Therefore, he ordered his workers to follow the basic reversed "T" design used by nobles and officials at the time. First came an open courtyard or garden. From here a narrow passageway led into a broad hall. A second passageway—

Rekhmire

POSITION

Vizier of Egypt

ACTIVE DATES

About 1460 B.C.

ACCOMPLISHMENTS

Fulfilled the duties of vizier—legal, military, economic, and social—during the second half of the rule of Thutmose III and the beginning of the rule of Amenhotep II; superintended the collection of tribute from conquered peoples, gifts from allies, and taxes from Egyptians; built a large tomb at Sheikh Abd el Qurna; left on his tomb walls a listing of the duties of a vizier, which has proved to be one of the most important surviving documents from ancient Egypt

When I judged a defendant, I was unbiased; nor did I act in any way for the purpose of a reward.

—Inscription from the tomb of Rekhmire

also very narrow—connected the hall to a corridor approximately 88 feet long. At the end was another chamber with a recessed area where, following custom, Rekhmire would have workers place a statue of himself. Behind the statue, workers painted the traditional "false door" through which Rekhmire's *ka* (life force) could reenter the world of the living and obtain whatever it needed for its survival.

Excavation teams have not found Rekhmire's burial chamber or his mummy, but they did notice the damaged condition of the wall paintings. Because the damage appears to be a form of vandalism, some historians think that Thutmose turned against Rekhmire, and as a result, Rekhmire's mummy never entered this tomb.

Along the walls of the corridor, which was larger and grander than those found in tombs belonging to others of his rank, Rekhmire had artisans list his duties and responsibilities as vizier. He also had them adorn the walls with scenes of events and incidents that had taken place while he held the office. Included are detailed descriptions of how, where, and with whom a vizier should prepare himself to receive petitioners. The inscriptions also make it clear that no vizier could pass new laws or rescind old ones—such rights belonged solely to the king. However, it was a vizier's duty to make sure everyone obeyed the laws and that those who did not were punished.

As to Rekhmire's role at the judicial hearings, the hieroglyphs are quite specific:

> While holding hearings, the vizier [as the Chief Judge] shall sit on a [special] chair, with a reed mat on the floor . . . a cushion under his back, a cushion under his feet . . . a scepter in his hand and the 40 leather straps shall be open before him. Then the chiefs of the South [Upper Egypt] shall stand . . . in front of him, with the Overseer of the Cabinet on his right, the Supervisor of Clients on his left, and the scribes of the vizier at either side—each man at his proper place. Let one petitioner be heard after another, without allowing the petitioner who is behind to be heard before the one who is in front.

The text continues with more instructions for Rekhmire: After he seated himself and listened to the petitioners and then to the overseers, he was to make his daily report to the king, if the king was in residence at Thebes at the time. When Thutmose was away, Rekhmire kept the king informed through messages sent by a courier.

Rekhmire's duties included collecting taxes and foreign tribute, receiving foreign envoys, settling boundary lines, overseeing the grain supplies, and surveying the land along the Nile after the flood season so that his engineers could re-mark the boundary lines and reopen irrigation canals. Rekhmire was not expected to accomplish all these tasks by himself. Following the example of his

Going forth over the land every morning to do the daily favors . . . not preferring the great above the humble, rewarding the oppressed . . . bringing the evil to him who committed it.

—Inscription on Rekhmire's tomb

predecessors, he used assistants to gather the information he needed to make wise and unbiased decisions. Rekhmire also depended on his aides for news of problems and internal conflicts.

Because his role in tax- and tribute-collecting was important, Rekhmire had the artisans decorate the walls of the great hall in his burial complex with paintings of envoys and taxpayers bringing their goods. He also had himself pictured with scribes who were responsible for recording the items presented, the name of each presenter, and the country of origin. Much of this list has survived, and the entries include huge jars of honey, strips of cedarwood, weights of gold, apes, bows, oxen, jewelry, bead necklaces, chests of linen material, pigeons, grain, and bread. A Nubian holds a panther on a leash. Two other Nubians appear to be coaxing a giraffe with a monkey climbing on its neck to move forward. A fourth Nubian carries a great elephant tusk across his shoulders. Syrian envoys offer beautiful vases and horse-drawn chariots.

The inscriptions on another wall area in the tomb focus on Rekhmire's responsibilities as inspector of all crafts. Here the artisans depict Rekhmire reviewing the work of jewelers, goldsmiths, coppersmiths, carpenters and cabinetmakers, crafters of stone vases, and sculptors. A scene in a goldsmith shop shows a scribe recording the weight of each piece of gold given a goldsmith. (To prevent thievery, officials weighed every object the goldsmith fashioned to make sure the weight of the finished product matched the weight of the original piece of gold.)

Carpentry was another trade that required skill and talent. In Rekhmire's painted "carpenter's shop," carpenters work with adzes and saws. They also

brush walls with plaster or a similar substance. Round about their shops lie finished objects, including a fan handle, a headrest, and a table. Other scenes show carpenters busily crafting shrines and objects for temple use. An accompanying inscription names Rekhmire as the source of inspiration for the designs the carpenters will produce. It was Rekhmire's responsibility to make sure that all workers observed the prescribed standards of quality.

Rekhmire worked many hours at his job, but he also spent time relaxing. And it was these happy times that he also wanted with him in the next life. For this reason, he commissioned scenes of festival celebrations to be painted on the walls of the long corridor. In some, he relaxes at a banquet with his wife Meryt and their sons and daughters. In others, dancers whirl about as musicians play the harp, lute, and drum.

To ensure a smooth passage from this world to the next, Rekhmire asked his artisans to depict the traditional funeral and burial rites along the hall and corridor walls. One scene shows his children bringing the traditional offerings of food and drink. Another depicts the most important burial ritual—the Opening of the Mouth ceremony. The tomb designs that pay eternal tribute to Rekhmire's achievements have also given Egyptologists invaluable information.

FURTHER READING

Lichtheim, Miriam. *Ancient Egyptian Literature: A Book of Readings*, vol. 2, pp. 21–24. Berkeley: University of California Press, 1976.

Tooley, Angela M. J. *Egyptian Models and Scenes.* Buckinghamshire, England: Shire, 1995.

More Ancient Egyptians to Remember

Seqenenre Tao II (active about 1574 B.C.) ruled from Thebes, the chief city in Upper Egypt. Determined to drive the Hyksos who controlled Lower Egypt from Egyptian soil, he advanced against these foreigners. A later folktale gives a reason for the conflict between Seqenenre and the Hyksos king Apepi I (also known as Apophis). According to the tale, Apepi was upset because the roaring of the hippopotamuses in Thebes was keeping him awake—from 500 miles away at his palace in Lower Egypt! He wanted Seqenenre to attend to the matter.

Seqenenre's mummy, uncovered in the royal cache at Deir el Bahri in 1881, reveals that he died in a violent struggle. His skull bears the marks of terrible wounds—gouges inflicted most likely by one or more enemies wielding a dagger, ax, spear, and maybe even a mace. Seqenenre's two sons, Kamose and Ahmose, continued the struggle against the Hyksos. Kamose also led forces north and succeeded in extending Egyptian control as far the Hyksos capital at Avaris. Inscriptions at Karnak tell of Kamose launching an offensive against Nubia. His intent was probably to prevent the Nubian king from helping Apepi by attacking the Egyptians from the South. Under Ahmose's rule, Seqenenre's goal of expelling the Hyksos became a reality.

Ahmose I (active about 1570–46 B.C.) was quite young when he succeeded Kamose on the throne. His mother, Queen Ahhotep, most likely ruled as regent for a while. The Hyksos took advantage of the situation and began retaking land they had lost to Kamose. When Ahmose came of age he quickly proved himself a strong leader. In a series of campaigns, he captured Memphis, the traditional capital of Upper and Lower Egypt, and forced the Hyksos to retreat farther north into the Delta region. Ahmose then laid siege to Avaris. After taking the city, Ahmose drove the intruders

The Egyptians often used wooden sledges on rollers drawn by oxen to transport medium-size stone blocks. Ahmose's workmen would have used this method in temple restoration.

The images on this painted limestone honor Ahmose-Nefertari (right), and her son Amenhotep I (left). It is thought that the term "pharaoh" was first used to refer to Egypt's ruler during the reign of Ahmose-Nefertari's husband, Ahmose I.

out of Egypt and pursued the retreating army to Sharuhen, a Hyksos stronghold in Palestine. After a six-year siege, Sharuhen finally surrendered to Ahmose. Years later, one of Ahmose I's naval officers, Ahmose, son of Ebana, recorded on the walls of his tomb details of these battles and of Ahmose's other campaigns. Ahmose also advanced his troops into Nubia and reestablished Egyptian control south of the Second Cataract. To the east, Ahmose sought Egyptian access to trade routes that crisscrossed the Mediterranean Sea and marched into southern Palestine. Ahmose then turned his attention to domestic matters. He rebuilt irrigation systems, restored temples, and appointed people whom he could trust to positions of authority.

After a reign of approximately 25 years, Ahmose I died. History remembers him as the founder of the 18th Dynasty and credits him with establishing the foundation on which the Egyptian Empire would be built. Ahmose's tomb site remains to be discovered, but in 1881, at Deir el Bahri, archaeologists uncovered his mummy, garlanded with pale blue delphinium flowers. Further examination revealed that he was a thin person with excellent teeth but that he suffered from arthritis, especially in his knees.

Ahmose-Nefertari (active about 1580–40 B.C.) was the wife of Ahmose I, the mother of Amenhotep I, and the mother-in-law of Thutmose I. Most likely she was also the daughter of Seqenenre Tao II and his Great Royal

Wife. After Ahmose died, she served as regent for Amenhotep. Later, Amenhotep showed her great respect and, after her death, established a religious cult in her honor. The people of Deir el Medina, the village established to house the skilled artisans who worked on the royal tombs in the Valley of the Kings, looked to Ahmose-Nefertari as their patron deity. For approximately 500 years, her name was included in the inscriptions carved into the walls of private tombs and on public monuments.

In 1881, in the burial chamber now numbered Tomb DB320 (at Deir el Bahri), archaeologists found the enormous coffin of Ahmose-Nefertari. It was fashioned, as was the custom at the time, in the shape of a human figure, with feet together, arms crossed over the chest, and an ankh in each hand. The *cartonnage* (a combination of mainly linen and plaster) cover on her face had been shaped to resemble a head and shoulders and was painted with an idealized picture of the queen. Because Egyptian priests some 450 years after Ahmose-Nefertari's death reburied many royal mummies in DB320, it is unclear whether the remains found inside the coffin are actually those of the queen. Further research and testing, especially of DNA samples, may someday provide the answers.

Thutmose I (active about 1524–18 B.C.) followed Amenhotep I on the throne of Egypt. He had served as Amenhotep's co-regent during the last years of his reign. He was not the king's son, but he may have been a relative. To protect Egypt's interests in Nubia, he advanced his troops as far as the Fourth Cataract on the Nile. Thutmose

A black granite sculpture of Thutmose I, in a traditional royal pose: seated with his hands on his lap.

then looked east, followed the route the retreating Hyksos had taken into Syria, and led his troops as far as the Euphrates River.

In thanksgiving to the gods, Thutmose placed the master architect Ineni in charge of refurbishing the great temple complex dedicated to Amun-Re at Karnak. Thutmose also placed Ineni in charge of building his tomb. Ineni chose a new site—a secluded ravine that is known today as the Valley of the Kings. Nearby, in Deir el Medina, a village was established for the skilled workers on his tomb and mortuary temple.

Thutmose's reign had been feverish with activity both on the battlefield and throughout Egypt. Yet it was a short reign, lasting just over six years. To ensure the line of succession, especially considering that both his sons by his Great Royal Wife had predeceased him, Thutmose married Hatshepsut, his daughter by his Great Royal Wife, to a son he had fathered with a minor queen.

4 Splendor and Revolution (New Kingdom, about 1440–1293 B.C.)

 The cities and the rocky cliffs that rose above the sands bordering the Nile River hummed with construction. Trade caravans and graceful boats crafted to take advantage of the Nile's current and light winds crisscrossed Upper Egypt and Lower Egypt with imports and exports. Egypt's merchants traveled the trade routes of the eastern Mediterranean world as well, and envoys from the Aegean islands brought gifts to Egypt's rulers. It was a time of prosperity and strength. Egypt had an abundance of goods such as grains, papyrus, textiles, and dried fish. With these, Egyptian merchants could barter for whatever goods they needed or wanted. Although rich in natural resources, Egypt did lack such resources as gold and hardwoods, both of which were critical to maintaining the high standard of living the Egyptians now enjoyed.

Later historians would refer to this period, the 18th Dynasty, as one of the grandest of the New Kingdom and, indeed, one of the greatest periods in Egyptian history. Thutmose III had extended Egypt's power and influence east to the banks of the Euphrates and south to the Fourth Cataract. As a result, tribute from conquered nations and gifts from those who wished to ally themselves with so powerful a neighbor added to the country's wealth. Thutmose's son, Amenhotep II, had continued his father's policies, although he was more ruthless and vindictive toward those whom he considered enemies.

However, as Egypt changed from a land centered on activity along the Nile to an international power, its economy and the lifestyle of its people changed as well. Because foreign traders and a growing number of prisoners and slaves from other lands now made their way up the Nile, Egyptians were constantly being introduced to new languages, new religious ideas, and new customs.

Two constants, however, remained: the annual flooding of the Nile and the worship of the sun god. Although irrigation canals and other technology had increased the amount of arable land, a good harvest depended on the annual deposit of silt left by the floodwaters. The building of new temples and the refurbishing of old temples at Karnak and Heliopolis reflected the Egyptian belief that life depended on the sun god Amun-Re. The king was no longer regarded as a divine being, but he was still considered the human representative of the sun god here on Earth.

Part 4 of *Ancient Egyptians* profiles people who inherited a strong and prosperous kingdom and continued the policies that had transformed the Two Lands along the Nile into a strong empire. It also focuses on a brief period in Egyptian history when a king's belief in the Aten rather than in Amun-Re temporarily changed the basic principles of Egyptian tradition.

This relief of Asian and Nubian soldiers was uncovered in Akhenaten's city of Akhetaten. As Egyptian control extended farther south and east, the troops in Egyptian armies came from many parts of the region.

Amenhotep III

THE MAGNIFICENT

Amenhotep was about 12 years old when he succeeded his father, Thutmose IV. Because of his youth, his mother, Mutemwia, was named regent. Although she was not of royal blood, she was, according to most Egyptologists, the daughter of Egyptians who had close ties to the royal family. The tradition that the Great Royal Wife had to be a member of the royal family was no longer as important. The same was true when Amenhotep's mother and his advisers made arrangements for him to marry Tiye. Like Mutemwia, Tiye was a nonroyal and the daughter of influential Egyptians who held high-ranking government positions. In the years to come, Tiye herself would become adept at handling government matters and at advising her husband. Amenhotep and Tiye had at least two sons and four daughters. After the death of their oldest son, their second son became Amenhotep's heir and successor. This son would ascend the throne as Amenhotep IV, although history would remember him by the name he later chose for himself—Akhenaten.

Unlike his predecessors, Amenhotep III did not need to prove Egypt's military might. Egypt had become the dominant force in the eastern Mediterranean, and few rulers dared oppose him. Records tell of some unrest in Year 5 at Ibhet, in Nubia, that was quickly quelled. On a stele honoring this victory, Amenhotep had workers carve the following:

> [A messenger] came to tell his majesty: "Kush [the Egyptian name for Upper Nubia] has planned rebellion in . . . his heart." His majesty [Amenhotep] led on unto his victory and completed it on his first victorious campaign. His majesty went forth . . . like Montu [the Theban god of war] . . . [Amenhotep] was a fierce-eyed lion and he seized Kush.

Amenhotep also recorded other events—neither political nor military—on the underside of large stone scarabs. Other kings had commissioned artisans to inscribe two or three words honoring a significant event or achievement on a scarab, but Amenhotep seems to have been the only one who issued a series of these scarabs, each with an inscription recording a specific event. Actually, Amenhotep used his stone scarabs much like news bulletins, and excavators have unearthed them at sites as far south as Soleb in the Sudan and as far north as Ras Sharma in Syria.

The scarab as an art form was an Egyptian tradition. For centuries, Egyptians had worn amulets (charms with magical powers thought to ward off evil), and the scarab was one of the most popular. Made of a hard material such as stone, gold, or gems, the scarab was shaped to resemble a dung beetle and was identified with the all-powerful, life-giving sun. The Egyptians saw a beetle push a ball of dung into a hole

Live . . . Amenhotep, ruler of Thebes; beloved lord of Amun . . . given life . . . that he may rule the Two Lands, like Re, forever.

—Inscription on the monument in Amenhotep's mortuary temple at Thebes

The battered and worn ruins of this 60-foot statue of a seated Amenhotep III attest to the lasting craftsmanship of the sculptors.

from which young beetles later emerged. They did not realize that the mother beetle laid her eggs in the dung. For the ancient Egyptians, the beetle represented the daily rebirth of the sun because they saw a parallel between the sun's rise each day and what they believed was the rebirth of the beetle. Thus they came to depict the sun as a round ball being pushed across the sky by a beetle.

Amenhotep's first scarab dates to Year 2 of his reign and commemorates his marriage to Tiye. The second dates to the same year and records Amenhotep's prowess as a hunter of wild cattle. Here he followed precedent —his father and grandfather had both been great sportsmen.

Amenhotep's favorite sport, however, seems to have been lion hunting.

In Year 10, Amenhotep ordered a third scarab issued. This time, the inscription carved onto the flat underside read as follows: "Number of lions which his majesty brought down with his own arrows from Year 1 to Year 10: fierce lions, 102."

The fourth scarab was also commissioned in Year 10. This one honored Amenhotep's marriage to Gilukhepa, the daughter of Shuttarna II, king of Mitanni. Because the Mitannians and the Egyptians had been archenemies for years, the marriage must have been a political one. It does not seem to have affected Queen Tiye's position, especially since Amenhotep had Tiye's name and title linked with his own on this scarab.

The fifth and final scarab told of Amenhotep's command in "Year 11,

On the underside of Amenhotep III's third commemorative scarab (a stone beetle), an inscription records that he killed 102 lions in the first 10 years of his reign. The scarab is about 2 1/4 inches long.

third month of the first season [akhet, the time when the Nile overflowed its banks], day 1 . . . to make a lake for the Great King's Wife, Tiye. . . . His majesty celebrated the feast of the opening of the lake [two weeks later] when he sailed on the lake in the royal barge *Aten-Gleams*." (The Egyptians considered the god Aten a form of the sun god Amun-Re.) If the inscription is accurate, then the laborers must have completed the entire project in 15 days! Quite an accomplishment, considering that the lake was just over a mile long and about a quarter of a mile wide. Its exact location has been debated for years, but many historians believe it lay on the west bank of the Nile at Thebes.

Temples were also important to Amenhotep, just as they been to his predecessors. And Amenhotep did not confine to Egypt his building of new temples and repairing of old ones. He ordered several temples built in Nubia, including one at Soleb, which he dedicated to himself, Tiye, and the god Amun-Re. This identification of the royal couple as deities whom the Nubians should worship set a precedent that his successors would follow.

The focus of Amenhotep's building efforts, however, was at Karnak. Records credit him and his architects—especially the twin brothers Suti and Hor—with the construction of the main portion of the temple at Luxor and with the great processional avenue linking this temple with the Karnak temple to Amun-Re. Bordering each side of the great avenue was a row of ram-headed stone sphinxes. The ram heads were appropriate because the ram was sacred to Amun-Re.

Amenhotep also added the Third Pylon (a massive ornamental gateway) at the entrance to the Karnak temple. In front of the pylon, workers began construction on the great hypostyle hall (a roofed area supported by rows of pillars) with a central aisle of massive stone columns that artisans later decorated with brilliantly colored designs. Skilled craftsmen crowned the columns with capitals carved to resemble lotus buds. Once a year, as part of the Festival of Opet rituals, priests carried Amun-Re's statue from the Karnak temple to the Luxor temple.

Amenhotep and his architects seem to have had a special preference for size, particularly oversize statues. The ram-headed sphinxes are only one example. To adorn the colonnade of the temple at Luxor, Amenhotep had his artisans sculpt a six-foot-high pink-quartzite statue of himself. When it was rediscovered in 1989, the statue was still intact, its head crowned with the double crown of Lower and Upper Egypt and its stance that of a powerful, confident ruler.

To adorn the temple at Karnak that was dedicated to Mut, the great goddess and wife of Amun-Re, Amenhotep had 600 black granite statues fashioned in the likeness of the lion-headed goddess Sekhmet. At Soleb in Nubia, two enormous rose-granite lions—both in a reclining position—stood guard before the temple Amenhotep dedicated to himself, his wife, and Amun-Re. The effect must have been breathtaking, especially if one considers that an ancient inscription described the temple as "finished with fine white sandstone . . . its floor adorned with silver, and all its portals are of gold." Two enormous stone statues of baboons that Amenhotep ordered erected at Hermopolis-Magna in Upper Egypt also still stand.

Amenhotep also took time to focus on his personal needs, and he chose a site at Malkata on the west bank of the Nile for his palace. This was not, however, to be a single compound with rooms only for Amenhotep and his

Amenhotep III

POSITION
King of Egypt

REIGN
About 1886–49 B.C.

ACCOMPLISHMENTS
Ended a revolt in Kush (Lower Nubia); kept peace throughout the Egyptian Empire and with foreign rulers; promoted international trade; refurbished many temples and monuments throughout Egypt and the lands controlled by Egypt; built a new temple to Amun at Thebes; ordered the avenue linking Karnak and Thebes lined on both sides with huge reclining ram-headed sphinxes; built an enormous mortuary temple on the west bank at Thebes and had two colossal seated statues of himself (the so-called Colossi of Memnon) placed before the entrance; built an enormous palace at Malkata

His eye is the sun, making brightness for all . . . his two hands hold power, his word bears victory.

—Inscription on the pylon Amenhotep erected at Karnak

immediate family, but instead a small city covering more than 80 acres and including several royal residences. Most likely one was for Queen Tiye. Another may have been for his daughter Sitamun, whom records suggest he also married. Here, too, were administrative quarters, houses for senior palace officials, and quarters specially designed for the minor royal wives and other wives in Amenhotep's harem. One of the most important areas was the festival hall where the Sed, or Heb-Sed, celebration was held. He even had his architects design guest rooms for all high-ranking Egyptian officials who would be attending the festival, as well as for ambassadors from conquered territories and from nations whose leaders had pledged their allegiance to Egypt. As was the custom, Amenhotep celebrated his first Sed jubilee in the 30th year of his reign. He celebrated his second in Year 34, and a third in Year 37. He died before he could celebrate another Heb-Sed in this life.

The palace buildings were mostly one level. Because they were made of mud bricks and not stone, little has survived. Yet here, too, size and grandeur were the chief characteristics. Decorating the walls were delightful scenes of animals and flowers. The design shows a preference for fine illustration and reflects an Eastern influence.

More important to Amenhotep than his royal palace, however, was his burial complex. Like his father, he, too, had his mortuary temple built on the west bank of the Nile, in an area that was separated by rock cliffs from his tomb in the Valley of the Kings. On a black granite stele positioned within the mortuary temple Amenhotep had workers carve the following inscription:

[Amenhotep] made it [the temple] as his monument for his father, Amun, lord of Thebes . . . an eternal, everlasting fortress of fine white sandstone, adorned with gold throughout. Its floor is decorated with silver, all the portals with electrum. . . . It resembles the horizon in . . . heaven when Re rises therein. . . . Its storehouse is filled with male and female slaves, with children of the princes of all the countries of the captivity of his . . . majesty. Its storehouses contain all good things, whose number is not known.

For Amenhotep, as for his predecessors, his mortuary temple was exactly what its name indicated, a "house of millions of years." Unfortunately, some 150 years after his death, a king named Merneptah ordered his workers to use Amenhotep's temple as a quarry. Because Merneptah had chosen to build his mortuary temple on land just northeast of Amenhotep's temple, it was easier to have his workers dismantle Amenhotep's temple than to have them quarry new stone blocks and columns. Merneptah did not, however, touch the two colossal statues of a seated Amenhotep placed directly before the entrance to the temple. Cut from a single block of stone, each statue measured approximately 68 feet in height and weighed about 270 tons.

Today the statues still stand, but in a much battered state. And they are not associated with Amenhotep anymore. Centuries after the king's death, Greek travelers to Thebes began calling the statues "the Colossi of Memnon." According to Greek mythology, Memnon was the king of the Ethiopians and the son of Eos, the Greek goddess of the dawn. In the great war fought between the Greeks and the Trojans (the Trojan War is traditionally dated to around 1180 B.C.), Memnon allied himself with the Trojans and was killed by the Greek hero Achilles. His body was supposedly buried at the feet of the two statues.

When an earthquake shook the ground beneath the statues in 27 B.C., it created a crack in the stone of the more northerly statue. Soon after, visitors began noticing that, when the rays of the sun first fell upon this statue in the morning, it gave a sound like the twang of a harp. Imagination came into play, and the story spread that the sound was Memnon's voice calling a morning greeting to his mother Eos. Around A.D. 200, the Roman emperor Septimus Severus learned of the crack and ordered it filled. No records survive to tell of his reaction when he learned the statue no longer "moaned" at dawn. (The scientific explanation of the "moan" is much different: The noise was probably the result of the sun's heat drying up the moisture that had formed in the crack during the cooler night hours.)

Amenhotep did not follow precedent when he chose his burial site. Instead of the East Valley in the Valley of the Kings, he opted for the West Valley. But he did have his architects use the traditional tomb plan and adorn the walls of the burial chamber with scenes from the *Amduat*. Adjoining the principal burial chamber were two other burial chambers. One was most likely intended for Queen Tiye and the other for Queen Sitamun. More than 3,000 years later, in 1799, engineers assigned to accompany the French emperor Napoleon to Egypt discovered Amenhotep's tomb, but no mummy. In the 1880s, Egyptologists discovered two burial places where ancient Egyptian priests reburied royal mummies to keep them from robbers. Amenhotep's mummy is believed to be one of the mummies found in these tombs. Positive identification is difficult, as his mummy suffered much abuse through the years and is in poor condition. The head is now completely detached, and the front part of the body is missing. Ancient robbers, in their ruthless search for treasures, often used an adze to hack a hole through the wrappings around the head and in the center of the chest. Also, the priests had placed the body thought to be Amenhotep's in a coffin inscribed with the name of Ramesses III (a much later ruler). Even the lid on this sarcophagus does not belong to Amenhotep, but to Seti II (another later ruler).

Further study of Amenhotep's mummy has revealed that he was about 50 years old when he died, an age that supports surviving accounts that credit him with a rule of approximately 38 years. His teeth were in terrible condition—full of holes as a result of cavities that had, in turn, caused abscesses in his gums. Amenhotep once asked his father-in-law, the Mitannian king Tushratta, to loan him a special statue of the goddess Ishtar that supposedly had healing properties. Surviving records indicate that Tushratta agreed to the request on the condition that Amenhotep return it to him when he was finished. Unfortunately for Amenhotep, the statue's "power" did not work, and his condition worsened. Amenhotep IV succeeded his father.

Archaeologists have uncovered more than 337 tablets that date from the last years of Amenhotep III's rule through some 20 years later, when Tutankhamun was king. Known as the Amarna Letters, because they were discovered at the excavation site called Tell el Amarna, these tablets are diplomatic correspondence between Amenhotep and his successors and rulers in the East. They are not written in hieroglyphs or hieratic script (a simplified system of writing also used by the Egyptians), but in cuneiform (wedge-shaped characters used in ancient Akkadian, Babylonian, and Persian inscriptions). The texts on these tablets clearly indicate that Amenhotep's successors followed his example in foreign policy. Full of details not found in any other records, they provide a unique glimpse into the lives of peoples and nations subdued by the Egyptians. In one, a man named Lab'ayu proclaims himself innocent of the charge that he had rebelled against Amenhotep III. He swears that he had merely defended himself against overaggressive neighbors. As proof of his unfailing loyalty, Lab'ayu states that he would kill himself should Amenhotep command that of him.

FURTHER READING

Fletcher, Joann. *Chronicle of a Pharaoh: The Intimate Life of Amenhotep III*. New York: Oxford University Press, 2000.

Lichtheim, Miriam. *Ancient Egyptian Literature: A Book of Readings*, vol. 2, pp. 43–48. Berkeley: University of California Press, 1976.

Tiye

![eye of Horus symbol]

THE QUEEN
AS DIPLOMAT

Love and marriage were not always synonymous in ancient Egypt, especially for members of the royal family. And Amenhotep III was no exception. Sometime in the second year of his rule, his advisers arranged for him to marry Tiye. Both were quite young—too young, in fact, to make such a decision for themselves. Amenhotep was about 14 years old, Tiye about 12. Although the match proved to be an excellent one, it did not conform to the rules observed by many of Egypt's kings.

This face and the *uraeus* (the cobra shape on the royal head-dress) belong to Queen Tiye, but the statue represents the goddess Isis, who sometimes was given the features of the reigning queen. The cow's horns circling the solar disk are symbols of the goddess Hathor.

Although robbers in ancient times had entered the tomb of Tiye's parents, Yuya and Tjuya, the ancients had resealed the tomb and excavators found many magnificent objects within, including Tjuya's gilded, inlaid funerary mask.

Tiye was not Amenhotep's sister, or even his half-sister. She was not even of royal blood. Tiye's parents came from Akhmim in Upper Egypt, which was a religious center for the fertility god Min. Tiye's father, a nobleman named Yuya, was the overseer of the royal stables and held the position of priest at the temple at Akhmim. Tiye's mother, Tjuya, held the honored post of Mistress of the Robes in Min's temple. Both were nonroyals, but their influence was considerable, and they wielded much power.

In 1905, archaeologists excavating in the Valley of the Kings made a surprising discovery. In the area reserved for Egypt's kings, they found the tomb of Yuya and Tjuya. Further digging brought the archaeologists face-to-face with Yuya and Tjuya. Both mummies were in good condition—actually, they are two of the best-preserved mummies thus far discovered in ancient Egypt. Tests indicate that Yuya was probably in his 60s when he died and Tjuya in her 50s. The embalming process had turned their hair yellow, but the faces still had a gentle and serene look. Yuya's body measured approximately five feet four inches; Tjuya's body approximately four feet nine inches. Both Tjuya's ears appeared to have been pierced twice for earrings, and her bones showed signs of arthritis.

Each coffin was beautifully decorated with thin hammered sheets of gold and silver. About the chamber were glass inlays, a jewel box, wooden containers painted to imitate decorated glass vases, bedsteads painted and decorated with gold and silver leaf, a chariot, and a wig basket. The finds provide a glimpse into the world in which Tiye lived, a world where artisans crafted objects of great beauty and

had ready access to the resources needed to create them.

Tiye lived a very comfortable life and had wanted for nothing. Her childhood had been privileged, and so, too, was her adulthood. Yet as Amenhotep's Great Royal Wife, she proved herself a queen who welcomed duties and responsibilities. Soon after their marriage, Amenhotep commissioned his artisans to record the event on the flat side of a large stone scarab. And it must have been on his orders that the names of her parents, Yuya and Tjuya, were also carved on the scarab. Another scarab describes a pleasure lake that Amenhotep had dug so that Tiye might enjoy a pleasant sail. Inscriptions tell of the royal couple attending the dedication ceremonies and enjoying an outing on the royal barge.

Tiye bore Amenhotep at least six children, two boys and four girls. Their oldest son died young, so it was their second son, Amenhotep, who became heir to the throne and succeeded Amenhotep as Amenhotep IV (he later changed his named to Akhenaten). Because surviving records refer to their daughters Isis and Sitamun as queens, many Egyptologists believe that Amenhotep III married both of them. If he did, the two marriages indicate a revival of the practice of keeping the royal bloodline in the family.

Tiye appears to have approved and even encouraged such unions, because her name accompanies Amenhotep's on an inscription announcing his marriage to Sitamun. Tiye's name also appears with her husband's on the scarab that announces the arrival of the Mitannian princess Gilukhepa and Amenhotep's marriage to her. All records indicate that Tiye was her husband's political confidante and ally as well as a dutiful and caring wife. Surviving official documents prove that Amenhotep often ordered Tiye's name inscribed together with his. He even commissioned sculptors to fashion a great sphinx with its head modeled after Tiye's. At Sedeinga, which lay between the Second and Third Cataracts in Nubia, Amenhotep had a temple built and dedicated to her. He also granted Tiye the honor of participating in religious ceremonies and royal rituals that were traditionally reserved for kings, including the Heb-Sed jubilee festival.

Tiye's name appears on several tablets in the Amarna Letters, a collection of clay tablets uncovered in 1887—a definite indication that she was personally involved in foreign affairs. Written in cuneiform, the "letters" were correspondence that rulers in the area known today as the Middle East had sent to Amenhotep and two of his successors, Amenhotep IV and Tutankhamun. These show that foreign rulers addressed letters directly to Tiye as well.

Archaeologists have also uncovered a letter that Tushratta, king of Mitanni, wrote to Tiye after the death of her husband. In it, Tushratta expressed his sincere hope that the good relations he had had with Amenhotep III would continue under the new king, Tiye's son Amenhotep IV. In a letter to the young Amenhotep, Tushratta wrote, "Your mother, Tiye, knows all the words that I discussed with your father; no one else knows them." In another passage, Tushratta expressed anger when he referred to two solid gold statues that Amenhotep III had promised to send him. He noted that, when the statues finally arrived in the Mitannian court, Amenhotep was dead and Amenhotep IV was on the throne.

He made it very clear that he suspected the new king of deceit because the statues were made of wood with only a gold overlay. Wary of trusting Amenhotep IV, Tushratta asked Tiye to involve herself in the problem so that the matter would be resolved fairly and according to the original agreement. No records have surfaced to tell how this misunderstanding was resolved.

Tiye's political influence most likely continued during the early part of Amenhotep IV's reign, and she may even have acted as regent for Amenhotep IV for several years. Sometime around Year 12 of her son's rule, she moved to the new palace he had built on the east bank of the Nile at Akhetaten (present-day el Amarna). When she died, Amenhotep IV (now Akhenaten) had her buried near this new city. Although no proof supports these details, most Egyptologists agree that Tiye spent her last years with Akhenaten.

Nevertheless, Tiye's stay in the Akhetaten tomb was quite brief. Egyptologists believe that after Akhenaten died, his successor Tutankhamun had Tiye's mummy reburied in the Valley of the Kings, probably in the tomb known today as Tomb 55. One of the most celebrated tomb sites ever discovered, Tomb 55 is also referred to as KV55. (The present system of numbering tombs in the Valley of the Kings is based on the system devised by the English Egyptologist John Gardner Wilkinson in 1827.) When excavators uncovered the entrance to this tomb in 1907, they found within it a large wooden panel that had formed part of a shrine. Covered in gold, it was inscribed with Tiye's name and had been shaped to represent the queen. A mummy was found nearby, but scientific

Tiye

POSITION
Queen of Egypt

REIGN
Around 1370 B.C.

ACCOMPLISHMENTS
Mothered six children, one of whom, Amenhotep IV (later called Akhenaten), succeeded their father, Amenhotep III, as king; won the respect of Egyptians and foreign rulers who were both allies and leaders of areas subject to Egyptian rule

Live—the Great King's Wife Tiye, the wife of a mighty king whose southern boundary is as far as Karoy [in Nubia] and whose northern boundary is as far as Naharin [Mitanni].

—Inscription on the scarab Amenhotep III commissioned to commemorate his marriage with Tiye

tests proved it was that of a young man. His identity remains a mystery.

Because the tomb held no body that could be identified as Tiye's and none of the traditional funerary equipment that would have accompanied her mummy in death, Egyptologists now believe that the queen's remains were buried a third time to protect them from robbers—probably in tomb KV35.

Just nine years before the 1907 discovery, a French archaeologist named Victor Loret was working in the East Valley of the Valley of the Kings and uncovered an entrance to tomb KV35. Inscriptions and other artifacts soon proved it to be the tomb of Amenhotep II. In fact, Loret even found the king's mummy still in the sarcophagus. Further digging led Loret and his workers into side chambers where they found 16 mummies—10 royal and 6 whose remains have not yet been positively identified. Like the cache of mummies uncovered at Deir el Bahri in 1881, these, too, had been reburied by ancient Egyptian priests in an attempt to protect them from further desecration by robbers.

When Loret entered the side chamber with the three unwrapped mummies, he noticed that one had long (almost one foot in length), curly dark brown hair. With no other identifying characteristics, she came to be

known as the "elder woman." Results from later testing suggest that the mummy is that of Queen Tiye. Recent analysis of the mummy's hair also seems to confirm this theory. Scientists found that her hair strands match exactly the strands found in a locket in Tutankhamun's tomb that are believed to be Tiye's.

The features of the mummy are quite fine, with a slightly pointed nose and chin. The teeth are very worn—a common problem in ancient Egypt because tiny particles of sand constantly became mixed with grain that was being ground to make bread. Unfortunately, ancient robbers had treated the remains with little respect. In their attempt to steal the treasures buried in the wrappings, they pierced the chest and left a large gaping hole. Despite their callous actions, the mummy's face still reflects a royal dignity that Tiye certainly would have had when she helped her husband rule Egypt more than 3,000 years ago.

FURTHER READING

El Mahdy, Christine. *Mummies, Myth and Magic in Ancient Egypt*, pp. 39, 46–47. London: Thames & Hudson, 1989.

Akhenaten

THE HERETIC KING

The life and ideas of the Egyptian king who called himself Akhenaten have intrigued Egyptologists and others for decades. Who was this king who tried to radically alter the religious practices of his people? What motivated him to do so? And why did his successors reverse his decisions and strike his name from the king list? Archaeologists and Egyptologists are working to find the answers to these questions. Certain facts, however, are indisputable.

Akhenaten was the name he gave himself after he had ascended to the throne as Amenhotep IV. His parents had called him Amenhotep, but not with the intention that he should follow his father, Amenhotep III, to the throne. His older brother, Thutmose, was in line for that honor. Nevertheless, both boys were raised to follow the example set by their ancestors, a long line of distinguished kings who had extended Egypt's boundaries and made the nation the center of a powerful empire. Life took an unexpected turn when Thutmose died. With little time to reflect on his changed circumstances, Amenhotep suddenly became the heir to the throne of Egypt. How he accepted his new role is unknown,

This head from a colossal sandstone statue of Akhenaten bears characteristics of Amarna art in its elongated face, the shape of the mouth, and the great curve from the nape of the neck to the chin.

Beautiful you are, appearing in the horizon of heaven, you living Aten, the one who gives life.

—"Hymn to Aten," thought to be written by Akhenaten

as no personal letters or documents have survived. Whether he shared the rule with his father as co-regent before becoming sole ruler is also an unknown.

Tablets uncovered in the 1880s reveal that his mother, Queen Tiye, outlived her husband and continued as a strong political presence during the first years of her son's reign. A second dominant personality in Amenhotep's life was his wife, the beautiful Nefertiti, who, like Queen Tiye, was a nonroyal. Nefertiti, however, was not a stranger to the royal family; nor was she an outsider. Records indicate that she may been have been a close relative of Tiye.

For the coronation ceremony, Amenhotep followed the traditional customs and rituals. And during the months that followed, he commissioned architects to design buildings in the same massive style that had come to characterize Egyptian architecture. At Soleb, in Nubia, he ordered workers to complete the decoration of his father's temple. To commemorate his opening of the sandstone quarries at Gebel el Silsila in Upper Egypt, Amenhotep commissioned artisans to craft reliefs of him worshiping Amun-Re.

Gradually, however, Amenhotep began to focus increasing attention on another deity, the Aten. Like Amun-Re, the Aten was also associated with the sun. For more than 500 years, the Egyptians had honored the Aten. In fact, Amenhotep's grandfather, Thutmose IV, worshiped the Aten as a war god, and his father, Amenhotep III, promoted worship of the solar aspect of the Aten's nature. Amenhotep III had even named the magnificent royal barge *Tehen-Aten,* or "Aten Gleams."

For Amenhotep IV, the Aten was the force that produced life itself, the creative power that extended its warmth and kindness to the earth. For him, the Aten was the only deity. He saw it as the sun's disk that rolled across the sky every day, rising in the east and setting in the west. In time, this belief became the focus of his thoughts, and he could no longer rule or live as he had been living. New rules, new rituals, new styles had to be developed to embrace this "new religion."

First came the name change from Amenhotep, meaning "Amun is satisfied," to Akhenaten, meaning "He who is beneficial for the Aten." As Akhenaten, he ordered the name Amun erased from memory. To do this, he had statues of Amun destroyed and the hieroglyphic symbols representing Amun's name and the word "gods" cut out of records, inscriptions, and reliefs. Nor did Akhenaten confine this order to the lands of Egypt, as he also commanded that the same "erasure" procedures be carried out in Nubia and beyond the desert sands to the East as well. His directions even included chiseling out the "Amen" in his father's name.

To represent the Aten, Akhenaten chose a disk. Sculptors and artists drew a series of straight lines extending downward from this disk to represent the life-giving rays of the sun. At the end of each ray was a little hand that "gave" to Akhenaten and his family the goodness of the Aten in return for the family's devotion and worship. Some hands were represented holding an ankh ♀, the ancient Egyptian symbol for life. Akhenaten's intent was clear. He considered himself the Aten's personal representative on Earth and the only one to whom the Aten revealed himself. Thus he, Akhenaten, was to serve as the mediator between the Aten and the Egyptians. No longer were Egyptians to honor or make offerings to Amun or the other gods. Rather, they were to worship the Aten by addressing their prayers to Akhenaten, because only Akhenaten, Nefertiti, and their daughters received the goodness of the Aten directly.

As a result of Akhenaten's focus on the Aten, Egypt's economy began to suffer, and the normal routines of daily life were seriously interrupted. Akhenaten's predecessors had used much of the tribute and taxes that poured into Egypt's coffers to adorn Amun-Re's temples. They had also granted tracts of land to the priests of Amun-Re. These priests, in turn, rented some of these lands to Egyptian farmers. Thus, thousands of Egyptians worked, so to speak, for Amun-Re, and their welfare was directly tied to the prosperity and well-being of the deity's temples. The temple sites also included areas that served as schools, offices, and hospitals where Egyptians could seek the aid of physician-priests to cure their ills. As a result, the power of Amun-Re's priests had increased steadily through the years.

Because this situation could lead to rivalry between the priests and the king, Akhenaten might have felt that he had to take measures to curb the priests' power. Although historians do

not agree on Akhenaten's motives for worshiping only the Aten, they do agree that Akhenaten's actions robbed Amun-Re's priests of their power. Just as Akhenaten had eliminated the name of Amun from view, now he eliminated the god's worship by closing all the temples dedicated to Amun-Re. Because Amun-Re's priests were no longer able to rent out temple lands or employ workers in a variety of jobs, many Egyptians suddenly found themselves out of work. How the people felt about Akhenaten is not known. At several sites, including a village built to house those working on Akhenaten's

Akhenaten relaxes with his wife Nefertiti and their daughters. The rays extending downward from the Aten (the sun disk) represent the abundance of goodness the Aten pours down on the royal family.

construction projects, excavators have found graffiti that suggest many Egyptians continued to worship Amun-Re.

Still, the changes continued. Images disappeared of gods that shared human characteristics and seemed approachable. Gone, too, were the animal-headed figures of gods. Akhenaten preferred the impersonal sun disk as the representation of his god, the Aten. Because the sun was readily visible to all, statues were no longer needed. The traditional temple form with its open court leading into closed-in areas and dark recessed spaces reserved only for priests and the king also had no place in his religion.

For centuries, the Egyptian people had gathered at the great religious festivals to watch the priests carry Amun's statue in a sacred barque during the great procession. At all other times, the boat and statue were inaccessible to them. Akhenaten wanted no mystery, no secrecy. His Aten could be seen daily—one had only to look at the sky and watch as the Aten rolled by on its daily journey. To reflect this belief, Akhenaten ordered his workers to build the Aten's temples with an entranceway that led to a columned hall area and a series of inner courtyards. These courtyards were to have no roofs, but instead be open to the sky, to the goodness of the Aten. This openness allowed the food and drink offerings placed on the many stone altars set up in the courtyards to be clearly visible to the Aten passing above.

Unfortunately, none of Akhenaten's temples have survived, not even as ruins. However, recent excavations have uncovered some of the blocks used to build at least two of the temples dedicated to the Aten. While digging at Karnak and Thebes, archaeologists found more than 36,000 small

sandstone blocks (known as *talatat*, the local Arabic nickname for the blocks). It is the size of the blocks that is especially interesting. Egyptologists theorize that Akhenaten and his architects ordered small blocks because the workforce included many unskilled men who found it easier to work with this size of block than with the traditional large blocks of stone.

Religion, however, was not Akhenaten's only concern. He also turned his attention to government policy. The changes he made in this area must have caused some uneasiness, especially among nobles and administrative officials. Instead of restricting his appointments to members of the royal family and others of the "inner circle," Akhenaten named new people, people without political and religious ties, to the highest offices in Egypt. Although this new policy was fairer, it came too quickly and did not allow the newcomers enough time to develop and broaden their diplomatic skills. As a result, the practice weakened Egypt's influence, especially in the conquered lands under its control.

One of Akhenaten's most radical decisions was to abandon Thebes and Memphis, the traditional religious and political centers of Egypt. He also abandoned the royal palace his father had built at Malkata. As the capital of his empire, Akhenaten chose an area that lay about halfway between Thebes and Memphis and had no ties with any Egyptian tradition. In fact, no town or city had ever been built on the land. Akhenaten named his city Akhetaten, meaning "Horizon of the Aten" or "Horizon of the Sun Disk."

To mark the boundaries of this city, Akhenaten rode about the perimeter of the area in his "great chariot of electrum." He had large stelae carved at intervals in the rock cliffs that formed a protective arc east of the city limits. On each stele was a relief that depicted the king, with his wife and daughters by his side, worshiping the Aten. The accompanying inscriptions stated that the land was sacred and that all were to be buried within the boundaries marked by the stelae.

In 1887, a great find was made at Akhetaten. An Egyptian woman was searching the area for old mud bricks to use as fertilizer on her fields and uncovered a collection of baked clay tablets inscribed with wedge-shaped writing. At first, no one considered them genuine. Testing, however, proved that they were diplomatic correspondence addressed to the king of Egypt by officials in Syria, Palestine, Phoenicia, and other neighboring lands. Some were addressed to Akhenaten; others to his father Amenhotep III; and several to his successor Tutankhamun. Today they are known as the Amarna Letters, from el Amarna, the modern name of Akhenaten's city Akhetaten. Egyptologists had first called the site Tell el Amarna, a combination of el Till (a neighboring village) and Beni Amran (a local tribe). Today historians also use Amarna to refer to this period in Egyptian history.

The Amarna Letters reveal unrest in the lands conquered by Akhenaten's predecessors. Unable to protect themselves against the Hittites (a warrior tribe from northern Syria and Asia Minor), officials in these lands were pleading with the Egyptian king to send help. The officials also wanted Egypt's king to take action against Egyptians who were extorting unjust sums from the people they were sent to govern. The urgency of their requests is made clear in a letter written by Ribaddi of Gebal (later Byblos): "If no help

comes, then I am a dead man." This was the last of several pleas marked "urgent" that he had sent to Akhenaten. Although no historical records have surfaced that tell of Ribaddi's fate, accounts do indicate that Akhenaten preferred to focus his attention on Akhetaten and on promoting the worship of the Aten.

In a few reliefs Akhenaten is dressed as a warrior and grasps captives by the hair with one hand while preparing to strike them with a mace, or heavy metal war club, with the other. In one relief Nefertiti strikes the same pose. Yet we have no indication that Akhenaten ever assumed the role of a warrior-king. In fact, Akhenaten seems to have spent most, if not all, of his time in Akhetaten.

Some 10 years after the Amarna Letters were uncovered, the renowned English archaeologist Sir Flinders Petrie and his assistant Howard Carter began digging at el Amarna. Their work has provided Egyptologists with a rare glimpse of city life in ancient Egypt. Because no one had lived in Akhetaten before Akhenaten and because the city was abandoned soon after Akhenaten's death, all the finds reflect life during one particular time period—and a very unique period it was.

To complete the city quickly, Akhenaten's builders must have worked at a feverish pace. The Great Royal Palace had a magnificent throne room, and the North Palace had a pool and a small zoo that included an aviary and animal pens. Akhetaten had temple complexes, residential areas, business areas, and to the south, the Maruaten with its great garden area set aside for pleasure and worship. A road, known today as the Royal Road, ran parallel to the Nile and connected the main areas of the city.

Akhenaten

POSITION

King of Egypt

REIGN

About 1350–34 B.C.

ACCOMPLISHMENTS

Changed the focus of Egyptian religion from the worship of Amun-Re to the worship of the Aten, the sun disk; proclaimed himself the mediator between humans and the Aten; built a new capital city north of Thebes and named it Akhetaten; kept correspondence from subject states in the East at Akhetaten

In the desert sands, a short distance from the main city, was a small square-shaped village area. Archaeologists believe it probably housed the workers (and their families) who cut and decorated the tombs in the rock cliffs that bordered the city to the east. A wall surrounded the entire village, with just one gate for residents to enter and leave. Sixty-eight of the sixty-nine houses were the same size and starkly simple, especially in contrast to the royal residences and private homes of the city's officials. (The larger house probably belonged to the foreman.)

Cut into the wall of one of the tombs, excavators found the "Hymn to the Aten":

> You rise in the eastern horizon and fill
> every land with your beauty.
> You are beautiful and great, and
> gleam. You rise high above every land.
> Your rays, they encircle the lands, so
> far as all that you have created.

So unlike the "Hymn of Victory," written about 100 years earlier during the reign of Thutmose III, Akhenaten's song of praise did not speak of crushing the enemy but of the greatness of the Aten. It told, too, how the Aten's rays brought life and beauty to everyone and everything, not only in Egypt but throughout the world.

In reliefs, houses and temples are brightly painted. Designs on the walls of buildings and private houses picture bakers busily kneading bread dough, women spinning and weaving, and other typical everyday scenes. Along the base of many walls, artists painted graceful illustrations of gardens, and near the ceiling, they painted bouquets of flowers. Designs of local plant life decorated the floor. It is almost as if el Amarna is a window on ancient Egypt.

Such scenes, however, were not the predominant focus of the artists. Everywhere were illustrations of Akhenaten and his family receiving the goodness of the Aten. The royal family had become the icons of the age and had replaced all the gods in the Egyptian pantheon. There were no scenes of the afterlife. Rather, the focus was on the present—on Akhenaten's accomplishments and his role as representative and interpreter of the Aten's will.

The art of the period also reflected Akhenaten's dislike of the staid and solemn images of the past and his preference for topics of a more personal nature. Thus, we see royal family members pictured as they never had been before: Akhenaten gently cradling a daughter in his arms, Nefertiti playing with her daughters, and the family at the dinner table with Akhenaten gnawing on a bone. Always present in these illustrations is the round disk symbolizing the Aten, with its rays extending downward to the royal family.

Nor was subject matter the only area in which the painted images at Akhetaten differed from those of previous decades. A fluidity of movement carried the curving, wavy lines from one image to the next. Colors were more subdued and more delicate, and there were more of them. As artists sought to capture scenes from everyday life, they included birds soaring in flight and papyrus plants waving in the breeze.

One design element, however, did not change. Artists continued to portray the human figure partly in profile form: a side view of the head and neck, a front view of the torso, and a side view of the legs. What did change was the way they depicted the human form, especially the bodies of the king and the royal family. No longer was the king represented as a powerful, perfectly formed warrior and leader. No longer was his expression regal and almost impassive as he gazed out over his world. Realism and naturalism were key elements of the design at Akhetaten. Actually, this was quite appropriate because Akhenaten wanted the emphasis on *ma'at* (justice), truth, and the right order of the universe. A stele inscription tells how Bek, Akhenaten's chief sculptor and Master of Works, followed the king's instructions to draw exactly what he saw.

Yet whether the elongated skulls and distorted limbs that are found so frequently in Amarna art represent a new style or portray reality is a question. Some scientists think that Akhenaten suffered from Fröhlich's disease, which causes the pituitary gland to malfunction. If this is true, then Akhenaten's body would have looked similar to the way it was depicted in the art style of the period: an abnormally long, egg-shaped face and head, slanting eyes, thin neck, sloping shoulders, pot belly, and wide thighs. The artists may have painted others with the same physical characteristics so as not to accentuate the king's abnormalities. Whatever the case, the unique culture of this period represents the only real break from tradition in the long history of ancient Egypt.

Akhenaten's rule of about 17 years was too short for him to implement all his ideas. Many of the structures and tombs at Akhetaten were never finished. Several members of the royal family, however, including Akhenaten's mother, Tiye, and his young daughter, Mekeaten, were buried in the complex.

Give him very many jubilees with years of peace.

—Prayer for Akhenaten found at Akhetaten

The design of Akhenaten's tomb may also have reflected his belief in the Aten. The straight axis of the tomb was positioned in such a way that the sun's rays entered the doorway, "flowed" down a ramp that had a set of stairs on either side (the first ancient Egyptian tomb to have a step-ramp-step entryway), then down the long corridor, another step-ramp-step passageway, and into the burial chamber where they would rest on his sarcophagus. According to present-day observations, however, the Aten's rays could not shine directly on the sarcophagus because the latter was a little off center.

Soon after Akhenaten's death, a royal decree ordered the statues of Akhenaten toppled and the names of Akhenaten and the Aten cut from all reliefs, inscriptions, and statuary. His city was abandoned, and later kings and architects even used it as a quarry for their building projects. No mention is made of Akhenaten's mummy, and its whereabouts remains a mystery.

FURTHER READING

Aldred, Cyril. *Akhenaten: King of Egypt.* London: Thames & Hudson, 1988.

Freed, Rita E., Yvonne J. Markowitz, and Sue H. D'Auria, eds. *Pharaohs of the Sun: Akhenaten, Nefertiti, Tutankhamun.* Boston: Bulfinch, 1999.

James, T. G. H. *Akhenaten: Egypt's False Prophet.* London: Thames & Hudson, 2001.

Nefertiti

THE BEAUTIFUL
ONE IS COME

The sculptor Thutmose spent many long hours chipping away at the limestone block he had specially chosen for the bust of Nefertiti, the Great Royal Wife of Akhenaten. And the result was a masterpiece. The face was beauty personified, and the calm expression told of an inner sense of security and accomplishment. The painted features gave it life—black eyebrows perfectly curved and shaped, gentle but determined dark eyes rimmed with black eyeliner, as was the custom, and full red lips. For a headdress, Thutmose had fashioned a tall blue crown that tilted slightly backward. He painted a simple, vertically striped band around the middle of the crown. This was not the traditional crown of Upper Egypt or of Lower Egypt, but one specially

Among the most famous of ancient Egyptian archaeological finds is this painted head of Nefertiti that was uncovered in the artist Thutmose's studio at Akhetaten.

designed for Nefertiti. Other artists had done the same with their images of the queen. Thutmose's creation, however, never left his studio.

In 1914, more than 3,000 years after Thutmose had sculpted the bust, members of the German Oriental Society were clearing the sand and other debris that had covered the eastern residential section of Akhenaten's city. In a workshop they identified as belonging to the sculptor named Thutmose they found the statue. Part of the right ear and most of the left were missing, and so, too, was the left eye.

As the digging continued, more statuary was uncovered, including a second bust of Nefertiti. This one was unfinished and had no crown and no ears. Still visible were the lines an ancient sculptor had drawn on the stone to mark the eye area and the nostrils above the lip. Another line ran straight down the forehead, across the nose, and over the middle of the lips and chin. Most Egyptologists agree that this statue was probably one of many that Thutmose had used to teach pupils the art of sculpting. Yet even in its half-finished form, the beauty of Nefertiti is ever present. And anyone who looks at it is left without any doubt that this queen of Egypt did indeed live up to her name, which means "the beautiful one is come."

Although few facts have survived about Nefertiti's life, it seems certain that she was a nonroyal. Most likely, she was a commoner whose parents and grandparents held high-ranking government positions. Nefertiti's father may even have been the well-respected and influential vizier Ay, the brother of Queen Tiye. Relief inscriptions refer to Tey, Ay's wife, as Nefertiti's "nurse" and "governess." Thus, from childhood, Nefertiti was well acquainted with men and women who wielded considerable power.

Although Egypt's rulers, by tradition, were men, several royal wives had proved themselves extremely capable leaders and advisers. In fact, Egyptian laws regarding women's rights were far more liberal than those of many other nations in the eastern Mediterranean at the time. Egyptian women could own property, inherit property, and bring legal suit in the law courts. They also held religious positions and played an active role in the rituals and rites governing daily life throughout the Two Lands. Nefertiti definitely followed the precedent set by several of her predecessors.

Sometime in her early teens, Nefertiti married the son of Amenhotep III. At the time of their marriage, her husband still used his given name, Amenhotep. Surviving reliefs and uncovered bits of evidence suggest that Nefertiti and Amenhotep were approximately the same age.

When Amenhotep succeeded his father to the throne, Nefertiti became the Great Royal Wife. All Egypt now looked to her as the mother of their next king. The longed-for son, however, did not arrive. Nefertiti and Amenhotep had six children—all of them girls.

During the first years of marriage, Nefertiti lived at Malkata, the royal palace Amenhotep III had built at Thebes. Life there must have been quite pleasant because the palace had every amenity, even an artificial lake that had been created specially for Queen Tiye's pleasure. Delightful painted scenes covered the walls of the huge complex, and servants were ready to satisfy any request a royal might have. When Amenhotep succeeded his father as Amenhotep IV, the royal family remained at Malkata. But there were hints of change.

Nefertiti and her husband had been questioning Egypt's religious beliefs for some time and were beginning to feel uncomfortable worshiping the many gods in the Egyptian pantheon. They also disapproved of the tremendous

Nefertiti

POSITION
Queen of Egypt

REIGN
About 1345 B.C.

ACCOMPLISHMENTS
With her husband, Akhenaten (Amenhotep IV), ended the worship of Amun-Re and promoted the worship of the Aten; with Akhenaten oversaw the construction of a new capital city, Akhetaten, on the east bank of the Nile; encouraged a new art form, known today as the Amarna style

The elongated torso and wide thighs are unmistakable traits of the Amarna style during the reign of Akhenaten. So, too, is the realism evident in this beautiful female torso, thought to be that of Nefertiti.

power wielded by the priests of the great god Amun-Re. For them, the Aten was the only deity deserving of worship. Depicted as the round disk of the sun, the Aten had been honored for centuries, but as one of many deities. In recent years, however, several rulers, including Amenhotep's father, had paid more attention to the Aten.

Nefertiti seems to have been especially keen on promoting the worship of the Aten, and some Egyptologists believe that she, more than her husband, was responsible for the religious reforms that followed. As the royal couple's feelings toward the Aten intensified, both began to feel that changes were necessary in their personal lives.

First, a new capital city was needed, one that had no association with the traditional Egyptian deities. Their choice was an area about eight miles long and three miles wide on the east side of the Nile River, where no one had ever built before. They called the city Akhetaten in honor of the Aten.

Unconcerned about acting contrary to custom, the royal couple had their tombs cut into the rock cliffs to the east of the city. This was the first time an Egyptian ruler had chosen a site that was not located on the west bank of the Nile River. Nefertiti and Amenhotep had followed their own beliefs and chosen the east side of the river, the direction of the rising sun.

It was around this time also that Amenhotep took the name Akhenaten, which means "He who is beneficial for the Aten." Because Nefertiti's name had no connection with any deity, she kept it, but she added a second name that was more descriptive—Nefernefruaten, meaning "Beautiful is the beauty of the Aten." The royal couple also

incorporated the name of the Aten into the names of each of their first four daughters: Meritaten, Meketaten, Ankhesenpaaten, and Nefernefruaten (the two youngest were Nefernefrura and Setepenra).

In the years that followed, the changes continued as Nefertiti and Akhenaten sought to concentrate all religious rituals on the Aten. A new law stated that sculptors and artists could no longer draw or carve figures of Amun-Re or any other deities. Only the Aten, represented as a sun disk with lines extending downward, was to be revered. Pictured beneath the lines, which represented the sun's rays, were the figures of the royal family receiving the goodness of the Aten. Many Egyptians, particularly officials and nobles, adopted the practice of placing images of Nefertiti, Akhenaten, and the royal princesses receiving the rays of the sun disk in chapels in their homes and in other places of worship. As a result, sculptors, like Thutmose, were kept busy fashioning images of the royal family.

Along with these changes in religious practices came a change in the way artists depicted the human figure. Long narrow heads now sat atop long thin necks; stomachs were round and full like potbellies; and legs resembled sticks. Artists, however, did not exaggerate these areas when drawing Nefertiti's form as much as they did with Akhenaten's figure. Another characteristic of this new style—the Amarna style—was its informality. The traditional stiff, rigid pose was replaced by one that radiated warmth and sensitivity. Under previous rulers, scenes of the royal family at rest or enjoying each other's company had been considered inappropriate subject matter for artists.

In Amarna reliefs, we see Nefertiti as a loving mother—cradling a daughter in her arms, playing with another daughter, and crying at the death of Meketaten. We also see her as a faithful wife—riding in the royal chariot with Akhenaten, walking hand-in-hand with Akhenaten to a service, and standing with her husband as he grants rewards to faithful officials. In other reliefs, she is represented as a devoted follower of the Aten—worshiping the Aten with her family, receiving the Aten's goodness, and officiating at ceremonies.

Because the image of Nefertiti figures prominently in most reliefs, some Egyptologists have suggested that she played the dominant role in the new religion. To confirm their claim, they point to several reliefs of Nefertiti, accompanied only by a daughter, worshiping the Aten.

Around Year 12 of Akhenaten's reign, Nefertiti exits the royal scene and is mentioned no more. No records survive to tell us why. Some believe that she fell ill and/or died. Others think that she had to withdraw from public view after Akhenaten chose their daughter Meritaten as his chief wife. Still others consider her "disappearance" an indication that the royal couple disagreed about official policy.

Although Nefertiti's disappearance does not seem to have affected Egyptian life or the worship of the Aten, the kings who succeeded Akhenaten quickly reinstated the worship of Amun-Re and the other deities of the Egyptian pantheon. They also ordered the names and images of Akhenaten and Nefertiti cut from all stone inscriptions and reliefs. Soon, even the city of Akhetaten was abandoned.

Egyptologists have located the royal tomb at Akhetaten, but they found within it only traces of paint along the lower and upper edges of the walls in the main burial chamber. Close examination of these areas has revealed that the scenes near the ceiling once showed the Aten as the sun disk with lines representing rays extending downward. The scenes near the floor depicted Nefertiti and her husband sacrificing to the Aten.

For centuries, tales of the "heretic king and queen" were told and retold. However, it was the rediscovery of Akhetaten that sparked a genuine interest in this period and in the royal couple. News of finding Nefertiti's sculptured head focused worldwide attention on ancient Egypt, and soon her beauty became a symbol of the civilization itself. At Akhetaten and in museums around the world, her graceful figure continues to revere the Aten, the deity she considered supreme.

The great crown princess . . . with whose existence the lord of the Two Lands is well pleased . . . his beloved Great Royal Wife.

—Inscription on a boundary stele at el Amarna

FURTHER READING

Aldred, Cyril. *Akhenaten and Nefertiti*. New York: Viking, 1973.

Tyldesley, Joyce A. *Nefertiti, Egypt's Sun Queen*. New York: Penguin, 2000.

Tutankh-amun

THE BOY-KING

On November 26, 1922, a news bulletin read as follows: HOWARD CARTER AND LORD CARNARVON BREAK THE 3,000-YEAR-OLD SEALS TO TUTANKHAMUN'S TOMB IN THE VALLEY OF THE KINGS. Soon word of their discovery was racing about the world, exciting an interest in Egyptology that continues today.

This was not a chance discovery. For years, Carter had been digging in Egypt, but the tomb of this little-known king had eluded him. Nevertheless, he had refused to stop searching. In 1922, Egyptian officials finally granted Carter permission to search a small triangular area that lay close to Ramesses VI's tomb. Carter was optimistic. In 1907 American archaeologists had uncovered linen wrappings and several large pots in that same area. The fact that one of the pots had Tutankhamun's throne name (Nebkheprure) inscribed on it seemed positive proof to Carter that the king's tomb lay nearby. He believed that the pots were the remains of a funerary banquet held in honor of the king and that the linens were some of those the priests had used during the mummification process of the king's body.

This time Carter's instinct brought almost instant success. During the first few days of digging, he and his crew uncovered a step. More digging uncovered a flight of 16 stairs, then a sealed door. Seventeen days later, Lord Carnarvon stood with Carter at the bottom of the stairwell staring at the seals of Nebkheprure on the lower part of the doorway. The room looked in order except for signs of some ancient replastering in the top left-hand corner.

After the team passed through the doorway, they entered a descending corridor that was more than 26 feet in length and packed with limestone chips. Again they met signs of intruders—the chips had been tunneled through and the empty areas later refilled. The team slowly cleared the corridor of chips and came to a second doorway. This, too, had been sealed and showed signs of having been entered illegally and patched over. When Carter peered through an opening he had made in the plastered doorway, he quickly answered Carnarvon's question, "Can you see anything?" with "Yes, wonderful things."

And, indeed, he did, for Carter had uncovered a tomb that was virtually untouched. Soon after the king's burial, robbers had broken the seals on the two doorways and entered the antechamber, taking mostly linens, oils, and perfumes. When officials learned of the theft, they immediately ordered workmen to fill the entrance corridor with limestone chips—originally the corridor had been left empty—and then to reseal the doorways. Tomb robbery, however, was

Inlaid with colored glass and carnelian (a semiprecious red stone), this small gold coffin was of one of four used to hold Tutankhamun's internal organs.

At last I have made wonderful discovery in Valley; a magnificent tomb with seals intact.

—Howard Carter's 1922 telegram to Lord Carnarvon after uncovering a staircase leading to a blocked and sealed doorway

and sand they tossed onto the ground below obscured the entrance to Tutankhamun's tomb.

For Carter, the discovery was just the beginning of 10 long years of work—clearing, sorting, labeling, and moving the incredible treasures he had uncovered. But there was one great disappointment—nowhere in the four rooms of the burial complex did Carter find any papyrus rolls, any literature, any documents that referred specifically to Tutankhamun and the times in which he lived. The hieroglyphs, symbols, and inscriptions carved into the walls and on the various artifacts uncovered in the tomb were the same traditional religious formulas and rituals found in other tombs. All were intended to help the deceased make the journey from this life to the next with the greatest ease. As a result, many of the questions Egyptologists had about Tutankhamun remained unanswered.

Indeed, who was this boy-king who came to the throne at an early age—perhaps at only eight or nine? Some say his father was Amenhotep III; others name Akhenaten. Many Egyptologists believe his mother, Kiya, was a minor wife of Akhenaten. Because Kiya's

such a profitable profession that these measures failed to deter criminals, and a second break-in occurred. This time, the thieves took jewelry and other precious objects, but evidence suggests that they were caught in the tomb. In the antechamber, Carter found a scarf wrapped and knotted around eight gold rings—proof, it appears, that the robbers, in their haste to escape capture, did not leave with all they had managed to grab. Carter also found the

name Djehutymose inscribed on the bottom of one of the jars. Having seen traces of this name in other tombs from the same time period, Carter guessed that Djehutymose was one of the scribes responsible for repacking the contents of the plundered tomb.

Some 200 years after Tutankhamun's death, workers preparing the tomb of the pharaoh Ramesses VI cut away at the rock cliff above Tutankhamun's tomb. The shovelfuls of rock

During his lifetime, Tutankhamun wore this amulet, found under the 12th layer of bandages on his mummy's chest. The vulture goddess Nekhbet (left) and the snake goddess Wadjet (right) flank the Sacred Eye of Horus, or Wadjet eye, which symbolized good health and prosperity and was thought to protect the wearer against evil.

name disappears from the records at about the same time Tutankhamun is born, many believe that she died in childbirth or shortly thereafter.

While there is uncertainty about which ruler Tutankhamun succeeded—Akhenaten or Smenkhkare—evidence links Tutankhamun with Akhenaten, Nefertiti, and the city of Akhetaten.

Tutankhamun's birth name, Tutankhaten, which means "living image of the Aten," suggests a close association with Akhenaten and Nefertiti, the royal couple who worshiped only the Aten and not Amun-Re and the other traditional Egyptian deities. As a member of the royal family, Tutankhaten most likely spent his early childhood playing in the palaces and gardens of Akhenaten's new city, Akhetaten. However, once he became pharaoh, his advisers had him spend many hours learning about Egypt and the lands he now controlled in Nubia, Syria, and Palestine. His advisers also arranged his marriage to Ankhesenpaaten, Akhenaten's eldest surviving daughter by his Great Royal Wife, Nefertiti.

Chief among these advisers were the vizier Ay and the general Horemheb. Young Tutankhaten's power to

make decisions was limited, and in matters of religion, Tutankhaten probably played no significant role in reinstating the worship of Amun-Re and the other deities of the Egyptian pantheon. The credit for the return to the traditional religious practices goes to Ay, Horemheb, and those officials who believed that worship of the Aten did not serve the needs of Egypt or the Egyptians.

In Year 2 of his reign, Tutankhaten changed his name to Tutankhamun, meaning "living image of Amun," and Ankhesenpaaten changed her name to Ankhesenamun. Name changing, however, was not enough. A royal decree followed, ordering architects to design new temples dedicated to Amun-Re and to refurbish those that had fallen into disrepair. Another decree commissioned a great "Restoration" that would commemorate the return to traditional religious practices and to the rebuilding of Amun-Re's temples. The Aten continued to be worshiped, but not as the only deity.

On the recommendation of his advisers, Tutankhamun left Akhetaten with Ankhesenamun and other members of the court. Amenhotep III's old palace at Malkata was reopened, and Tutankhamun stayed there whenever his presence was required at religious festivals in Thebes. The royal residence in Memphis was also made ready, and Tutankhamun stayed there when government matters required his attention. Tutankhamun, however, was still only a figurehead. Ay and Horemheb shared the responsibilities of governing. Each had a central office: Ay's was in Thebes, and Horemheb's was in Memphis. Helping them to implement these changes were loyal Egyptians whom they appointed to key posts in Egypt and in the subject territories. In an attempt to associate Tutankhamun more closely with Akhenaten's predecessors, Egyptian engineers and workers were ordered to complete several of the projects begun under Amenhotep III. These included the colonnade at the temple of Thebes, with its beautiful scenes of the Opet festival and the second of a pair of granite lions at Soleb in Nubia.

Egypt waged successful military expeditions in both Nubia and Syria during Tutankhamun's reign. In a relief in the tomb of Huy, Tutankhamun's vizier of Nubia, envoys from the South and the East offer great amounts of tribute to the king. On a box in the king's tomb, Howard Carter found reliefs of the young monarch hunting lions and gazelles in the desert. In other scenes Tutankhamun attacks Nubians and Syrians who fall dead, pierced by well-aimed royal arrows. Egyptologists find it highly improbable that Tutankhamun ever participated in campaigns against Egypt's southern neighbors or against the Syrians.

Sometime around Year 9 of his rule, Tutankhamun died. We know the number of years he reigned from seals found on wine jars in his tomb. The highest year listed is Year 9. Using this date and analyses of other evidence, Egyptologists have concluded that Tutankhamun was about 17 when he died.

Although surviving inscriptions do not hint at the cause of his death, it appears to have been completely unexpected. The news spread quickly, as priests, embalmers, and others were notified. The mummification process took approximately 70 days, leaving those in charge of the burial little time to prepare a royal tomb. What they needed was a tomb that was already finished,

> *The seals [of the tomb] were those of a king—King Tutankhamun. And then beyond all doubt we knew we were on the edge of a great discovery.*
>
> —Howard Carter's notes about uncovering the stairway and sealed doorway, November 1922

or close to being finished. Most likely the chosen tomb was the one Ay had prepared for himself. The tomb's size is appropriate for a noble or high-ranking state official—not for a king. The fact that Ay was allowed to construct his tomb in the Valley of the Kings indicates his high rank and the respect Tutankhamun's government had for him.

Tutankhamun left no heirs. The two mummified fetuses Carter found in the young king's tomb were most likely his children by Ankhesenamun. Recent analysis of the two mummies suggests that both were female and that one died before birth and the other at or shortly after birth. Each had been carefully embalmed and placed in an inner coffin that was enclosed in an outer coffin.

With no direct heir to succeed Tutankhamun, Ankhesenamun seems to have formed a plan. Archaeologists working in Hattusas, the capital city of the Hittites (archenemies of the ancient Egyptians) found records of a letter sent by a recently widowed Egyptian queen to the Hittite king Suppiluliumas. Although there has been some question as to whether Ankhesen-amun or Nefertiti wrote the letter, most Egyptologists believe it was Ankhesenamun.

In the letter, the widowed queen explained that her husband had died and that she had no son. Because she had heard that Suppiluliumas had many sons, she was asking him to send "one of your sons that he might become my husband. I do not wish to take one of my subjects and make him my husband."

Suppiluliumas naturally questioned the queen's motives and sent an official named Hattu-zitis to Egypt to investigate the matter. Upon learning that the queen did wish to wed his son and make him king of Egypt, Suppiluliumas agreed to her request. Unfortunately, the son was murdered before he entered Egypt.

Again from the records, it seems that after this plan failed, Ankhesenamun married Ay. For Ay, who had no royal blood flowing through his veins, marriage to Ankhesenamun provided the legitimacy he needed to claim the throne. On the north wall of Tutankhamun's burial chamber, Ay had the tomb artists paint his image wearing the blue war helmet of Egypt's kings and performing the Opening of the Mouth ceremony for Tutankhamun. According to religious tradition, only the son and heir of the dead king could perform this ceremony. By appointing himself to the task, Ay named himself Tutankhamun's son and heir.

Ay's reign, however, was brief—only four years. Horemheb then took command, and in an effort to erase from history all those connected with Akhetaten and Akhenaten, he ordered the names of his three predecessors—Akhenaten, Tutankhamun, and Ay—removed from the records. He listed himself as Amenhotep III's successor.

As a result of Horemheb's actions and those of subsequent kings, Egyptologists knew very little about Tutankhamun. Thus it was with great anticipation that Carter entered the boy-king's tomb. Within, Carter found signs of haste. With so little time to do their job, the artists had decorated only the walls of the burial chamber. In addition, the tomb appeared to have been sealed before the paint had completely dried. The result was a rise in the humidity, which, in turn, damaged some of the objects that had been placed in the tomb. And these objects represented everything Tutankhamun might need in the afterlife, including chests, stools, boxes, beds, headrests, chairs, and even the Golden Throne. The back panel of this throne was fashioned mostly of gold, with a relief design of Ankhesenamun anointing Tutankhamun with perfumed oil. Above the couple is the round sun disk of the Aten with its rays extending goodness to the royal couple.

Here, too, were throwing sticks, which the Egyptians used to hunt birds and other small animals. It is thought that Tutankhamun probably used these sticks, as inscriptions and surviving images all indicate that he enjoyed hunting. Also in the tomb were 35 boat models and 6 of the king's chariots.

There were also items of a more personal nature. One was a wooden form of the king's body, which Egyptologists think a tailor might have used when making the king's garments.

Another was a pair of beautiful sandals, fashioned with a bound Asian depicted on one instep and a bound Nubian on the other. The symbolism is clear—with every step Tutankhamun took he was crushing a bitter foe to death. Other finds included a sling bandage and a baby's robe with a rolled hem of incredibly fine hand-sewn needlework. The robe was just one of 50 or so pieces of children's clothing that had been carefully laid to rest with the king.

Dominating the room now called the Treasury was one of the most remarkable finds in the tomb—the canopic shrine that held Tutankhamun's embalmed internal organs. Six-and-a-half-feet high, five feet long, and four feet wide, the enormous box-like wooden container stood majestically on a wooden sledge. Inside were four finely crafted canopic jars, each fitted with a stopper that had been shaped to resemble the head of a king. Inscribed on each was the name of Horus's son protecting the organ within—Imsety, the liver; Hapy, the lungs; Duamutef, the stomach; and Qebhsenuef, the intestines. As with so many of the other items in the tomb, the stoppers had been fashioned to hold someone else's remains, but Tutankhamun's sudden death had forced officials to use what was available at the time.

As Carter and his crew began working on the burial shrines that enclosed Tutankhamun's body, a feeling of intense excitement filled the tomb. No royal mummy had ever been found intact or untouched. The task, however, proved extremely difficult. Measuring 16 feet long, 11 feet wide, and 9 feet high, the outer burial shrine almost filled the chamber, leaving just enough room for a person to squeeze around the side.

With great care, Carter disassembled the first (the outer) shrine. Within he found a second shrine, then a third, and a fourth—all were floorless and slightly different in design, but all exquisitely decorated in gold.

After months of work clearing and recording every find, Carter came to the king's magnificent sarcophagus, carved from a single block of hard yellow-gold quartzite. Time constraints again seemed to have forced those in charge of the tomb to improvise, because they used a red granite lid but painted it yellow to match the sarcophagus.

To lift the lid, Carter used an intricate pulley system specially designed for the task. Inside he found a coffin measuring more than seven feet long and draped with two pieces of linen cloth. The coffin had been shaped to resemble a human figure, as was the custom, and was made of wood that had been covered with gesso (a plaster of Paris that is mixed with glue and applied to a surface) and then covered with a layer of gold. The face was that of Tutankhamun, but the arms were positioned to represent him as Osiris, the god of the Underworld. That is, the arms were crossed over the chest area, and the right hand held a crook and the left hand a flail.

When Carter lifted the lid of the outermost coffin, he saw a linen shroud covered with wreaths of flowers. Adorning the forehead area was a beautiful wreath fashioned of olive leaves, blue lotus petals, cornflowers, and celery leaves. The colors were so vibrant that the flowers seemed almost fresh. They were also very brittle, and some crumbled to dust when touched. The basic design of this second coffin was similar to the first. The facial features, however, did not resemble those of Tutankhamun. Once again, tomb workers had used previously prepared funerary items.

Inside the second coffin lay a third coffin that was quite similar to the other two in shape and design, but with even finer and more elaborately wrought details. Around the coffin's "face" was a magnificent floral collar, made of blue and yellow flowers with tiny blue-green faience rings and red and yellow fruits. The royal *nemes* headdress was of linen, and over the coffin from the neck area to the feet lay a red linen cloth. When Carter lifted the cloth, he saw that the ancients had poured a thick, dark resin over the middle and bottom portion of the third coffin. Hours of painstaking work followed as Carter chipped away at the hardened resin and uncovered the inner coffin. Made of gold, it measured just over six feet in length and weighed approximately 223 pounds.

Using the golden handles the ancients had attached to the coffin's lid, Carter and his crew lifted the lid and beheld the boy-king Tutankhamun. Covering his face was a magnificent mask crafted of two separate sheets of gold with the traditional royal beard attached to the chin and the royal *nemes* headdress. The ancient artisans had used inlays of blue glass to make the stripes on the *nemes* and to define the king's eyebrows and eyes. They had also placed a floral collar about the chest and neck area and fashioned two hands made of sheet gold. The hands, one holding a crook and the other a flail, had been sewn to the mummy wrappings in the traditional crossed position. Between the hands was a scarab made of black resin. As Carter carefully unwrapped the burial shroud, he found 170 items, including amulets, wreaths, bracelets, an iron dagger—each designed to help Tutankhamun

pass from this life to life eternal in the underworld.

Tutankhamun's embalmers followed the traditional rules. After removing the internal organs and drying the body with natron, they stuffed the cadaver with padding so that it resembled its original shape. However, because they poured so much of the resin-based oils over the wrappings, the wrappings had stuck to the coffin, making Carter's task extremely difficult. The areas covered with gold—Tutankhamun's face, fingers, and toes—suffered less damage. Each finger and toe had been bound and fitted into a gold case. Scientific analysis of the mummy has revealed that Tutankhamun had a slight build, that he measured about five and a half feet in height, and that his third molars had only just broken through the gums. His head had been completely shaved, and he wore a beautifully worked close-fitting beaded cap.

FURTHER READING

Brier, Bob. *The Murder of Tutankhamen: A True Story*. New York: Putnam, 1998.

Caselli, Giovanni. *In Search of Tutankhamun: The Discovery of a King's Tomb*. New York: Peter Bedrick, 1999.

Green, Robert. *Tutankhamun*. Danbury, Conn.: Franklin Watts, 1996.

Hepper, F. N. *Pharaoh's Flowers, the Botanical Treasures of Tutankhamun*. London: HMSO, 1990.

James, T. G. H. *Tutankhamun*. New York: Friedman/Fairfax, 2000.

Reeves, Nicholas. *The Complete Tutankhamun*. London: Thames & Hudson, 1990.

Ventura, Piero, and Gian Paolo Ceserani. *In Search of Tutankhamun*. Morristown, N.J.: Silver Burdett, 1985.

Tutankh-amun

POSITION
King of Egypt

REIGN
About 1334–25 B.C.

ACCOMPLISHMENTS
On the advice of advisers, left Akhetaten and had Memphis serve as the capital city for political matters and Thebes as the capital city for religious matters; reinstated the worship of Amun-Re and of the traditional gods of the Egyptian pantheon; rebuilt many religious structures; with his advisers, promoted international trade

Horemheb

GENERAL
TURNED KING

Horemheb was not a member of Egypt's royal family, nor was he a nobleman. None of his family had ever distinguished themselves in the service of the king or of the nation. Home was a small provincial town just south of the Faiyum oasis. Horemheb's military prowess, however, had quickly brought him to the attention of his superiors, and the promotions came swiftly.

Horemheb served first under Amenhotep III. When Amenhotep IV followed his father on the throne, he also listened to reports about Horemheb's military skills and continued to approve his advancement through the ranks. Even after Amenhotep changed his name to Akhenaten and withdrew to a new capital city, Akhenaten turned to Horemheb as his commander-in-chief of the army. When Tutankhamun ascended the throne after Akhenaten's death, Horemheb became one of the young boy-king's closest advisers. In the months that followed, Horemheb's responsibilities steadily increased, and so, too, did his power. Egyptologists believe that Tutankhamun's reinstatement of Egypt's traditional gods and goddesses was the direct result of advice from Horemheb and another senior adviser named Ay. Both men understood the difficulties Akhenaten's policies had caused and now sought to return Egypt to the mighty power it had been under Amenhotep III.

Horemheb led military campaigns into Syria and Palestine and a diplomatic mission to Nubia that was aimed at resolving differences between the two nations. In his Saqqara tomb, scenes depict victories on the battlefield, Egyptian soldiers cleaning and provisioning Horemheb's tent in a military encampment, ambassadors from the East pleading before Tutankhamun for mercy, and Asiatic prisoners of war being paraded before the king and queen.

In recognition of Horemheb's many achievements, Tutankhamun granted him many titles—hereditary prince, king's messenger in front of his army to the foreign countries, fan bearer on the right of the king, wearer of the royal seal, sole companion (of the king), and overseer of all divine offices. Tutankhamun also conferred many honors on Horemheb, including the privilege of building his tomb at Saqqara. Horemheb's tomb site was positioned high on the plateau and at a distance from the other tombs in the area. Within were wall paintings that told of his many accomplishments and promotions. The scenes were realistic in design and replaced the staid, traditional figures and decorative patterns of the past. Following his instruction, the workers listed the positions Horemheb had held in the government, the military, and the priesthood. Around Horemheb's neck, the artists painted gold collars, the traditional reward for anyone who achieved great success. They also depicted the "Window of Appearance" on one wall. By tradition, Egypt's king stood at this window in the palace during certain festivals and distributed awards to those who had performed noteworthy deeds. For his loyalty and accomplishments, Horemheb had been summoned to pass by the window and receive his rewards.

Horemheb continued as Tutankhamun's adviser even as the boy-king grew into his teens. But then the unexpected happened. After ruling for about nine years, Tutankhamun died and left no heirs. Ay took Tutankhamun's Great Royal Wife as his bride and claimed the throne.

Within four years of taking command, Ay, too, was dead. This time, Horemheb claimed the right to rule. Because no royal blood flowed through his veins, Horemheb cited his kinship with royalty. Records suggest that his wife, Mutnodjmet, was a close relative of Ay and of Nefertiti, Akhenaten's wife.

Yet royal bloodlines and proper hereditary lines were no longer critical in the selection of a new king. What Egypt needed now was a strong ruler, one who would foster stability and prosperity throughout the empire. The fact that no inscriptions or reliefs even hint of trouble or dissent when Horemheb came to the throne suggest that all approved his kingship.

Using the same determination and foresight he had shown on the battlefield, Horemheb now pressed to implement his reforms. First came orders to complete the restoration of the temples of Amun-Re and the traditional gods and goddesses of ancient Egypt. Horemheb also reinstated the power once held by Amun-Re's priests. However, aware of the need to control the priests' power, he chose priests from the army. Because of his close connections

with the military, these were priests he knew he could trust.

Horemheb also looked to the army for political appointments. To avoid granting too much power to one military officer, he retained his title of commander-in-chief and created two additional posts: Commander of the Forces in Upper Egypt and Commander of the Forces in Lower Egypt. Before naming anyone to these positions, Horemheb determined the duties of each post and studied the qualifications of potential candidates. Loyalty to him was just one prerequisite; achievement and ability were the others.

This relief scene depicts a funeral dance in Horemheb's tomb at Saqqara. He never used the tomb. The reason is unknown, but today workers continue to clear the site, seeking additional clues to his personal life and rise to kingship.

A bound captive, one of the many prisoners of war Horemheb and his troops captured in the Syria-Palestine campaigns. This relief was found in Horemheb's tomb at Saqqara.

Horemheb saw that centralization of power in the hands of one person did not work well unless that person had loyal and responsible officials to whom he could delegate duties. Therefore, he made himself that central power and chose loyal officials to keep him informed about what was happening throughout the kingdom. Once again, he divided the authority and named two viziers to oversee the Two Lands. One vizier was to take charge of Upper Egypt; the other, of Lower Egypt. Each vizier was to follow Horemheb's example and appoint loyal, hardworking people to positions in his area. For Horemheb, division of authority was the key to success, but two positions he did not divide—his own as king and the office of Chief Priest of Amun.

To curb unrest among the common people, who felt harassed by tax collectors, Horemheb enacted a series of measures aimed at restoring order and justice throughout the land. He was determined to prevent tax collectors and other officials from demanding more than the law required, according to surviving fragments of his decree.

Known today as the Edict of Horemheb, the decree begins "[H]is majesty took counsel with his heart . . . to expel evil and suppress lying . . . his majesty spent the whole time seeking the welfare of Egypt and searching out instances [of oppression]. . . . Then he seized [his writing materials] and put it into writing." The list of cases is simple but direct, and each is accompanied by prescribed punishments for various offenses. For example, "[I]f the poor man made himself a craft with sails in order to be able to serve the king . . . [and he was robbed of the craft] and stood without any goods and stripped of his many labors . . . the law shall be executed against the officer [who took his dues] and took the craft, in that his nose shall be cut off and he shall be sent to Tharu [the marsh country in the Delta]."

Although few records tell of Horemheb's involvement in overseas ventures, some refer to successful military campaigns both against the Asiatics to the East and against the Nubians to the South. There are also scenes of young men being inducted into the army, and inscriptions that tell of Horemheb encouraging trading expeditions, including one to the fabled land of Punt. In a wall relief the chiefs of Punt present Horemheb with sacks of gold dust, ostrich feathers, and other prized trading items.

Horemheb removed the names of Akhenaten and the three kings (Smenkhkare, Tutankhamun, and Ay) from the king lists and official records. His name now followed Amenhotep III's, and Year 1 of Horemheb's reign referred to the year immediately following Amenhotep's death.

Horemheb also claimed responsibility for the structures built under Tutankhamun and Ay, including the Restoration Stele that Tutankhamun had ordered to celebrate the return to the worship of the god Amun-Re. Horemheb had the Aten's Great Temple at Karnak dismantled block by block and used these blocks as fill for the Ninth and Tenth Pylons (monumental gateways) he had built to adorn Amun-Re's temple at Karnak. (Almost 3,000 years later, archaeologists digging at Karnak uncovered the blocks, and with the aid of computer technology, they are now attempting to re-create an image of the Aten's temple.) Horemheb then focused his attention on the construction of the great hypostyle hall (a roofed area supported by rows of pillars) at Karnak.

Following the policies initiated during Tutankhamun's reign, Horemheb kept Thebes as the religious capital of the Two Lands and made Memphis in Lower Egypt his political capital. Thebes was also the city he chose for his coronation ceremony. And to make the occasion even more meaningful, Horemheb scheduled it to coincide with the Opet festival. This was the time when the god Amun-Re "visited" the Opet (Inner Chambers of the South—the temple dedicated to Amun-Re at Thebes). A yearly celebration lasting 11 days (later it was lengthened to around 27 days), Opet took place during the second month of the inundation season when the Nile flooded its riverbanks.

Opet began with Horemheb traveling in a great royal procession up the Nile from Memphis to Thebes. The scene was one of majesty and pomp as Horemheb sat in the state barge, which had been specially decorated for the occasion. At Thebes another procession followed. The priests of Amun-Re put the sacred barque that held the cult statue of the god onto a frame attached to carrying poles. Placing the poles on

Horemheb

POSITION

King of Egypt

REIGN

About 1321–1293 B.C.

ACCOMPLISHMENTS

Returned Egypt to the worship of Amun-Re and reinstated the priesthood of Amun-Re; led expeditions into Syria and Nubia; sent a trading expedition to Punt and restored trade relations with the South and the East; issued the Edict of Horemheb to address the abuses suffered by the poor, especially excessive taxation; reestablished Memphis as the political capital of Egypt; inaugurated a building program, including a great hypostyle hall in honor of Amun-Re their shoulders, they solemnly walked along one of the grand processional routes paved with stone and lined with huge reclining statues of sphinxes. The ram-headed sphinxes along one avenue linking Amun-Re's temple at Karnak with the smaller temple of Mut, Amun-Re's wife, had been added at Horemheb's request. In fact, the sphinxes he commissioned started at the Tenth Pylon—the pylon that contained the blocks from Akhenaten's temple to the Aten.

Of all the rituals associated with the Opet festival, one of the most solemn was the king's visit to the dark inner precinct of the temple at Thebes. There, according to custom, he united himself in a mystical manner with Amun-Re. For all Egyptians, this ritual symbolized the divine relationship between their ruler and the god Amun-Re. For Horemheb, it validated his kingship; it identified him, in a way no other event or decree could, as the legitimate heir to the throne of Egypt. To identify himself even further with the rituals of Opet, Horemheb commissioned artisans working on a temple at Gebel el Silsila in Upper Egypt to include in the reliefs a scene of 12 attendants carrying him in the procession on a frame-like platform.

To further reflect his position as king, Horemheb ordered a new tomb site built in the Valley of the Kings. He did not, however, forget the Saqqara tomb, and sent artisans to Saqqara with orders to add a *uraeus*, a royal symbol in the shape of a rearing cobra, to the forehead of every wall image of himself. Archaeologists think that two of Horemheb's queens may have been buried in the Saqqara tomb.

When archaeologists discovered the entrance to Horemheb's tomb in the Valley of the Kings in 1908, all the treasures that Horemheb had had buried with him were gone, and debris was everywhere. Even the lid of his pink granite sarcophagus lay in pieces on the floor. Only the wall paintings were intact. Of special interest were passages from the *Book of Gates*, a new royal guide designed to help the deceased pass more easily from this world to the next. (The name refers to the gates that were believed to divide the hours of night.)

As archaeologists continued their study of the tomb and its wall paintings, they realized that Horemheb's tomb had been left unfinished. The skill of the artists, however, is clearly evident. Master draftsmen had drawn each scene to scale before enlarging it to fit the planned wall space. Less-experienced artisans simply cut the designs onto the tomb walls and painted them. To ensure the quality of the work, these draftsmen regularly checked the work of the artisans, and their corrections are clearly evident on Horemheb's walls. For Egyptologists, Horemheb's tomb provides a unique glimpse of a work in progress.

During Horemheb's long reign—27 to 30 years—Egypt enjoyed continued prosperity and stability. Because he had no sons or heirs, Horemheb turned, as he had so often in the past, to the army. He named as his successor Pramesse, a career officer whom he had recently promoted. Time would prove Horemheb's decision a wise one because Ramesses (the name Pramesse took as king) founded one of the greatest dynasties ever to rule Egypt. It also proved that Horemheb did indeed live up to the meaning of his name "Powerful bull with wise decisions."

FURTHER READING

Lichtheim, Miriam. *Ancient Egyptian Literature: A Book of Readings*, vol. 2, pp. 100–3. Berkeley: University of California Press, 1976.

Reeves, Nicholas and Richard H. Wilkinson. *The Complete Valley of the Kings*, pp. 130–33. London: Thames & Hudson, 1996.

More Ancient Egyptians to Remember

Amenhotep, Son of Hapu (active about 1370 B.C.) won the admiration and respect of generations of Egyptians. Approximately 1,000 years after his death, the Egyptians proclaimed him a god of healing, dedicated a temple to him at Deir el Bahri, and instituted religious rituals in his honor. Amenhotep was most likely born in Athribis, a town in the Delta region of Lower Egypt, and may have been a commoner. He studied to be a scribe, which was one of the most respected professions in ancient Egypt, as scribes were among the few who could read and write. He was also an architect with a keen sense of design. Amenhotep III commissioned him to design a royal mortuary temple on the west bank of the Nile. This temple did not survive the centuries, but the two gigantic, seated statues that Amenhotep, son of Hapu, had carved of the king—the Colossi of Memnon—remain. Other designs credited to him are a temple to Amun-Re at Thebes and additions to the great temple at Karnak. He is also believed to have played a major role in planning the magnificent royal palace at Malkata.

To show his appreciation of Amenhotep, son of Hapu, Amenhotep III granted him the great honor of building a mortuary temple in Thebes, just a short distance from his own. Amenhotep III also allowed the son of Hapu to set up several statues of himself at Karnak. Amenhotep, son of Hapu, had inscribed on one statue that the king "adorned my city [of Athribis] greatly and my family on earth as well." And, indeed, Amenhotep, son of Hapu, loved his native city of Athribis. As he grew older—records show that he lived to about 80 years of age—Amenhotep, son of Hapu, preferred the duties of priest at the temple at Athribis to official, public duties.

Surviving statues of Amenhotep, son of Hapu, depict him in the traditional pose of a scribe—sitting cross-legged with a writing tablet spread out on his kilt. In his left hand he holds the edge of the tablet; in his right, a pen. A scribe's palette hangs from a strap on his left shoulder.

The statues of Ramesses II and Nefertari cut into rock on either side of the entrance to the queen's tomb at Abu Simbel dwarf their visitors. Nefertari is dressed as the sky-goddess Hathor, who was represented with a solar disk between cow horns crowning her head.

5 Conquest and Decline
(New Kingdom–Ptolemaic Period, about 1325–245 B.C.)

Horemheb's decision to groom Pramesse for the throne was a wise one. Pramesse took the name Ramesses and became the founder of the 19th Dynasty. His son Seti I and grandson Ramesses II would be honored as two of Egypt's greatest kings. Golden ages, however, do not last forever, and periods of unrest began to plague the Two Lands. The reasons were varied, but the one that threatened even the king himself was the ever-increasing power wielded by the priests of Amun-Re. Approximately 130 years after Ramesses II's death, a priest of Amun-Re named Herihor proclaimed himself king. Such internal conflicts weakened the government, but external problems also threatened the unity of Egypt itself.

Wars far beyond Egypt's borders had forced many to leave their cities and towns and seek a new homeland. Many of these refugees, some known as the Sea Peoples, set out for Egypt. Others, especially to the west in Libya and to the south in Nubia, looked to Egypt not as a place of refuge but instead as a place to conquer. To them, the unrest in Egypt caused by its internal problems presented an opportunity to further their own goals. Under such pressures, the Two Lands could not resist and yielded to foreign control.

Part 5 of *Ancient Egyptians* focuses on those who were responsible for ancient Egypt's last great Golden Age and then on those who guided the nation through the problems, both internal and external, that beset the Two Lands in the centuries that followed.

Seti I

A RETURN TO GREATNESS

eti's two years as co-regent with his father, Ramesses I, had provided him with invaluable experience. As sole ruler, he had to rely on his own foresight to set goals and to develop the means to achieve them. Timing was critical; but even more important was not to waste time.

Aware of Egypt's illustrious past, Seti wanted the family line begun by his father to rival those of Egypt's greatest kings. As his coronation name, he chose Menmaatre—a combination of Ma'at (the goddess of justice and truth) and Re (the all-powerful sun god). His choice of deities was significant, for both Ma'at and Re were among the oldest deities worshiped by the Egyptians.

Two rope-bound prisoners—an Asiatic (left) and a Nubian—are painted on a panel representing sandal soles. The wearer reinforced the subservience of these people to Egypt.

As a native of Lower Egypt, Seti felt closer to this region and issued decrees from the capital city of Memphis. He even maintained a palace in Avaris. Yet he understood that unity was key to Egypt's stability and never treated Upper Egypt, especially the religious center at Thebes, as a less important area. He often had scribes follow his given name Seti with the epithet, "Beloved of Amun," the chief god at Thebes.

Seti also concerned himself with foreign policy. He considered himself the commander-in-chief of all military forces, but he placed the troops in Upper Egypt under one military officer and those in Lower Egypt under another. He did the same with the office of vizier, and with other offices as well. Like his predecessor Horemheb, Seti divided power and responsibility because it prevented anyone from becoming his equal in authority in any field.

Both Horemheb and Ramesses I had focused on retaking the lands in the Syria-Palestine area that had been lost to foreign invaders under Akhenaten and his successors. Seti resolved to complete the task. His Nebti, or Two Ladies royal name, "The strong-armed one who renews births and recaptures the Nine Bows," clearly told the nation of his intention to be a warrior king who would provide Egypt with powerful descendants.

Soon after his coronation, Seti assembled an army and marched east from the border town of Tjel. Almost immediately, he found himself facing Shasu Bedouin who were determined to prevent his passage. Decades earlier, Egyptian troops had dug nine wells across the Sinai Peninsula and built garrisons to protect them. With a supply of fresh water guaranteed, Egyptian commanders could cross this desert area. Rallying his forces to battle, Seti wrested control of first one well and then the next until he had reclaimed all nine and arrived in southern Palestine.

Grant that my monuments may endure for me, and my name may abide upon them.

—Temple inscription, Year 9 of Seti I's reign

Here, too, the welcome was unfriendly. But Seti urged his men to prove their skills and determination under attack. Later, he would have artisans carve an inscription at Karnak to commemorate his bravery. "His majesty marched against [the enemy] like a fierce-eyed lion, making them carcasses in their valleys." Victory followed victory as Seti marched across Palestine, taking the key cities of Gaza, Pella, Yenoam, Acre, and Tyre. Fearing defeat, the rulers in Lebanon sought an alliance with Seti rather than face him on the battlefield. Seti agreed, but he demanded that they send timber—the prized so-called cedars of Lebanon—as tribute to the temples in Egypt.

Seti gave the command to bind the scores of prisoners he had taken in battle and begin the long march home. Artisans would later carve on Seti's monuments: "The heart of his majesty . . . rejoices to begin battle . . . his heart is satisfied at seeing blood; he cuts off the heads of the rebellious-hearted; he loves an hour of battle more than a day of rejoicing." This gory statement would make any potential enemy consider the consequences of opposing so powerful a king.

Still, one Syrian stronghold had not yielded to Seti's might: Kadesh, a city well known for its rebellious attitude toward the Egyptians. More than 150 years earlier, Thutmose III had managed to take Kadesh, although with great difficulty. Kadesh stood high on a hill, and its massive walls with only one entrance made it almost impregnable. Siege tactics did not work because two moats circled the city and provided the defenders with a ready supply of water from the nearby Orontes River. Such obstacles, however, were not enough to deter Seti.

Once again, he set out for Syria, and again he met victory. He followed this first campaign with three more. On the fourth and final campaign, the historic first encounter between Egyptians and Hittites occurred. The Hittites occupied the land north of Syria and had allied themselves with the people of Kadesh. For years the Hittites had sought to expand their area of influence and had been encroaching on Egyptian territory. Determined to eliminate the Hittite threat to his country's interests, Seti marched his troops north against the enemy. Soon after, he sent word home of an Egyptian victory. The Hittites, however, seem to have done the same, for official records show that Seti and the Hittite king Mursilis signed a treaty drawing the line of Egypt's northern border just south of Kadesh. Seti's "victory" gave Egypt control of Palestine and Syria, plus a pledge of no more Hittite attacks. The Hittite "victory" stopped the northward advance of the Egyptians and kept Kadesh free of Egyptian control.

Seti now turned his attention west and marched against Libya. Here, too, just as in Syria, he was successful and returned home with bound prisoners in tow to give thanks to Amun-Re. Under a relief of Amun's foot on a monument commemorating Seti's achievements, artisans inscribed, "I give you all lands, every country is beneath your sandals."

Records indicate that Seti also led his army south into Nubia and defeated the chiefs of Kush. An inscription reads: "[They] fall in their blood by the might of your father, Amun, who has decreed for you might and victory."

Egypt was gradually regaining the power it once had, but there was still much to be done. To increase trade, Seti ordered garrisons built to protect Egyptian interests in the Sinai's turquoise mines. He also ordered the mines to the east of Edfu in Upper Egypt brought up to full operation. This hot desert area lacked wells or places where a traveler or worker might quench his thirst. Seti had remarked, "How evil is the way without water! . . . I will make a supply [of water to keep the workers and travelers here alive] so that they will thank [Amun] in my name." Seti also ordered a small village and a temple built for the workers near the site.

Seti had inscribed on the temple walls a series of warnings aimed at anyone who neglected or tampered with the mines, water stations, or revenue from the mines that he had set aside for the upkeep of his mortuary complex: "The monument of the violator [of my monuments and policies] shall itself be violated . . . the lords of my house shall punish in an appropriate manner anyone who acts contrary to the interests of my people."

One key to Seti's success was his Nauri Decree, a series of laws that were drawn up in Year 4 of his reign to help officials maintain justice and peace throughout the land. These laws were quite harsh and unforgiving toward anyone who disobeyed them. Most applied to workers on estates that belonged to the temple of the great god Osiris, at Abydos.

Abydos, a city just west of the Nile, was the site of one of Egypt's ancient royal cemeteries. In keeping with his emphasis on tradition, Seti built a mortuary temple at Abydos. To ensure that the workers assigned to this construction project remained on the job,

In front of the king list that begins with Menes and ends with Seti, Seti I (left) and his son Ramesses II recite hymns from a papyrus roll. This relief is carved in the Gallery of Kings in Seti I's temple at Abydos.

he decreed that no official could take a worker from Abydos and assign him to another construction site. Reassignments seem to have been a common practice, and it may have been the only way to make sure a huge building project was completed on time.

In the Nauri Decree, Seti stated that any official, any overseer of the fields, any herdsman—in short, anyone—who attempted to change the boundary lines for the estates belonging to the temple at Abydos would be demoted to the position of field worker at the temple and lose both his ears. As for the "criminal" who prevented a worker at the temple from snaring his marshes or catching fish in the pond, he was to receive 100 lashes and five open wounds. The person who "kidnaps" a herdsman from the temple and forcibly moves him to another place would be subject to 200 whiplashes and had to replace every head of cattle that the herdsman lost during the time he was away—at a ratio of 100 to 1.

Seti's choice of Abydos was politically and religiously wise. Abydos was the religious center of worship for Osiris, the god of the dead. Since the Middle Kingdom, some 500 years earlier, all Egyptians had looked forward to triumphing over death, just as Osiris had done. Kings also honored Osiris and believed that, in death, they became a divine representation of Osiris, and that their successor on the throne was the earthly representation of Osiris's son, Horus.

For centuries, Egyptians had looked to Abydos as a sacred burial place and the area had become a pilgrimage site. Seti, in an effort to associate himself more closely with tradition and with the practices of his royal predecessors, commissioned his architects to design two structures at Abydos. Instead of dedicating the principal structure to himself or to one deity, as was the custom, he dedicated the building to himself and six other deities (Ptah, Re-Harakhte, Amun, Osiris, Isis, and Horus). Considered one of the most beautiful buildings ever constructed in ancient Egypt, Seti's temple at Abydos was made of fine limestone on a sandstone foundation. The scenes painted along the walls depict the daily rituals performed in the temple to honor the six deities. Here, the artists paid great attention to such detail as the folds of a garment, the intricate interlocking of neckwear fashioned of gold and precious jewels, the leaves and petals of flowers and plants, and the feathers used to fashion fans.

Contrary to custom, the temple's storerooms were built to the left of the sanctuaries, not directly behind them. As a result, the temple resembled a reversed, upside-down letter L. Why is unknown, but the architects may have wished to avoid the site symbolically honored as Osiris's tomb. Known as the Osireion, this structure lay directly behind the sanctuaries. Seti and his architects may have wanted the "false" doors in the temple to lead directly to the Osireion. Traditionally painted on the rear wall of sanctuaries, these doors

allowed the *ka* (life force) of the deceased to pass back and forth between this world and the next.

Over the centuries, architects had designed various structures to house Osiris's tomb, but Seti's was the most dramatic. Entrance to the underground tomb was by a shaft that reached down approximately 30 feet. This, in turn, led to a long tunnel approximately 336 feet long. On the west wall, Seti's artisans painted scenes and passages from the *Book of Gates* and other burial texts.

Seti's mummified body would rest in the Osireion before being transferred to his tomb in the Valley of the Kings. His stay here would be brief but significant, because his body would lie close to the sacred tomb of Osiris himself. And, just as the Osireion was Osiris's *cenotaph* (an empty tomb designed to honor a particular person or deity), so it was, according to some Egyptologists, also Seti's cenotaph. For centuries, Egyptian kings had often built their cenotaph near Abydos and laid their mummy to rest in a royal tomb elsewhere.

Seti, however, did not want his mortuary complex to focus solely on the next life. Because Egyptians valued tradition, Seti felt it only appropriate to include past and future in the reliefs along the temple walls and had the artisans list the kings of Egypt on the wall. Each was to be represented by his cartouche, which meant that the hieroglyphs for each king's birth name and throne name would be enclosed in an oval circle, bordered by a rope that was drawn in the shape of a loop with tied ends.

Seti had strong feelings about which rulers were to be included in the list. The first name was Menes, the ruler credited with uniting Upper and

Lower Egypt some 1,800 years earlier; the last name was his own. Among those missing were Hatshepsut and the four royals associated with the rebel belief in the Aten—Akhenaten, Smenkhkare, Tutankhamun, and Ay. Later kings would take this list as the official royal record and have it inscribed in their temples and on their monuments. Thus, it was Seti's rewrite of history that persisted for generations.

To connect himself even more closely with Egypt's royal line, Seti had the artisans carve his image to the left of the list. His figure on the same wall as the king list implied that he respected and honored these 75 great rulers, and he saw them as his ancestors. Yet making himself a royal descendant was not enough. Seti wished to establish a long line of rulers. To do so, he needed to align his family with past royal families.

Unlike many of his predecessors who had married daughters of kings, Seti had married the daughter of a military officer, a girl named Tuya. Seti saw a possible successor in their third child, named Ramesses after his grandfather. (Seti's and Tuya's first child, a boy, died young, and their second child was a girl.) To link his son with the past, Seti had artisans carve the figure of young Ramesses next to his figure on the wall with the king list. To show that Ramesses was still a youth, the artisans pictured his head shaved except for the traditional lock of hair hanging down the side of his head. (According to custom, this sidelock was cut off when a child reached adulthood.)

To pay for the upkeep of his temple, Seti decreed that the income from certain royal lands and resources go directly to the temple. Even though some of these lands lay beyond Egypt's

Seti I

borders and in areas that Seti had conquered, the rules set forth in the Nauri Decree applied to all workers on the temple's lands.

Karnak was also humming with activity. There workers were constructing the latest addition to the great temple dedicated to the god Amun-Re—a hypostyle hall (a roofed area supported by rows of pillars) that was grander in size and design than any ever built in Egypt. Seti's father, Ramesses I, had started it and his son, Ramesses II, would oversee the completion of the work.

One project still remained unfinished—Seti's tomb in the Valley of the Kings and his mortuary temple just to the southeast of the Valley at el Qurna. The temple was massive, although not as grand as the one at Abydos. The tomb, too, was massive, and of all the Egyptian royal tombs thus far uncovered, Seti's is still considered the grandest and its wall paintings the finest.

In October of 1817, an Italian by the name of Giovanni Battista Belzoni rediscovered Seti's tomb. The wall paintings so delighted his wife, Sarah, who was on-site with him, that the couple—so it is said—made the tomb their living quarters for several weeks.

Along the corridors were reliefs representing the rituals involved in passing from this world to the next. Astronomical texts decorated one side of the ceiling; images of the constellations and of the deities of the Egyptian pantheon adorned the other side. With the background painted a deep blue and the constellations gold, the effect was breathtaking. In his journal, Belzoni noted that the colors were bright and fresh and that the figures so fine and perfect that "one would think they had been drawn only the day before," not 2,200 years earlier.

The greatest find, however, was Seti's alabaster sarcophagus. Shaped to resemble the human form, as was the tradition, the sarcophagus measured nine feet five inches in length and three feet seven inches in width. By design, the alabaster was only two inches thick, and was of such a fine quality that when Belzoni placed a light inside the sarcophagus, it could be seen shining brightly from the outside. Artisans had carved scenes and passages from the *Book of Gates* directly into the alabaster. To highlight these designs, they filled them in with a blue paint-like mixture.

What Belzoni did not find was Seti himself. It was not until 1881 that Seti's mummy was discovered among 40 royal mummies that ancient Egyptian priests had reburied at Deir el Bahri. Close examination has revealed that Seti was about five feet tall, with pierced ears and a hooked nose. The latter seems to have been a family trait, because the mummies of both his father and his son suggest the same nose shape. Seti's features suggest the personality of a man who was strong-willed and determined, a person who commanded the respect of those about him but was, at the same time, at peace with himself and with the world.

FURTHER READING

Lichtheim, Miriam. *Ancient Egyptian Literature: A Book of Readings*, vol. 2, pp. 52–57. Berkeley: University of California Press, 1976.

Pritchard, James B., ed. *The Ancient Near East: An Anthology of Texts and Pictures*, pp. 182–83. Princeton, N.J.: Princeton University Press, 1958.

POSITION

King of Egypt

REIGN

About 1291–78 B.C.

ACCOMPLISHMENTS

Vizier and commander-in-chief of the military under his father Ramesses I; crushed Shasu opposition in the Sinai; led a series of successful military campaigns in Palestine and Syria; led the Egyptians for the first time into battle against the Hittites and settled Egypt's northern boundary just south of Kadesh; ended Libyan raids into Egypt; led a successful expedition against the Kushites; inaugurated a massive building program; built a mortuary temple at el Qurna; built a great temple to himself and six deities at Abydos; rebuilt the Osireion; built a temple at Abydos dedicated to his father; principally responsible for the enormous hypostyle hall in the temple of Amun-Re at Karnak; built the grandest and finest tomb thus far discovered in the Valley of the Kings

Ramesses II

KING OF KINGS

I met a traveler from an antique land
Who said: Two vast and trunkless legs of stone
Stand in the desert. Near them, on the sand,
Half sunk, a shattered visage lies, whose frown,
and wrinkled lip, and sneer of cold command,
Tell that its sculptor well those passions read
Which yet survive, stamped on these lifeless things,
The hand that mocked them and the heart that fed;
And on the pedestal these words appear:
"My name is Ozymandias, king of kings:
Look on my works, ye Mighty, and despair!"
Nothing besides remains. Round the decay
Of that colossal wreck, boundless and bare
The lone and level sands stretch far away.

Ramesses II might question the name "Ozymandias" in this sonnet by the nineteenth-century English poet Percy Bysshe Shelley. However, once he realized that Ozymandias was the ancient Greek adaptation of his throne name User-maat-re, he would have liked the "king of kings" phrase, for it reflected exactly how he saw himself and his reign.

Since the death of his older brother, Ramesses had been groomed by his father, Seti I, to inherit the throne. When Ramesses was about 10, Seti named him commander-in-chief of Egypt's armed forces. At the time this was an honorary title, but a few years later Seti would order Ramesses to accompany him on military expeditions in the Syria-Palestine area.

Ramesses was probably in his early 20s when he succeeded his father. Soon after, he attended the annual Opet festival at Thebes in honor of Amun-Re. There he performed the ritual that officially reinforced his right to inherit the throne and reestablished his identity as the divine representative of the gods on Earth.

The Opet festival, however, mattered little to those beyond Egypt's borders. Of far greater interest was how Ramesses would act politically and militarily. For Egypt's enemies, it was a time to watch and wait for an opportunity to strike. The first conflict came in Year 2. A people known as the Sherden crossed the Mediterranean Sea and invaded the Delta region. This was not the first time "Sea Peoples" (for thus they are known to history) raided the Delta, nor would it be the last. Ramesses easily defeated the Sherden, but he did not take the surviving males as captives. Because he would need additional troops to battle his opponents in the Syria-Palestine area, Ramesses ordered these foreign soldiers to join his army. He later commissioned the artisans decorating his temples and other buildings to depict the Sherden dressed in their traditional battle armor—round shields and helmets adorned with two horns.

Every country is beneath your feet, O king, ruler of the Nine Bows, Lord of the Two Lands, Ramesses II.

—Inscription on the walls of the temple to Amun, at Karnak

Farther east toward Palestine, trouble had been brewing, especially after Seti died. The rulers in lands abutting those controlled by Egypt began extending their own borders. Determined to control the situation, Ramesses advanced against the Hittites, a powerful people to the north of Syria. Ramesses believed Egyptian control of the strategically located city of Kadesh would enhance Egyptian might throughout the region. Kadesh, however, was a long-term goal. Retaking the area south of Kadesh was a more immediate concern because Ramesses wanted allies behind him as he marched north against the enemy.

After leaving the Egyptian border town of Tjel, Ramesses moved his army across the Sinai and into Palestine, where he returned the lands of Canaan, Tyre, Byblos, and Amurru to Egyptian control. Winning the allegiance of Prince Benteshina of Amurru was important because the prince of Amurru had previously allied himself with the Hittites, and his land acted as a buffer between Hittite territory and Egyptian territory.

But Ramesses was not one to act hastily or on impulse. For him, caution and preparedness spelled success, and so he halted his march at Nahr al Kelb (Dog River) near present-day Beirut and returned to Egypt. In the approaching winter months he planned a new offensive. When spring and warmer weather arrived, Ramesses was ready.

Year 5 saw Ramesses marching east, then north, toward Kadesh. Although he could not rely on the element of surprise because enemy scouts were reporting his position to the Hittites, he could still keep the Hittites wondering where and when he would attack, and which route he would choose. Records prove that Ramesses did indeed gain the advantage, for the Hittites seem to have been unaware of Ramesses's decision to send a contingent of elite troops by a more westerly route. This division was to march along

Seti I trained Ramesses, shown here as a child, in the arts of war and peace. The first lessons were simple, but they built Ramesses's confidence and instilled in him a sense of how and when to use authority.

This gold ring, often called the "horse ring," belonged to Ramesses II. The Egyptians enjoyed wearing jewelry and often placed it on the dead and on statues of the deities.

the coast of Palestine until they were well north of Kadesh. There they were to turn east, then south. If all went well, these troops and those with Ramesses would crush Kadesh in a pincer-like maneuver.

As Ramesses marched north, he divided his troops into the four traditional divisions. Each consisted of approximately 5,000 soldiers and was named after a powerful Egyptian deity—Amun, Re, Ptah, and Seth.

As king and commander-in-chief, Ramesses led the first division, the division of Amun.

Ramesses ordered his men to capture anyone who might be a Hittite messenger, spy, or scout. When two Hittites were caught, and both told the same tale—that the Hittites had set up camp about 120 miles from Kadesh—Ramesses felt he could advance without fear, but he had made one tactical error. With his thoughts only on victory, Ramesses had neglected to verify or even challenge the information revealed by the Hittites.

As he approached Kadesh, he ordered the troops to veer a little to the west and set up camp just outside the city walls. Joy soon turned to dismay after two more Hittites were captured. Under torture, they admitted that the first two Hittites were spies and that the great Hittite army of King Muwatallis, which was "more numerous than the sand of the shore," was encamped just beyond the city walls to the east. Ramesses immediately summoned a council of war. It was a small council, as only the troops belonging to his division were with him. The other three divisions were still on their way north.

The Hittites, meanwhile, stood ready and in position. As soon as the division of Re crossed the Orontes River and was quickening its pace to reach Ramesses, Hittite chariots burst onto the plain from the east and attacked the middle of the division. The Egyptians had no time to arm themselves or even to position themselves in a formation that might withstand an attack. And they could expect no help from Ramesses, whose division was some five miles to the north.

Yet even if the soldiers of Re had had more time to prepare, the odds of surviving a surprise Hittite chariot attack were slim. The two armies relied on very different tactics for success. By custom, each Hittite chariot carried three men—a driver, a shield bearer, and a warrior with a spear or javelin. The Egyptian chariot, on the other hand, had only two men—the driver and a bowman. In addition, the Hittites seemed to prefer hand-to-hand combat, using chariots as the means of advance, whereas the Egyptians preferred to have their archers send a volley of arrows from moving chariots, hit as many targets as possible, and then allow the foot soldiers to engage in hand-to-hand combat.

Unaware of the defeat his division of Re had just suffered, Ramesses was still meeting with his officers when survivors from Re's division burst into the meeting. They had barely finished their report when Hittite troops broke through the defensive wall around Ramesses's camp and headed straight for the royal tent. Ramesses wasted no time considering his options. For him, there was only one choice: defeat the enemy.

"When his majesty saw them, he was enraged against them, like his father, Montu, god of Thebes. He seized the adornments of battle, and arrayed himself in his coat of mail. . . . Then he mounted his horse and led quickly on." In such a way did the artisan commissioned by Ramesses later tell the story—not just once, but many times. Another account reads, "His majesty . . . charged into the midst of the foe . . . while he was alone himself, and no other with him." Ramesses also had the artisans record his conversation with his chariot driver, Menna: "When Menna saw so great a number of chariots had ringed about me, he felt faint, and fear entered his limbs. Thus he spoke to his majesty, 'We stand alone in the middle of the enemy. The infantry and the chariots have abandoned us. . . . Let us also leave unharmed.'" But Ramesses answered: "Steady your heart, Menna. I shall move in among them just as a hawk." With these words, Ramesses charged the Hittites again and again, "so great was the faith he had in himself and in his father Amun."

Although the accounts may be somewhat exaggerated, Ramesses's bravery certainly must have rallied the bewildered Egyptian troops. It definitely won the Egyptians time—time that allowed the elite forces that had traveled by the more westerly route to reach the battleground. To the surprise of the Egyptians, the Hittite soldiers slowed their assault. Tempted by the riches of the royal tent and the supplies abandoned by the Egyptian soldiers, they ran about snatching what plunder they could.

Soon, what had seemed an easy Hittite victory turned into a retreat. As the elite reinforcements joined the main divisions, Ramesses's troops regained their composure, steadied their weapons, and regrouped to attack. By day's end, a calm had settled on the battlefield and both sides rested. The following day, the two armies again took to the battlefield, but neither side was able to gain the advantage. Recognizing that continued fighting meant only more death and destruction, Muwatallis sued for peace and asked, "O victorious king, peace is better than war. Give us breath."

Although Ramesses did not take Kadesh, he considered Egypt's action victorious and had his version of the battle inscribed on monuments, temple walls, and papyrus rolls throughout Egypt. Often he is shown charging the enemy in a chariot and has the horses' reins tied about his waist so that he can freely use his bow and arrow.

For centuries, historians had only Ramesses's version of the battle. Then clay tablets detailing the same battle were uncovered in the ancient Hittite capital of Hattusas. The Hittites told a different story. They claimed that they, not the Egyptians, had won Kadesh. The version on the Hattusas tablets seems closer to the truth, considering that Kadesh continued under Hittite control. But the battle did establish Ramesses as a warrior king and a ruler who feared no enemy.

Nevertheless, Ramesses's reputation did not stop the Libyans from attacking Egypt's western border. To stop these border raids, Ramesses ordered a line of garrisons constructed from Rakotis (present-day Alexandria) to west of what today is el Alamein. Confident that the restless Libyans were contained within their own borders, Ramesses again looked east.

In Year 7, he marched north against the kingdoms of Jericho, Jerusalem, and Moab. Year 8 and Year 9 saw two more campaigns, each of which succeeded in extending the frontier of Ramesses's empire. This time, it was Tunip, Kadesh, and northern Amurru that fell before Ramesses's might. Then came news that Muwatallis had died, and that Muwatallis's son Urhi-Teshub (Mursilis III) and his uncle Hattusilis were locked in a bitter struggle for power.

After deciding that Egyptian interests would benefit more under Hattusilis, in Year 21 Ramesses's signed a treaty of cooperation with Hattusilis that brought a lasting peace between the two nations. He immediately commissioned artisans to carve the terms of the agreement on temple walls. Hattusilis did the same. Texts uncovered both in Egypt and in the Hittite capital make this the earliest recorded treaty to have survived in its entirety. According to the provisions, "There shall be no hostilities between [the Hittites and the Egyptians] forever." Should a ruler dare violate these terms, the treaty promised that "the thousand gods of the land of [the Hittites], and the thousand gods of the land of Egypt shall desolate his house, his land, and his subjects."

To further strengthen the bond between the two nations, Ramesses married one of Hattusilis's daughters. This was not Ramesses's first marriage. Egyptologists estimate that he had as many as eight principal wives and numerous offspring, for whom he commissioned a gigantic tomb complex diagonally opposite his own burial site in the Valley of the Kings.

Ramesses's favorite wife was Nefertari, whom he had married years before he ascended the throne. They had several children, including at least four sons. Istnofret was another of Ramesses's principal wives, and the accomplishments of two of her sons by Ramesses are well recorded. One was Khaemwaset, whose dedication to restoring the temples and monuments of Egypt's early kings won him renown

Ramesses II

POSITION

King of Egypt

REIGN

About 1279–12 B.C.

ACCOMPLISHMENTS

Reconquered the lands in Palestine and Syria; signed a peace treaty with the Hittite king Hattusilis; ended Libyan raids and ordered a line of garrisons established along the western edge of the Delta; improved trade relations with Nubia, the Sinai, Palestine-Lebanon-Syria, and the islands in the Mediterranean; oversaw a grand building program, including the hypostyle hall at Karnak and his mortuary temple at Abydos; ordered two temples cut into the rock cliffs at Abu Simbel, one in honor of himself and the other in honor of his wife Nefertari; ordered the building of his mortuary temple (the Ramesseum) on the west bank of the Nile near the Valley of the Kings; ordered his tomb complex built in the Valley of the Kings, along with a huge complex for the burial of his many children

Ramesses [II], who has made his monuments like the stars of heaven, whose works mingle with the sky, rejoicing over which Re rises in his house of millions of years.

—Inscription on an obelisk at Heliopolis

as one of the world's first archaeologists. The other was Merneptah, who succeeded Ramesses on the throne.

As soon as Ramesses heard that the Hittites had arranged for his new bride to make the journey in wintertime, he arranged for his army to meet her and her traveling companions in Palestine and escort the group to his palace in the new capital city of Pi-Ramesses.

Ramesses knew well the strategic importance of the site he had chosen for his capital. Because Egypt's political and economic welfare had become increasingly tied to affairs in the Syria-Palestine area, Ramesses considered Thebes too removed from the action. Even Memphis, which had served as Egypt's capital for centuries and lay at the entrance to the Delta, seemed distant. Pi-Ramesses, in the northeastern corner of the northern Delta region, seemed perfect.

Surviving contemporary accounts describe the palace as more magnificent than any ever built. Everywhere were inlays of gold, silver, lapis lazuli, and turquoise. Its rivers and lakes teemed with fish, and the surrounding fields produced an abundance of pomegranates, apples, olives, and figs. Because Pi-Ramesses lay close to a main waterway, the city was easily accessible to traders and enjoyed a plentiful supply of imported goods, both from other areas in Egypt and from abroad.

With the borders settled and no more wars to fight, Ramesses was able

to employ a large workforce that included both Egyptians and foreigners living in Egypt. Surviving Egyptian records mention a group of people known as the Apiru. Some worked in the stone quarries; others were responsible for transporting stone temple-blocks; still others made building bricks. Many historians believe that the Apiru were actually the Hebrews, and that the Biblical story of Moses petitioning a king of Egypt for the right to lead his people out of Egypt took place during Ramesses's reign. Today, archaeologists continue the search for more evidence in Egyptian inscriptions to confirm the Biblical story of the Exodus.

Ramesses concentrated on two building projects. One was a pair of temples at Abu Simbel in Nubia; the other was his mortuary temple on the west bank near the Valley of the Kings. At Abu Simbel he dedicated the Great Temple to Amun-Re, Re-Harakhte (another aspect of the sun god), and himself; the Small Temple he dedicated to the goddess Hathor and to Nefertari. The facade of the Great Temple rose to a height of 102 feet. On either side of the entrance were two gigantic statues of Ramesses in a sitting position. Each measured 60 feet tall. Smaller figures cut from the rock near each of the statue's feet represented Nefertari and their children.

A passageway more than 200 feet in length led from the entrance to the sanctuary deep within the rock cliff.

Along this corridor were eight standing statues of Ramesses—four on each side. They were carved to represent the king as the god Osiris with arms crossed over his chest and hands holding the royal symbols—the scepter and the flail. Mindful of his victory at Kadesh, Ramesses had artisans cover the walls with scenes of the battle.

At the rear of the temple were four seated statues. One was of Ramesses II; the others were of Amun-Re, Re-Harakhte, and Ptah. By design, twice a year—at the summer solstice (the longest day of the year) and at the winter solstice (the shortest day of the year), the rays of the sun stream down the corridor and rest on the statues of Ramesses II, Amun-Re, and Re-Harakhte. No rays shine on Ptah—quite fitting, as the Egyptians associated him with the underworld.

For centuries, Ramesses's temples at Abu Simbel stood as a tribute to himself and the nation's rich heritage. In 1955, Egypt's leaders approved the construction of a Great Dam near the First Cataract, to control the annual flooding of the Nile. To hold the waters backed up by this dam, the architects designed a lake site (Lake Nasser). Alarmed that many ancient sites would be "drowned," archaeologists met to discuss the possibility of saving some monuments, including the two temples at Abu Simbel. What followed was a modern engineering marvel—workers cut the two temples into large blocks, moved the blocks to a site just above the cliff where they had been situated originally, and then reassembled them.

Ramesses's mortuary temple was not so fortunate. Although not affected by Lake Nasser, it lies mostly in ruins. Surveys of the site show that the temple, known today as the Ramesseum, once measured about 910 feet by 550 feet. Surrounding the temple on all but the entrance side were administrative offices and huge vaulted storage areas. But it was the 1,000-ton statue Ramesses's sculptors had carved in his likeness that brought Ramesses everlasting fame—its toppled ruins moved Shelley to write the poem "Ozymandias." The poem and the ruins also inspired others to learn more about Ramesses, the ruler whose monumental structures won him the nickname "Ramesses the Great."

By the time Ramesses approached 90 years of age, he had celebrated 14 Heb-Sed jubilee festivals and had outlived many of his children. Merneptah was now next in line, and he was already in his 60s. For several years Merneptah had been assuming more and more responsibility as his father's health deteriorated. Ramesses's teeth, especially those in back, were quite worn and gave him considerable pain. The arthritis in his hip joints was also a source of much discomfort. He had problems walking, and his heart no longer beat as strongly or as regularly.

When Ramesses's mummy was discovered among those that ancient Egyptian priests had reburied at Deir el Bahri, Egyptologists came face-to-face with a man about six feet tall who showed signs of a great age. His ears were pierced, as was the custom, and his nose was hook-shape, which seems to have been a family trait. (Those responsible for mummifying his body had filled his nose with peppercorns to keep the arch shape.)

In 1976, fearing that the deterioration evident around Ramesses's neck might lead to the total disintegration of the mummy, Egyptian officials decided to fly the king to France to be treated by bacteria experts. When the plane carrying Ramesses's mummy landed in Paris, the French honored the ancient monarch in the same way they would any visiting royal. Government officials

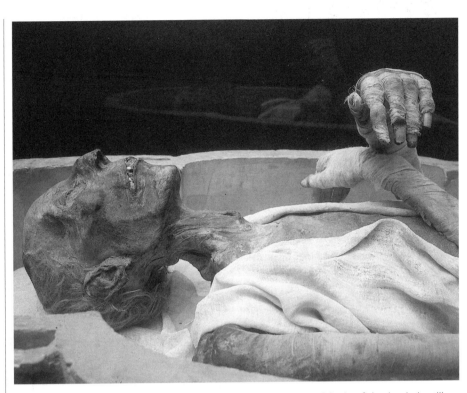

Ramesses II's mummy lies today in Cairo's Egyptian Museum. Much of the body is still wrapped in its original resin-soaked bandages.

met him with a full Presidential Guard of Honor. Following the successful treatment of his body and an appearance at a special exhibition, Ramesses made his final journey home, where a special room had been designed in Cairo's Egyptian Museum to house his remains.

FURTHER READING

Kitchen, K. A. *Pharaoh Triumphant: The Life and Times of Ramesses II.* Warminster, England: Aris and Phillips, 1981.

Menu, Bernadette. *Ramesses II: Greatest of the Pharaohs.* New York: Abrams, 1999.

Roberts, Russell. *Rulers of Ancient Egypt,* chap. 5. San Diego, Calif.: Lucent: 1999.

Nefertari

BELOVED WIFE

he temple Ramesses II commissioned architects to build at Abu Simbel in honor of his wife Nefertari was an architectural masterpiece. The inscriptions Ramesses's workers had carved into the stone were true: "of fine, white, and enduring sandstone—an eternal work" and "never was done the equal before."

The site, too, was breathtaking, situated as it was in a rock cliff just beyond the fertile strip of land that ran along the west bank of the Nile River. For Ramesses, however, what was more important was that a structure so massive and

For years the identity of this finely detailed bust was uncertain. In the late 20th century, the discovery of a similar, much larger statue helped Egyptologists solve the mystery. Both appear to be Meryetamun, daughter of Nefertari and Ramesses II, who later became Ramesses II's Great Royal Wife.

so magnificent was being built on Nubian, not Egyptian, soil. Thus, the temple clearly announced to all Nubians that Egypt, not Nubia, was the ruling power in the area.

Yet power was not the only message Ramesses hoped to convey. Ramesses saw the structure as proof of the great love and respect he had for Nefertari. Of all his wives—and he had quite a few—Nefertari was his favorite. Whether she was a royal is uncertain, as virtually nothing is known about her background. According to the records, Nefertari bore Ramesses several sons, but all died before Ramesses.

Her temple at Abu Simbel stood quite close to a larger one honoring Ramesses and the deities Amun-Re, Re-Harakhte, and Ptah—only a narrow, sandy gully separated the two temples. Because Nefertari's temple was also dedicated to Hathor, a sky goddess whom the Egyptians often associated with the goddess Isis, the symbolism was clear: According to tradition, Egypt's king was the earthly representative of Isis's son Horus, and the Great Royal Wife played a role similar to that of Isis. Thus, Nefertari and Isis were both mothers of sons whom the Egyptians honored as rulers of the two lands.

The facade of Nefertari's temple was approximately 88 feet wide and 39 feet high. On either side of the entrance stood two gigantic statues of Ramesses and one of Nefertari. Into the rock between these figures, sculptors had cut several smaller statues representing their children. While it was customary to represent royal families in such a manner, the scale and positioning of these figures against the rock cliff was awesome. To make certain that everyone knew exactly by whom and for whom the temple was built, Ramesses had his artisans carve above the entranceway that it was he, "strong in Truth . . . [who] made this divine place for his wife Nefertari, whom he loves."

The architects followed the traditional temple design for the interior. The central corridor led from the entranceway to the sanctuary at the rear of the complex. This room, known as the "holy of holies," was where the statue of the deity (or deities, in the case of Ramesses's temple) was placed. The magnificently adorned interior, however, gave little indication of how much work the actual construction had involved.

In the 1960s, when archaeologists from around the world joined together to save as many structures as possible before the new Lake Nasser flooded the area, all those working to rescue Nefertari's temple and Ramesses's temple gained a renewed appreciation for the engineering skills of the ancient Egyptians. Relying on an understanding of rock formation that had been acquired through the centuries, Ramesses's engineers pinpointed those areas in the rock cliffs at Abu Simbel where workers could cut deep into the rock. They then adapted their design to take advantage of hard sandstone banks that alternated with softer rock layers. Aware that the ceilings and the interior halls had to bear much weight, the architects made sure that their plans had these areas coincide with the hardest rock layers. The design also took into account how high the Nile's floodwaters reached. Exactness was possible here because for years the Egyptians had kept records of water-table and flood heights.

Nefertari may not have visited her temple many times, because her name disappears from the records around Year 24—the same year her temple seems to have been completed. Whether she died, became ill, or retired from public life is unknown. Most Egyptologists believe that she died at that time.

Architects also rank Nefertari's tomb among the most magnificent ever constructed in ancient Egypt. She and Ramesses chose an area known today as

Nefertari

POSITION
Queen of Egypt

REIGN
About 1270 B.C.

ACCOMPLISHMENTS
Gave much support to her husband Ramesses; her role as Chief Royal Wife and favorite wife led Ramesses to commission a magnificent temple built in her honor at Abu Simbel; her tomb complex in the Valley of the Queens, especially the wall paintings, was the most splendid yet uncovered as of 2001

One of several forms of Re, Khepri personified the young sun at dawn and thus became a symbol of renewal. Artists portrayed Khepri as a dung beetle (scarab) pushing a ball (the sun) or as a scarab-headed man (as in this wall painting).

the Valley of the Queens. The Egyptians called it "the Place of Beauty." A relatively new burial site, it lay on the west bank of the Nile River, a short distance southwest of the Valley of the Kings. Records suggest that Ramesses's grandfather was the first to bury his Great Royal Wife here.

Nefertari's pink granite sarcophagus was designed to lie for all eternity in a specially dug sunken area flanked by four square pillars that were decorated with finely executed scenes representing passages from the *Book of Gates*. Painted reliefs adorned the walls of the corridors and other chambers in the complex.

Ramesses II made as his monument for the Great King's Wife, Nefertari, beloved of Mut, a house cut into the pure mountain of Nubia.

—Inscription on the small temple at Abu Simbel

The warmth and realism they express make them among the most beautiful Egyptian artwork to have survived. The artists were masters of the task and drew the features of each figure with a sensitivity that brings the paintings to life. The colors are crisp and rich and the detail well defined.

A scene in the offering hall (the first room of the complex) shows Nefertari sitting regally on the throne. She holds the scepter of power with one hand and calmly moves a playing piece on a game board with the other. A wide tan band extends down the front of her long white dress. On either side are narrow, evenly spaced vertical bands. Decorating the free-flowing sleeves that reach to her elbows are narrow horizontal bands. A large collar-necklace covers her upper chest and her shoulders.

In the tomb's inner chamber (the third room in the complex), the reliefs on one wall show Nefertari offering a sacrifice to Osiris. Another scene shows the queen standing before Thoth, the ibis-headed god of wisdom and writing. At the same time, she is offering cloth to the god Ptah and honoring a bull with seven cows. With white as the background color of the walls and dark blue studded with gold stars on the ceiling, the ancient artisans created an effect that is still striking today.

Unfortunately, these magnificent structures tell few personal facts about Nefertari. We can only guess that she might have visited Set Maat ("the Place of Truth"). This village was home to the skilled tomb workers. Built more than 200 years earlier, Set Maat was located between the Valley of the Queens and the Valley of the Kings. The workers in the village ranked their position above that of the unskilled laborers. By custom, they were not conscripted to work on government projects for a specific period of time. Rather, Set Maat was their permanent, year-round home, and their job was a highly regarded profession, one that passed from father to son.

Over the centuries, the rising water table at Thebes has caused extensive damage to Nefertari's tomb, and the buildup of mineral salts in the walls is pushing the paint off of them. In an effort to reverse this situation, a group of concerned Egyptologists, archaeologists, and scientists has joined with the Egyptian government to launch an international project aimed at preventing further deterioration and, where possible, at restoring the paintings in Nefertari's tomb.

FURTHER READING

McDonald, John K. *House of Eternity: the Tomb of Nefertari*. Los Angeles, Calif.: J. Paul Getty Museum, 1996.

Siliotti, Alberto. *Guide to the Valley of the Kings*, pp. 80–93. London: Wiedenfeld & Nicolson, 1996.

Ramesses III

![Eye of Horus symbol]

IN THE FOOTSTEPS OF THE GREAT

In Year 5 of the reign of Ramesses III, messengers brought news to the royal court that the Libyans were advancing east across the desert sands. For centuries, Libyan tribes had looked with envy upon the fertile lands of the Delta in Lower Egypt. And for centuries they had heard reports of Egyptian granaries overflowing with surplus food crops. Now they too wanted some of this land.

About 30 years earlier, Merneptah, the son of Ramesses II (Ramesses the Great), had crushed a similar invasion, but the internal turmoil that followed Merneptah's death had allowed the Libyans to consider another advance on Egypt's western border. A new leader, an Egyptian named Seth-nakhte, came to power and restored order to the Two Lands. Historians list this ruler as the founder of the 20th Dynasty. After a rule of only three years, he died, and his son Ramesses III sat on Egypt's throne.

The Libyans did not consider themselves the aggressors. They claimed they attacked because Ramesses had interfered with the rights of the Tjemehu (a Libyan tribe) when he named a child to be their chief. The Libyans, however, had underestimated their opponent. Ramesses III knew well the history of his namesake Ramesses II and had chosen, as his personal goal, to emulate his distinguished predecessor. According to the inscription he later had workers carve on the outer north wall of his mortuary temple, he marched against

> those who shall invade his boundary . . . like a flame . . . in dry grass. [They flutter] like wild fowl in the middle of the net, with legs struggling in the basket. . . . Their loss is heavy. . . . Their leaders were carried off, slain. . . . They were made prisoners. . . . [Ramesses himself] is like a bull standing in the field, his eye and his two horns ready and prepared to ram their rear with his head. . . . He is like the lion with the deep roar upon the mountaintops, whose terror is feared from afar.

Unable to oppose this powerful "lion" successfully, the Libyans retreated. Ramesses, however, had little time to enjoy the victory. Trouble was brewing in the East. Migrant groups of people from different areas in Asia and other lands bordering the Mediterranean and Aegean Seas, including many refugees who were fleeing invasions of their own homelands, had begun pushing their way south—some by land, and some by sea. (History has referred to these groups as the "Sea Peoples.") Accompanying the warriors traveling by land were their wives and children, along with oxen pulling wagonloads of personal belongings.

Unwilling to divide his troops to counter both the attack by land and the one by sea, Ramesses took on the land forces first. He sent couriers with orders that the troops manning Egypt's garrisons along the eastern borders with Syria and Palestine should hold fast until he could march his army northward. Fearless in the face of the enemy, Ramesses "marched afar in his advance, smiting tens of thousands in the space of an hour. . . . He overwhelmed the combatants like fire, causing all those who confront him to become [ashes]."

Having met success on land, Ramesses now looked to do the same on sea. Because his fleet was not skilled in this type of fighting, he planned to draw the enemy into the waterways of the Delta. When the enemy entered a main Delta tributary, Ramesses ordered his fleet to block all escape routes. Thus "the net was made ready for them, to ensnare them . . . [and] they fell into it." Ramesses gave the signal for the archers he had positioned along the banks of the river to fire volleys of arrows. After the archers exhausted their supply of arrows, Ramesses ordered his sailors to snag the enemy's ships with huge grappling hooks and reel them alongside their own ships. Caught unawares and with many men already killed or wounded, the survivors found themselves overwhelmed and fell swiftly in hand-to-hand shipboard combat. Ramesses later had his artisans record the victory on his mortuary temple, "My arrow struck, and none escaped my arms or my hand. I flourished like a hawk among the fowl; my talons descended upon their heads. Amun-Re was upon my right and upon my left, his might and power were in my limbs."

After this sea offensive, which is often considered the first recorded naval battle in history, most of the Sea Peoples withdrew from the Delta region and settled in areas bordering the Mediterranean and Aegean Seas. Some settled in the Palestine area, and later became known as the Philistines.

Six years later, Libya's rulers again took up arms and marched east. Joined by other tribes, including the Meshwesh, the Libyans made a frontal assault on Egypt's border garrisons.

Brave and valiant king . . . his name has penetrated all hearts as far as the limit of the darkness.

—Inscription on Ramesses III's mortuary temple at Medinet Habu

Members of the court, far right, watch as Egyptian, Nubian, and Syrian wrestlers and stick fighters battle each other. This relief appears on a wall in Ramesses III's mortuary temple at Medinet Habu.

This is an excerpt from the lengthy Great Harris Papyrus. Written in hieratic script (writing derived from hieroglyphs), it includes records of Ramesses III's gifts to the gods, temple festivals, and military campaigns.

Ramesses quickly rallied his troops and fought "hand to hand, his voice upraised, shouting like a griffin [a mythical monster with the body and hind legs of a lion and the head, wings, and claws of an eagle]." In the face of such determination, the enemy "were scattered, overturned, brought to the ground; their blood was like a flood, their bodies [crushed on] the spot, trampled."

So reads the account Ramesses had inscribed on the walls of his mortuary temple. The sculptors accompanied the text with descriptive scenes of the confrontation. They showed Ramesses, his bow drawn, charging the enemy in his chariot. Two lines of Egyptian chariots accompany him, as do some foot soldiers. The Egyptian infantry, armed with sword and shield, march in perfect order ahead of the archers; the enemy, on the other hand, show no semblance of order, appearing scattered and confused. Some fall dead, pierced by the king's arrows; others scramble to escape their pursuers. After the battle, Ramesses leaves his chariot to help bind the captives.

Egypt certainly was not as powerful as it once had been, but Ramesses's victories brought a sense of security and stability to the empire. They also made

rulers in the lands beyond Egypt's borders aware that the king would not hesitate to march his army against them. On the walls of his mortuary temple, he proclaimed, "[T]he lands are in peace. . . . A woman goes about at her will, with her veil upon her head, her travels extending as far as she pleases."

Traders definitely benefited from Ramesses's firm rule, and merchants freely sent their wares up and down the Nile and across the Sinai Peninsula into Palestine, Syria, and Lebanon. Further exploration of the Sinai's copper mines was encouraged, and Nubia continued as one of Egypt's principal trading partners. Nubia's leaders even stopped their border raids and attacks on Egyptian garrisons. The most prized trading partner, however, was the fabled land of Punt. Following the example set by several of his predecessors, Ramesses sent a trading expedition to Punt—the last such expedition commissioned by an Egyptian king.

As the Two Lands regained some of their former strength, Ramesses looked to thank the gods for their help. He ordered his engineers to build several shrines and structures at Karnak and other sites. But he did not follow the example of his namesake Ramesses II and commission massive construction projects. Instead, Ramesses III preferred to focus most of his efforts on his mortuary temple. As the site, he chose land that lay approximately one half mile south of Ramesses II's mortuary temple, the Ramesseum, on the west bank of the Nile, and encouraged his architects to use the Ramesseum as a model. Today, the area is known as Medinet Habu ("town of Habu"), a name that refers to a community of Christians who, centuries later, lived in the same area. In Ramesses's time, the temple was called the "Mansion of Millions of Years of King Ramesses III" and "United with Eternity in the Estate of Amun."

Ramesses saw his temple as a means of recording both his achievements and his close association with the gods. Among the traditional elements were a series of shrines dedicated to the gods Amun, Mut, Khons, Ptah, Montu, and Re, and another series honoring Ramesses II and Ramesses III and his family. New to mortuary temple design was the 240-foot-high entrance gateway constructed of sandstone and mud brick. It resembled a *migdol*, the fortified gateway that served as an entrance to Syrian towns. To link the temple with the Nile River, workers built a canal and landing dock. Materials, supplies, and offerings could be brought directly to the site.

On the inside walls of the temple and on the thick outer wall, artisans carved and painted reliefs and inscriptions detailing Ramesses's exploits. Prayers and offerings of thanksgiving to the gods were also inscribed. A great calendar marked the festival days and offerings, and another relief recorded the religious holy days and rituals celebrated at the temple.

Egyptologists, however, question whether Ramesses III actually participated in all the campaigns or received all the honors credited to him in the reliefs. The artisans may have exaggerated details and fabricated a few facts, most likely to emphasize the greatness of their king's achievements and to associate him more closely with the gods. To reinforce the link between past, present, and future, Ramesses followed the example of Ramesses II and had artisans list the names of his sons on the walls of the west portico.

Ramesses saw his mortuary temple complex as a building for religious services and as a structure that could serve political needs as well. The great outer wall seems to have been a defensive wall. Should an emergency arise, such as a Libyan raid, those living in the area could take refuge behind the wall. The complex also became the administrative center for Thebes and the surrounding area. Here, too, was a brick palace and

the traditional Window of Appearance from which Ramesses distributed rewards to those who had achieved some notable accomplishment. On the south side of the complex stood another palace. This, however, was a model palace, designed to serve the dead king's *ka* (life force) in the afterlife.

Under Ramesses, Egypt experienced a mini–Golden Age. Tribute and taxes from the lands subject to or allied with the Two Lands continually increased Egypt's wealth. An account commissioned by Ramesses's son and successor listed the gifts Ramesses had presented to the gods during his reign of 31 years and 41 days. These records name specific parcels of land, slaves, various types of animals, grains, vegetables, fruits, ships and boats, and the number of linen cloth bolts and garments, weights of gold and silver, and individual pieces of jewelry presented.

From the length and detail of the list, Egyptologists think that Ramesses had the artisans include not only the gifts and offerings he gave the temples, but also those that previous rulers had given. Because the earlier gifts were now considered the property of the priests and temples, their accumulation of wealth clearly rivaled that of the king. According to the document, the priests of Amun owned 433 temples in Egypt, 83 ships, 46 temple workshops, approximately 500,000 heads of cattle, and 1,300 square miles of land. By some accounts, this meant that the temples and priests owned approximately 30 percent of all cultivable land and employed about 20 percent of Egypt's inhabitants. Because, as records suggest, both temples and priests were exempt from taxes, their wealth multiplied even more quickly. Such a policy did not have a positive effect on Egypt. Rather, it contributed significantly to the decline of royal power and to the destabilization of the government.

This account, which also includes a brief historical summary of Ramesses's

Ramesses III

POSITION

King of Egypt

REIGN

About 1182–51 B.C.

ACCOMPLISHMENTS

Defeated the Libyans in Year 5 of his reign and again in Year 11; defeated migrant peoples—the Sea Peoples preparing to invade Egypt; won battle against the Sea Peoples—history's first recorded naval battle; built a massive mortuary temple at Medinet Habu; first recorded labor union strike occurred during his reign; Harem Conspiracy may have resulted in his death

Ramesses III is kind-hearted toward Egypt, bearing the protection of the land on the height of his back without trouble; a wall, casting a shadow for the people.

—Inscription on Ramesses III's mortuary temple at Medinet Habu

reign, was written on papyrus and dated the day Ramesses died. It measures 133 feet in length and consists of 117 columns, each 12 to 13 lines in length. It was discovered in 1855 in a small private tomb in Deir el Bahri. After an Englishman named A. C. Harris bought the piece, it came to be called the Great Harris Papyrus. To date, it remains the longest papyrus ever uncovered in ancient Egypt and one of the most valuable.

Another uncovered document tells of Ramesses dismissing his vizier of Lower Egypt. Ramesses assigned himself the responsibility of regulating the gifts to be sent to the temples. Still another document details the world's first known labor strike.

Over the years, the tradition had developed of housing the skilled artisans, the scribes, and the foremen in charge of the royal tomb workers in villages close to the construction site. Those who worked at the royal tombs in the Valley of the Kings and the Valley of the Queens and the mortuary temples in western Thebes lived in Set Maat ("the Place of Truth"), better known today as Deir el Medina. According to surviving records, Thutmose I had established this village for the skilled artisans, the scribes, and the foremen of the workers on his mortuary complex.

Under Ramesses III, Deir el Medina housed about 50 artisans, although the numbers dwindled as his tomb and temple neared completion. The artisans actually spent little time there, except for holy days and festival days, because they worked nine days and were off on the tenth day. The nine nights they spent in a makeshift camp closer to the construction sites.

Living full-time at Deir el Medina were the families of the artisans and the scribes; gardeners who tended the small area granted the village to grow produce; fishermen; water-carriers; and others who cared for the business of the village. All, however, depended on the steady income of the workers to survive. This income was not money, but rather food and other necessities.

Since Ramesses wanted his tomb workers to be happy and content, Deir el Medina was well supplied. The enormous grain storerooms at the nearby temples were also kept full. However, in Year 25, a junior scribe named Neferhotep sent an official complaint to the office of the vizier stating that "all the supplies for us [at Deir el Medina] that come from the treasury, the granary, and the storehouse have been exhausted." The letter told how a large part of the monthly grain ration allotted to the village had been taken away and "we are dying."

Four years later, in Year 29, matters seem to have become considerably worse. This time, a senior scribe named Amennakht filed a complaint stating that the community had not received its wheat ration. He brought his grievance directly to officials whose offices were in the royal temple at Medinet Habu. Two days later, a shipment of wheat arrived at Deir el Medina.

The villagers' joy quickly turned to anger when their wages were again delayed. Their frustrations increased when only a fraction of what they were due did arrive. Having lost all confidence in the traditional methods of solving grievances, the workers took stronger action—they stopped all work on the burial complex, left the Valley of the Kings for the temple of Thutmose III, and there sat on the ground beside the granaries. After waiting 18 days for their wages to be delivered, the workers walked back to the village, but not to work.

Determined to have their grievances addressed, they again marched out of the village and headed for the Ramesseum. They stopped only when they reached the courtyards next to the enormous granaries. When no official approached to ask about their grievances, the men decided not to return home that evening but to continue their "sit-in" by the temple gate. The following day, temple officials met with the workers and listened to their grievances, "[we have] no clothing, no fat, no fish, no vegetables." Finally, the officials gave the workmen their overdue rations.

The matter seemed settled, but the strikes continued—an indication that the problem involved more than late wages. The workers were also upset because of the corruption among officials and temple personnel. Using the same tactics as they had before, the workers threatened to approach the High Priest of Amun, the vizier, and even Ramesses III himself if their concerns were not addressed. Again, the workers won. This time, new positions were created, and the new officials were charged with overseeing the arrival of all wages. Finally, after months of complaints and strikes, all was quiet.

Because Amun's priests had played a significant role in settling the strike, the workers looked to the priests, and not the government or state officials, as their champions. Ramesses recognized the increasing power of Amun's priests and of the priests associated with other religious buildings at Thebes. Because the priests also held considerable wealth, he named a non-Theban to the office of high priest of the Two Lands. Nevertheless, despite his precautions, the power of the priesthood continued to grow and so, too, did the relationship between the workers of Deir el Medina and the priests of Amun.

Religious power, however, was not Ramesses's most pressing problem. Trouble was brewing in the royal harem where, according to custom, Ramesses's wives lived. Because only the eldest living son of the Great Royal Wife inherited the right to succeed the king, all other royal offspring could only hope that their royal blood would win them a good position in the government. Tiy, one of Ramesses's minor wives, refused to accept this long-standing custom and found others within the palace who pledged to support her son as the rightful heir.

In the mid-1800s, Egyptologists uncovered several papyrus rolls that disclosed important details about a "Harem Conspiracy." According to the record, Ramesses was to be killed, and Tiy's son Pentewere was to ascend the throne. The plot, however, was discovered; the traitors were arrested, and

court proceedings were initiated. The defendants numbered around 40, many of whom Ramesses had considered loyal supporters. The document makes no mention of Tiy, not even if she was ever brought to trials. It does state that 24 of those tried were condemned to death. The others received lighter sentences.

Whether the conspirators actually killed Ramesses is unclear. The records do show that he was dead before the trial ended. The sentencing, however, continued without interruption, as did the preparations he had made for his son to succeed him. Ramesses's tomb in the Valley of the Kings was ready. His father, Sethnakhte, had originally ordered it, but had abandoned the site for a new tomb. Ramesses liked his father's first choice and had his workers complete the complex for himself. They encountered a few problems, the worst of which occurred when workers cutting the corridors of Ramesses III's tomb collided with the tomb of King Amenmesse (Ramesses II's grandson). After strengthening the walls of both tombs, the engineers reworked their design. Because surviving accounts include little about such "mistakes," Egyptologists believe they were rare and that architects and workers kept maps and plans of tombs in the valley. Still, the valley was becoming crowded, especially considering that rulers, Ramesses included, often opted for tombs larger than those of their predecessors. Ramesses had his tomb workers follow the traditional tomb design. However, he did have his artisans include scenes that were not usually found in a king's tomb—scenes that focused on everyday life in this world.

In 1881, Egyptologists found Ramesses's mummy along with many others that had been reburied by ancient Egyptian priests in Deir el Bahri. Detailed analysis of his mummy

I sat upon the throne with joy in my heart.

—Harris Papyrus

indicates that Ramesses was about 65 when he died. His mummy also bears witness to a new custom—the use of artificial eyes. The eyes looked gruesome, and makers of many horror films used Ramesses's mummy as their model. Ramesses's personality, however, seems the exact opposite, especially if we read the record of his reign as commissioned by his son and heir Ramesses IV:

> I planted the whole land with trees and verdure, and I made the people dwell in their shade. . . . I sustained the whole land, whether foreigners, common folk, citizens, or people, male or female. . . . The land was well satisfied with my reign. I did good to the gods, as well as to the people, and I had nothing at all belonging to any people. . . . Behold, I have gone to rest in the afterworld, like my father Re, I have mingled with the great gods in heaven, earth, and the afterworld. Amun-Re has established my son on my throne.

FURTHER READING

Newby, Percy Howard. *Warrior Pharaohs: The Rise and Fall of the Egyptian Empire*, pp. 194–96. London and Boston: Faber and Faber, 1980.

Siliotti, Alberto. *Guide to the Valley of the Kings*, pp. 62, 124–29. London: Wiedenfeld & Nicolson, 1996.

More Ancient Egyptians to Remember

Pa-wer-a'a (active about 1210 B.C.) served as the mayor of western Thebes and was responsible for overseeing the royal tombs in the Valley of the Kings. Tomb theft had long been a problem, and in the years following the reign of Ramesses III, the number of tomb robberies increased significantly. In Year 16 of Ramesses IX's reign, there broke a great scandal that involved high-ranking officials in Thebes and royal tomb workers. Among those accused of being an accessory was Pa-wer-a'a. According to uncovered documents, Paser, the mayor of the east bank, gave all the information he gathered about the case to his superior, the vizier Khaemwaset. Pa-wer-a'a, meanwhile, presented the vizier with a list that named eight robbers but did not include his own name. The court found Pa-wer-a'a not guilty of neglecting his duty to guard the tombs because the robbers confessed to the crime.

Sometime later Paser filed another complaint with the vizier, stating that more tomb robberies had occurred. For the second time, he implied that Pa-wer-a'a was involved. Once again, Pa-wer-a'a was found innocent. Months later, the officials reversed their decision and found Pa-wer-a'a guilty. The section that told the outcome of this trial is missing, but inspectors now knew how robbers had foiled them in the past. Aware that priests and those in charge of tomb sites only checked the seals at the entrance, robbers were entering these structures by burrowing their way in from behind.

Herihor (active about 1080–72 B.C.) welcomed his new role as High Priest of Amun. His climb to this position, the highest in the Egyptian priesthood, had been steady and determined. So, too, was his climb up the military and political ladder. Ramesses XI named him the general in charge of Upper Egypt, and records suggest Herihor married his sister Nodjmet. Even after Ramesses appointed Herihor governor of Kush, then vizier of the Upper Egypt, and high priest of Amun, Ramesses chose not to curb Herihor's influence in Upper Egypt. Instead, he seemed to welcome the opportunity to focus his attention on Lower Egypt and to spend more time in his palace at Pi-Ramesses in the Delta.

Herihor soon came to consider himself Ramesses's equal. For centuries, kings had allotted land, tribute, and taxes to the temples. Because those of Amun received the majority of grants, Amun's priests were by far the richest and the most powerful. It soon followed that Ramesses recognized what seemed inevitable and approved reliefs representing Herihor as king of Egypt. Two kings now ruled the Two Lands—Ramesses in Lower Egypt and Herihor in

Upper Egypt. And, according to the inscription on the temple walls at Karnak, both were sons of Amun.

Psamtik I (active about 664–10 B.C.) was determined to free Egypt from foreign rule. Freedom would be a new experience for his contemporaries because the Egyptian line of succession had ended some 300 years earlier, when first the Libyans and then the Nubians laid claim to the throne of Egypt. In 665 B.C., the Assyrian king Ashurbanipal recognized Psamtik's father, an Egyptian official named Necho, as king of Sais (present-day Sa el Hagan) in the Delta and named Psamtik king of Athribis, another city in the Delta. After the Nubians killed Necho in battle, Ashurbanipal recognized Psamtik as the king of all Egypt—with the provision that Psamtik regard Assyria as an overlord and incite no trouble against the Assyrians. Psamtik agreed, but he had no intention of serving Ashurbanipal and moved quickly to eliminate the opposition. Helping him were great numbers of mercenaries—foreign soldiers who hired themselves out to generals for pay. These included Nubians, Libyans, Phoenicians, Syrians, and Jews.

The Egyptians rejoiced in their new freedom, and Psamtik and his successors, who are known as the Saite kings because of their close association with the city of Sais, accepted reliance on foreigners as a fact. Some Egyptians, however, disapproved of the increasing numbers of "outsiders" settling in their lands. Therefore, to avoid any confrontation, Psamtik ordered his advisers and officials to establish special living areas for foreigners. One such area, the city of Naukratis (also spelled Naucratis) in the Delta region, was set up to accommodate Greeks. And in the years to come, Psamtik would come to be known more by the Greek form of his name—Psammetichus—than by his Egyptian name. Psamtik kept Sais as his official residence, but he moved the political capital of the Two Lands back to Memphis. Thebes continued as the center of religious celebrations. Trade prospects increased, and there was a return to prosperity. In fact, it was under Psamtik that Egypt began exporting large amounts of grain. In the decades to come, Egypt would become one of the chief producers of grain in the Mediterranean world. Psamtik ruled for 54 years and was succeeded by his son, Necho II, and then his grandson, Psamtik II, both of whom followed his policies and kept Egypt free and prosperous.

Amasis (also known as Ahmose II) (active 570–26 B.C.) was a general under Psamtik II's son, Apries. Amasis did not agree with his king's decision to send an army of mercenaries to fight the Libyans. After Apries suffered a terrible defeat on the battlefield, the Egyptians withdrew their support of him and his mercenaries and rallied around Amasis and his Egyptian troops. In 570 B.C., the two men—ruler and contender—met on the battlefield. Amasis's win brought him to the throne of Egypt.

Most Egyptians opposed extending the privileges granted to foreigners, and Amasis needed the mercenaries if Egypt was to remain an international power, so he stationed them at the border garrisons. To control the Greek merchant colony at Naukratis, he made the city a free trade zone and ruled that Greek merchants were to confine their business activities to Naukratis. Then, to win the support of the Greeks, he granted them special economic privileges. He did not, however, neglect Egyptian traditions and customs. He maintained close ties with Thebes, the chief religious center in Upper Egypt, and centered political and economic activity in the Delta region of Lower Egypt, especially in Sais. Persia remained an area of major concern for Amasis, and just one year after Amasis's death, the Persian king Cambyses II defeated Amasis's son and successor

Egyptians often represented the goddess Hathor as a cow and considered her the pharaoh Psamtik's nourisher and protector, especially in the afterlife. Carved from green schist (a type of rock), this sculpture of Hathor protecting Psamtik is three feet five inches long.

Isis (left) wears a headdress with the figure of a vulture. Nectanebo II is wearing the white crown of Upper Egypt with the cobra-shaped *uraeus*. His fourth and fifth royal names are carved in the two oval cartouches.

525 B.C., Udjahorresne had served King Amasis well, both as a naval officer and as his chief physician. Udjahorresne had also been attentive to his duties as priest of Neith, who was the wife of Khnum and one of Egypt's oldest goddesses.

When Psamtik III succeeded his father Amasis to the throne, Udjahorresne continued to hold the same official positions. Not a year had passed, however, before the Persian king Cambyses defeated Psamtik and took control of Egypt. Because the Persians were not showing proper respect to Neith's temple at Sais, Udjahorresne approached Cambyses and persuaded him to expel the foreigners living in the building. Udjahorresne even convinced Cambyses to honor Neith and to reinstate the priests previously assigned to the temple. Cambyses's son and successor, Darius I, also valued Udjahorresne's advice, especially his medical expertise. On Darius's orders, Udjahorresne began reorganizing the medical school associated with the temple at Sais. Darius even ordered Udjahorresne to accompany him back to Susa, the capital of Persia, and then provided Udjahorresne with a personal escort for the return trip home.

Nekhtnebef (better known as Nectanebo II) (active 360–42 B.C.) followed his father's orders and named himself king of Egypt. His grandfather Djedhor (also known as Teos) held the position officially but had left Egypt to defeat the Persians on the battlefield and then reconquer lands that his predecessors had taken centuries earlier. Few Egyptians approved the mission, especially the hike in taxes to pay its expenses. As king, Nectanebo promoted security, unity, and a feeling of nationalism. He commissioned several new construction projects and ordered temples restored. He also encouraged trade between Egypt and other foreign nations,

Psamtik III on the battlefield and took control of Egypt.

Udjahorresne (active about 525 B.C.) prepared to welcome the Persian conquerors of the Two Lands. A cultured and learned Egyptian, he believed that peace and prosperity could be maintained if the Egyptians worked with the Persians and explained their native ways to the conquering foreigners. Before the Persian takeover in

An antelope plays a board game with a lion, whose expression suggests he is winning. This scene from an uncovered painted papyrus dates to the late New Kingdom.

kept his Greek mercenaries paid and prepared for action, and sought to develop good relations with Persia's enemies.

When reports reached Nectanebo that Persia's new king, Artaxerxes III, was preparing to attack Egypt, he readied his army and marched to Pelusium, a strongly fortified garrison that stood at the eastern end of the Delta. But the Persian onslaught by land and by sea was too much for the Egyptians, and Pelusium fell. Artaxerxes then used captured Egyptian farmers to guide his troops through the Delta region. After learning that the major cities in the area had fallen to the advancing Persians, Nectanebo accepted defeat and fled south into Nubia. Once again, Egypt had fallen to foreigners. In the historical records, Nectanebo II would be listed as the last native ruler of Egypt in ancient times. Not until the revolution of 1952—more than 2,200 years later—would an Egyptian again rule the Two Lands.

Manetho (active about 280 B.C.) was an Egyptian priest from Sebennytos (present-day Samanud, in the central Delta region) who compiled a chronological list of Egypt's kings and accompanied each with a brief biography. Manetho could read the ancient Egyptian hieroglyphs and knew Greek as well. His work, the *Aegyptiaca* ("History of Egypt"), was written in Greek and presented a chronicle of ancient Egyptian history. In his research, Manetho used religious records, temple inscriptions, and royal records, as well as details from popular traditions and tales.

The first of Manetho's eight books listed Egypt's mythical rulers and the gods and demigods (half-human, half-god) of the Two Lands. Manetho then named Menes as the first historical king and dated his reign to around 3050 B.C. He listed Nectanebo II, whose rule ended in 342 B.C., as the last Egyptian to rule the Two Lands in ancient times. To make his list easier to

read and understand, Manetho subdivided the kings into family groupings, now called dynasties. Thus a dynasty consists of a founder and the descendants who follow him on the throne. Manetho grouped the ancient rulers into 30 dynasties. Later historians added two more dynasties—the 31st, which includes the Persian monarchs who claimed the right to the Egyptian throne, and the 32nd, which includes the Macedonian monarchs (Alexander the Great and the Ptolemies). Later historians grouped the dynasties into time periods—the Old Kingdom (around 2686–2181 B.C.); the Middle Kingdom (around 2040–1782 B.C.); and the New Kingdom (around 1570–1070 B.C.), with the years between these main subdivisions known as the First Intermediate Period (about 2181–2040 B.C.); the Second Intermediate Period (about 1782–1570 B.C.); and the Third Intermediate Period (about 1069–525 B.C.).

Appendix 1
An Egyptian Ruler's Five Names

An Egyptian ruler received official royal names at his or her coronation ceremony. This custom began during the Old Kingdom, and by the 12th Dynasty it reached the classic form of five royal names. The five-names tradition continued for about 2,000 years.

The first name, or the "Horus," meant that the ruler was the earthly representative of Horus, the sky god of Upper Egypt, whose symbol was the falcon. The Horus was written in a *serekh* panel, that is, within a picture of the front of the royal palace. The figure of Horus was perched at the top of the panel. The second name, or the "Nebti" ("Two Ladies" or "Favorite of the Two Goddesses"), represented a ruler's power over Upper and Lower Egypt. It also indicated that Nekhbet, the vulture goddess and goddess of Upper Egypt, and Wadjet, the cobra goddess and the goddess of Lower Egypt, watched over the ruler. The third name, or the "Golden Horus," symbolized the ruler's divinity. The fourth name was the "Prenomen," an official name a ruler assumed at the coronation ceremony. Preceded by the "Nisut-Bit," it represented the king's rule over the Two Lands. The fifth name was the "Nomen." It was the ruler's personal name—the one he had received at birth. By tradition the title "Son of Re" preceded this name and symbolized the fact that the ruler was also the son of the Egyptian sun god.

All five names were rarely used together. The first, fourth, and fifth were commonly used. During the reign of the 4th-Dynasty ruler Snefru, kings and queens began to wear rings inscribed with their fourth and fifth names. The hieroglyphic forms of the Prenomen and Nomen were outlined with a rope design, the ends of which were looped over each other. This elliptical figure is called a "cartouche."

Tutankhamun's Prenomen, or fourth royal name, engraved in the cartouche of a gold signet ring (left) and imprinted in a terracotta amulet mold.

Tutankhamun's Five Royal Names

Horus	Nebti	Golden Horus	Prenomen	Nomen
Ka-nakht tut-mesut	Nefer-hepu segeretawy sehetenetjer u nebu	Wetjes-khau sehetep-netjeru	Nisut-Bit: Nebkheperure	Sa-Re: Tutankhamun heqa-iunu-shema
Strong bull, fitting from created forms	Dynamic of laws, who calms the Two Lands, who propitiates all the gods	Who displays the regalia, who propitiates the gods	King of Upper and Lower Egypt; the Lordly Manifestation of Re	Son of Re: Living Image of Amun, Ruler of Upper Egyptian Heliopolis

Appendix 2
Foreign Rulers of Ancient Egypt

The decline of the Egyptian Empire that began during Ramesses III's reign (about 1182–51 B.C.) accelerated under his successors. When Ramesses XI, the last of Ramesses's line, came to the throne, the very unity of Egypt was at stake. At Thebes, the high priest of Amun, Herihor, had proclaimed himself king of Upper Egypt and made his post hereditary. This division of the Two Lands weakened Egypt's international position, and its neighbors began to extend their power into Egyptian territory. In this section, we present brief biographies of several foreign rulers who claimed the Egyptian throne.

Shoshenq I (ruled 945–24 B.C.)

Since the reign of Ramesses III, Egyptian kings and generals had become increasingly dependent on mercenaries. Many of these soldiers were Libyans who had settled in the Delta region. Through the years, several of their communities had prospered, including Pi-Bast (House of Bast, or Bubastis as the Greeks called it), the center for worship of the great cat goddess Bast. In 945 B.C., Bubastis's leading citizen was Shoshenq, a Libyan by birth, commander-in-chief of Egypt's armed forces, and adviser to Psusennes II, king of Lower Egypt. Shoshenq was also married to Psusennes's daughter, Maatkare. When Psusennes died with no son to inherit the throne, Shoshenq claimed the title.

Over the years, Lower Egypt had gradually surpassed Upper Egypt as the political and economic center of the Two Lands. Thebes had continued as the country's religious center, and Tanis, a northern city in the Delta, replaced Pi-Ramesses (city founded by Ramesses II) as the capital. Shoshenq kept the capital at Tanis; he made no plans to build a new capital closer to Upper Egypt. In the Syria-Palestine area, he reestablished trading ties with Byblos and marched against Judah, Jerusalem, and Israel. His northward drive ended at Megiddo, where he ordered a stele set up to honor his victories—just as Thutmose III had done 500 years earlier. Shoshenq was the first Libyan to rule Egypt, and his descendants would continue to rule the country for nearly 200 years. According to Manetho's king list, they were the kings of the 22nd, the 23rd, and the 24th Dynasties.

Piye (ruled 747–16 B.C.)

In the mid-700s B.C., Piye, also known as Piankhy, married the daughter of Alara, the ruling king of Napata, a city near the Fourth Cataract. When Alara died, Piye ascended to the throne of Kush and continued the northward advance his predecessors had begun. Piye battled the Egyptians for 10 years. A coalition of four kings ruled the Two Lands, making his struggle more difficult. These kings were descendants of Libyan rulers, and each claimed control of part of Lower Egypt. According to an inscription uncovered at Wadi Gasus, Piye had himself crowned king of the Two Lands at Thebes in Year 12 of his reign. Piye saw himself and the Nubians as the rightful preservers of Egypt's customs and religious practices, and assumed the coronation names used by the rulers of the New Kingdom. He adapted many Egyptian customs, including building a tomb pyramid. His was smaller and narrower than the traditional Egyptian pyramid, and its sides sloped to a peak that rose at a steeper angle. Eight of Piye's favorite horses were buried near his tomb.

Taharqa (ruled 690–64 B.C.)

According to the Egyptian historian Manetho, Piye's brother Shabaka succeeded him as the second ruler of the 25th Dynasty, also known as the Nubian or Kushite Dynasty. Piye's sons Shebitku and Taharqa succeeded their uncle. Taharqa came to the throne in 690 B.C. The first years of Taharqa's 26-year rule were relatively peaceful, and he devoted much of this time to grand building projects in Nubia and Egypt. Meanwhile, the Assyrian king Esarhaddon was pushing the frontier of his own empire farther south. Around 674 B.C. he faced Taharqa on the battlefield at Ashkelon, a city on the border of Egypt and Palestine. Esarhaddon lost, but in 671 B.C. he attacked again. This time, the Egyptians were unable to stop him, and he boldly advanced into Egypt. There his troops took control, seized the city of Memphis, and took the heir to the throne and members of the royal family as prisoners. Taharqa escaped to Thebes, reclaiming Memphis only after Esarhaddon returned to Assyria. When Esarhaddon died, his son, Ashurbanipal, advanced against Egypt and retook

Memphis. He allowed Necho to continue ruling as king of Sais and named Necho's son, Psamtik, to the throne of Athribis, another city in the Delta. Taharqa, meanwhile, retreated to Napata. He had lost control of the Two Lands, but he still ruled Nubia.

Cambyses II (ruled 525–22 B.C.)

Psamtik I's descendant and the last king of the 26th Dynasty, Psamtik III came to the Egyptian throne in 526 B.C. The following year, King Cambyses of Persia gave the order to attack Egypt. Cambyses's father, Cyrus, had begun the campaign four years earlier, but it was suspended when he unexpectedly died. Cambyses first took control of Phoenicia, a land that bordered the eastern Mediterranean and was known for its sailors. With the Phoenician fleet to supplement his land troops, Cambyses planned to attack Egypt by land and by sea. Psamtik III, meanwhile, led his troops east to Pelusium, a gateway city to Egypt. When the Persian army easily overwhelmed the Egyptians, Psamtik retreated to Memphis. Cambyses followed and took Memphis. Cambyses ordered Psamtik bound in chains and sent to Susa, the Persian capital. Surviving texts indicate that Cambyses liked Egypt and ordered temples and other structures built or restored. He adopted many Egyptian customs, encouraged the interchange of ideas between Egypt and Persia, and sent many Egyptian artisans and officials to work in Persia. His attempts to extend Persian control into Nubia met with defeat. When reports of unrest in Persia and Syria reached Cambyses, he named Aryandes governor of Egypt and returned home.

Darius I (ruled 522–486 B.C.)

Cambyses's son Darius commissioned several construction projects during his 35-year rule. Egypt was the richest of Persia's provinces. Darius reopened the great stone quarries at Wadi Hammamat in Upper Egypt and ordered the completion of a canal joining the Nile River with the Red Sea. This new sea route shortened travel time between Egypt and Persia and allowed messengers to keep Darius better informed about political developments in the province. When reports of Aryandes's cruel treatment of the Egyptians proved true, Darius quickly withdrew his support of this satrap (governor). Darius requested a list of the wisest Egyptian soldiers and priests, and assigned these people to compile and codify the laws of Egypt. Later generations of Egyptians would consider Darius one of their great lawgivers.

A renewed prosperity spread across the Two Lands while Darius sat on the Persian throne. After the Greeks defeated the Persians in 490 B.C., Darius focused all his efforts on his war with Greece. Four years later, the Egyptians revolted against their Persian overlords, but Darius's death that same year prevented any immediate action from being taken. Darius's son, Xerxes I, quelled the revolt.

Alexander the Great (ruled 332–23 B.C.)

In 332 B.C., Alexander set off to conquer Egypt. The Persian satrap surrendered the country without a fight. In recent years, Persian domination had become increasingly harsh, with the satraps showing little respect for Egyptian traditions and customs. For this reason, the Egyptians hailed Alexander as their liberator. Alexander named Kleomenes from the Greek colony of Naukratis to the post of satrap and appointed six governors. Two were Macedonians and were put in charge of military affairs. The other four—two Greeks and two Egyptians—were to rule in civil matters. Alexander also initiated a building program that included a new capital city to be named Alexandria. Alexander did not live to see it, but within decades of his death, Alexandria became one of the principal scientific and cultural centers in the ancient world.

Alexander visited Amun's temple in the Siwa Oasis to present his divine father with a petition. No records tell of Amun's reply, but tradition maintains that Alexander told his companions he had heard what he wanted to hear.

His hold on power threatened by Darius III, Alexander left Egypt just six months after taking control of the country. He was the first Macedonian to rule Egypt, and Macedonians would rule the Two Lands for nearly 300 years.

Ptolemy I (ruled 323–282 B.C.)

Alexander died unexpectedly in 323 B.C. without an heir. Two kings were named—Alexander's feeble-minded half-brother and Alexander's newborn son—but as neither one was capable of ruling the empire, Alexander's generals divided the regions among themselves. Ptolemy chose Egypt, Libya, and Arabia (the Sinai Peninsula). To strengthen his claim to the region, Ptolemy kidnapped the coffin carrying Alexander's body from Babylon back to Macedonia and brought it to Egypt. He claimed that Alexander had intended to be buried in Alexandria. In 305 B.C., Ptolemy proclaimed himself King Ptolemy I Soter (Savior) of Egypt. The founder of the Ptolemaic Dynasty, Ptolemy would be the first of 13 rulers with the same name to rule Egypt.

Ptolemy initiated a great building program, returned traditional responsibilities to temple priests and nobles, passed laws to protect Egypt's maritime rights, established the first coinage system, and had workers construct a gigantic lighthouse on the island of Pharos at the entrance to the port of Alexandria. This lighthouse, known as the Pharos of Alexandria, became known as one of the seven wonders of the ancient world.

Ptolemy never adopted Egyptian customs or dress. Nor did he learn the language. He welcomed Greek settlers in Egypt, and encouraged the exchange of ideas between Greeks and Egyptians. He commissioned the building of a gigantic library at Alexandria, as well as a museum with rooms and lecture halls where scholars from around the Mediterranean world could discuss their findings and consider new ideas. In 285 B.C., Ptolemy named his son as co-regent. Three years later, Ptolemy II Philadelphos succeeded his father.

Ptolemy II Philadelphos (ruled 285–47/46 B.C.)

During Ptolemy II's reign, Egypt's Greek population continued to increase. Ptolemy II weakened the influence of Egyptian nobles and the upper class by naming Greeks to high administrative positions. Ptolemy extended his rule into Syria, Asia Minor, and parts of the Aegean, and used political marriages to align himself with neighboring rulers. He followed a custom long practiced by Egyptian kings and married his sister, Arsinoe; each assumed the Greek name Philadelphos, meaning "brother-loving." Ptolemy's marriage shocked the Greeks living in Egypt. So did his fostering of religious practices that honored himself, Arsinoe, and his parents as "brother gods."

Ptolemy commissioned new irrigation projects to increase the amount of arable land, especially in the Faiyum district. To encourage trade, Ptolemy ordered his engineers to reopen the canal connecting the Nile River with the Red Sea. He established Greek farming communities in the Faiyum and exported much of their harvest to peoples around the Mediterranean world. Ptolemy also oversaw the completion in Alexandria of his father's unfinished commissions: the gigantic lighthouse at the harbor's entrance and the great library and museum.

Arsinoe II (ruled 275 B.C.)

Ptolemy I's daughter Arsinoe was first married to Lysimachos, bodyguard to Alexander the Great. After Alexander's death, Lysimachos was given control of Thrace and the lands bordering the northern Aegean Sea. Next, he extended his control into Asia Minor, Macedonia, and Thessaly. When Lysimachos died in 281 B.C., Arsinoe took control of the lands and riches he had amassed. She married her half-brother Ptolemy Ceraunus, but they soon divorced. Arsinoe convinced her brother Ptolemy II that his chief wife was conspiring to kill him. Ptolemy ordered this wife arrested and exiled from Egypt. Soon afterward, Ptolemy married Arsinoe. When she added her lands to Ptolemy's, Egypt once again became one of the richest and most powerful kingdoms in the world.

Arsinoe II was the first Egyptian to officially invite envoys from Rome to visit Alexandria and the royal court. Military veterans so appreciated her practice of granting retiring soldiers lands in the Faiyum district that they named the fertile lands there Arsinoite nome, or "Arsinoe's district." After Arsinoe's death, a cult was established in her honor at Alexandria, and a magnificent shrine, the Arsinoeion, was dedicated to her.

Cleopatra VII (ruled 51–30 B.C.)

Ptolemy XII's death in 51 B.C. brought 17-year-old Cleopatra, his daughter and heir, to the throne as Cleopatra VII. Egyptian control of its territories had begun to deteriorate with the reign of Ptolemy IV. Egypt had lost all of its former territories except Cyrene, on the coast of North Africa, and the island of Cyprus. In the meantime another Mediterranean power was gaining strength—Rome.

Following the wishes of her deceased father, Cleopatra married her brother, 15-year-old Ptolemy XIII. When Cleopatra learned that Ptolemy XIII's sympathizers were plotting to kill her, she fled to Syria. Rome's leader, Julius Caesar, supported Cleopatra, and in the battle that followed, Ptolemy XIII drowned while trying to escape. Cleopatra married her younger brother, Ptolemy XIV, and the two became king and queen of Egypt. She took her leadership role seriously. She learned the Egyptian language, the first Ptolemy to do so; and she joined with the Egyptians in worshiping their gods. She also aligned herself with Julius Caesar. Caesar's assassination in Rome in 44 B.C. was followed by a power struggle between Caesar's nephew Octavius (later Augustus) and Caesar's friend Antony. Cleopatra won Antony's affections and the support of his trained legions. Furthermore, Antony was willing to consider Egypt, not Rome, the center of the empire. On September 2, 31 B.C., Antony and Cleopatra lost a sea battle to Octavius at Actium, just off the western coast of Greece. He followed Cleopatra and Antony to Egypt. Determined to remain queen of Egypt, but unable to win Octavius to her side, Cleopatra took her own life (in 30 B.C.), and with it Egypt's independence.

Octavius

On August 31, 30 B.C., Octavius officially took control of Egypt and named himself king of the Two Lands. He had no plans for a royal court or capital city there. For Octavius, Egypt was only one area in a vast empire. However, because it produced a tremendous amount of grain, Egypt was essential to Rome. It would become known as the breadbasket of the Roman Empire. In order to keep Egypt free from political disturbances, Octavius treated the Two Lands as his personal property. By decree, he forbade Roman senators and members of his family from visiting the country without his formal permission.

Appendix 3
Timeline of Events in the Egyptian World

The number in parentheses after a king's name indicates his order as dynastic ruler (for example, Pepi I was the second ruler of the 6th Dynasty). All dates are B.C. *and are approximate.*

3050
Menes (1) unites Two Lands

2686–2181
Old Kingdom

2686–13
3rd Dynasty

2668–49
Djoser (2) rules Egypt

2660
Imhotep designs Step Pyramid

2613–2500
4th Dynasty

2613–2589
Snefru (1) rules Egypt

2600
Hetep-heres is queen of Egypt

2589–66
Khufu (2) rules Egypt

2570
Hemiumu designs Khufu's pyramid tomb

2558–32
Khafre (4) rules Egypt

2532–04
Menkaure (5) rules Egypt

2500–2345
5th Dynasty

2400
Ptahhotep writes his *Maxims*

2345–2181
6th Dynasty

2332–2283
Pepi I (2) rules Egypt

2300
Weni oversees digging of canals to bypass First Cataract on Nile

2278–2184
Pepi II (4) rules Egypt

2275
Harkhuf leads caravan expeditions into Nubia

2220
Pepinakht leads several military campaigns

2181–2040
1st Intermediate Period

2060–1991
11th Dynasty

2060–10
Nebhepetre Mentuhotep I (1) rules Egypt

2040–1782
Middle Kingdom

2030
Meketre oversees making of *ushebti* for his tomb

2030
Heqanakht is farmer and landowner

1991–1782
12th Dynasty

1991–62
Amenemhet I (1) rules Egypt

1971–28

Senwosret I (2) rules Egypt

1878–41

Senwosret III (5) rules Egypt

1842–1797

Amenemhet III (6) rules Egypt

1782–1570

2nd Intermediate Period

1663–1570

17th Dynasty

1574

Seqenenre Tao II (2) rules Egypt

1570–1070

New Kingdom

1570–1293

18th Dynasty

1570–46

Ahmose I (1) rules Egypt

1560

Ahmose Nefertari is queen of Egypt

1535

Ahmose, son of Ebana, captains vessel against Hyksos

1524–18

Thutmose I (3) rules Egypt

1504–1450

Thutmose III (5) rules Egypt

1498–83

Hatshepsut (6) rules Egypt as king

1490

Senenmut designs Hatshepsut's mortuary temple at Deir el Bahri

1460

Rekhmire records vizier's duties on his tomb walls

1386–49

Amenhotep III (9) rules Egypt

1370

Tiye (2) is queen of Egypt

Amenhotep, son of Hapu, designs Amenhotep III's mortuary temple and "Colossi of Memnon"

1350–34

Akhenaten (Amenhotep IV) (10) rules Egypt

1345

Nefertiti is queen of Egypt

1334–25

Tutankhamun (12) rules Egypt

1321–1293

Horemheb (14) rules Egypt

1293–1185

19th Dynasty

1291–78

Seti I (2) rules Egypt

1279–12

Ramesses II (3) rules Egypt

1270

Nefertari is queen of Egypt

1210

Pa-wer-a'a becomes involved in tomb robbery scandal

1185–1070

20th Dynasty

1182–51

Ramesses III (2) rules Egypt

1080–72

Herihor (8) rules Egypt

1069–525

3rd Intermediate Period

664–525

26th Dynasty

664–10

Psamtik I (1) rules Egypt

570–26

Amasis (Ahmose II) (5) rules Egypt

525–332

Late Period

525–404

27th Dynasty (1st Persian Period)

525

Udjahorresne persuades Cambyses to honor Egyptian customs and traditions

380–342

30th Dynasty

360–92

Nectanebo II (3) is last Egyptian to rule ancient Egypt

332–30

Ptolemaic Period

280

Manetho divides king list into dynasties

Glossary

adze—a cutting tool whose blade is at a right angle to its handle. Used in the "Opening of the Mouth" ceremony.

afterlife books—passages from religious texts that the ancient Egyptians inscribed on tomb walls and coffins to help ensure the deceased person's safe and easy passage from this world to the next. The books included the *Amduat* (also called "That Which Is in the Underworld" and "The Book of the Secret Chamber"), *Litany of Re, Book of Gates, Book of the Dead* (also called "The Book of Coming Forth by Day"), *Book of Caverns, Book of the Heavens,* and *Book of the Earth.*

ankh—an Egyptian cross with looped top; symbol of life. ☥

ba—often described as the "essence," or "soul," of a person. The *ba* was represented as a bird with a human head. It left the body at death and returned after the deceased had been mummified. The *ba* could visit the world of the living.

barque—a boat. In religious ceremonies, barques of all sizes carried cult statues of the gods. The boat symbolized the importance of the Nile River to Egyptian life. According to religious beliefs, sacred barques transported the dead from this world to the next.

canopic jar—one of four jars, usually buried with the mummy, in which a deceased person's liver, lungs, intestines, or stomach was preserved. Up to the 18th Dynasty, the stopper was in the shape of a human head. Afterward, the stopper represented one of Horus's four sons, a different one for each organ.

cartonnage—linen and plaster molded to form masks and coffins for mummies. These funerary items were formed by applying gesso (powdered chalk and glue) to sheets of linen cloth. The cartonnage was then painted and gilded.

cartouche—an oblong frame enclosing a ruler's birth name and throne name. The oblong is formed by a looped rope.

cataract—steep rapids in a river. There are six cataracts along the Nile between present-day Aswan, Egypt and Khartoum, Sudan. The First Cataract marked the original southern boundary of ancient Egypt, simply because its treacherous waters and rocks made boat travel beyond that point impossible. By building canals to bypass the cataracts, as well as taking control of the surrounding land, Egypt's kings were able to extend the country's southern boundary.

Coffin Texts—inscriptions on coffins meant to help deceased nonroyals pass from this life to the next.

cuneiform—wedge-shaped writing used by the Akkadians, Babylonians, Assyrians, and Persians.

demotic script—a form of writing dating from the end of the seventh century B.C. Easier to read and write than hieroglyphs, demotic script was used for everyday legal and administrative documents and for correspondence.

festival of Opet—annual Theban festival celebrated during the season of the Nile's overflowing its banks. At the high point of this festival, the king entered the temple, accompanied by priests, then proceeded alone into the chambers at the rear of the temple to reaffirm his divine link to the great god Amun, his "father."

Great Royal Wife—the principal wife of an Egyptian ruler. Although a ruler could have many wives, he had only one Great Royal Wife, or Chief Wife, at a time. A king's heir was usually his eldest son by his Great Royal Wife. In the Old Kingdom and Middle Kingdom, a king also married his sister. If a king had no sons by his Great Royal Wife, a son by a minor wife sometimes became king. This son then married a daughter of the Great Royal Wife—his half-sister—to provide legitimacy to the succession.

Heb-Sed festival—a celebration that sometimes lasted for two or more months to mark a king's "rebirth," or "recrowning." Also known as "Sed" and "jubilee." The practice began early in Egypt's royal history and continued for thousands of years. A king traditionally celebrated his first Heb-Sed in the 30th year of this reign, and others at shorter intervals thereafter. (Not all kings observed the waiting period of 30 years; several celebrated their first jubilee earlier in their reigns.) Because the celebrations were believed to continue in the next life, royal tomb complexes included Heb-Sed courts.

hieratic script—a form of writing derived from hieroglyphs, but simpler. Hieratic was used until the end of the New Kingdom, chiefly by priests and scribes for legal and business documents, but also for correspondence.

hieroglyphs—a pictorial script used principally for religious and literary texts, from the Greek word meaning "sacred writings." Hieroglyphs consist of sound values as well as picture signs that have no sound value.

jubilee—*see* Heb-Sed festival

ka—the everlasting life force of a person, or "another self." After the body died, a person's tomb was the ka's home. The ka subsisted on offerings brought to the tomb. The ka returned periodically to its other self (the mummy) or to a statue of the deceased body in the tomb. The hieroglyphic sign for ka is a human body with two upraised arms.

king lists—chronological lists of Egyptian rulers inscribed on temple walls, used in rituals honoring royal ancestors. A king did not always list every ruler who had preceded him; he often omitted those he considered illegitimate.

mastaba—a rectangular, mud-brick tomb resembling a bench (from the Arabic word for "bench"). The size and decoration of the below-ground burial chamber depended on the owner's circumstances and status in the community. A false door painted on one wall allowed the deceased's ka to pass between the tomb and the afterlife.

mummy—the preserved body of a dead person. To make a mummy, embalmers removed the deceased's internal organs. The rest of the body was dried until no moisture remained, then wrapped in layers of bandages between which religious symbols and amulets were placed.

obelisk—tall, four-sided stone pillar that tapers to a pyramid-shaped top. Kings often commissioned pairs of obelisks for religious centers throughout the Two Lands.

Opening of the Mouth ceremony—a ritual to bring the senses of a mummified body to life for eternity by touching its mouth, eyes, ears, and nose with an adze. When a king died, his son and heir performed the ceremony.

papyrus—a plant commonly found in the Nile Valley, and from which paper was made. To make paper, Egyptians first cut the stems of papyrus plants into thin strips. They layered strips, resin, and a second layer of strips perpendicular to the first, then pressed the layers together to form a fine paper. The Egyptians also used papyrus to make rope, sandals, skiffs, and baskets. The English word "paper" comes from "papyrus."

pharaoh—title of a king or ruler. The Egyptian phrase *Per wer*, referred originally to the royal palace, or "great house." Around the start of the New Kingdom (18th Dynasty), it also came to mean the "great person" who lived there.

pylon—a monumental stone entrance made by two trapezoidal towers flanking a temple's doorway. Artisans carved reliefs and flagpole holders into pylons.

pyramid—a stone structure having four triangular-shaped sides that slope upward until they meet at a point. Egyptian kings of the Old and Middle Kingdoms constructed huge pyramids as their tombs.

Pyramid Texts—a collection of sacred writings meant to help a deceased king pass easily from this life to the next. The Pyramid Texts are the earliest known religious texts in Egypt. They are carved into pyramid walls of the Old Kingdom, a time when only the king was believed to be immortal.

ruler of the Nine Bows—the ruler of the nations (represented by nine bows) subdued by Egypt.

scarab—dung beetle considered sacred by ancient Egyptians. The scarab pushes a ball of dung into a hole and enters it to lay eggs in the dung, which will feed the larvae; in time, new beetles emerge from the hole. Thus the beetle was a symbol of life to the Egyptians.

They imagined a great beetle rolling the sun across the sky. Scarabs were carved onto the flat side of stones, gems, gold, and faience. Cartouches were often inscribed on them. The "heart scarab" had a passage from the *Book of the Dead* inscribed on it and was placed between the mummified body and the bandaging to ensure life in the next world.

Sed—*see* Heb-Sed festival

serdab—a small, sealed chamber in an ancient tomb containing a statue of the deceased; Arabic for "cellar." One wall had a small opening in front of the statue's eyes so that it could see the offerings left and rituals performed in the adjoining offering hall.

stele (*plural* stelae)—a rectangular stone slab used for commemorative purposes. The upper part was usually a semicircle, and stelae were often inscribed with accounts of such accomplishments as treaties and victories on the battlefield. Nonroyal stelae are often found in private funerary chapels. These, too, were inscribed with praiseworthy information about the deceased, in order to ease his passage from this world to the next.

Two Lands—the lands that flank the Nile River north of the cataracts. In ancient times, this area was divided into two political entities—Upper Egypt and Lower Egypt.

ushebti—mummiform figures found in Middle Kingdom tombs of wealthy Egyptians; supposed to work on behalf of deceased in fields of Osiris. Originally made of wood, later of stone or ceramic.

vizier—an executive officer of the nation, ranked second to the king in power and prestige in the Two Lands. His duties were administrative as well as legislative and economic.

Further Reading and Websites

The books in this list vary in level of difficulty, but none is too technical for the interested reader. Titles preceded by an asterisk (*) are recommended for younger readers.

BOOKS

Archaeology

Arnold, Dorothea. *When the Pyramids Were Built: Egyptian Art of the Old Kingdom*. New York: Rizzoli International, 1999.

*Avi-Yonah, Michael. *Dig This! How Archaeologists Uncover Our Past*. Minneapolis: Runestone, 1993.

*Caselli, Giovanni. *In Search of Tutankhamun: The Discovery of a King's Tomb*. New York: Peter Bedrick, 1999.

David, Rosalie. *Discovering Ancient Egypt*. New York: Facts on File, 1993.

*Donoughue, Carol. *The Mystery of the Hieroglyphs*. New York: Oxford University Press, 1999.

Ford, Barbara. *Howard Carter: Searching for King Tut*. New York: Freeman, 1995.

*Giblin, James Cross. *The Riddle of the Rosetta Stone: Key to Ancient Egypt*. New York: HarperCollins, 1990.

Hobson, Christine. *Exploring the World of the Pharaohs*. London: Thames & Hudson, 1987.

*Ikram, Salima. *Egyptology*. Washington, D.C.: Amideast, 1997.

Lehner, Mark. *The Complete Pyramids*. New York: Thames & Hudson, 1997.

*Moloney, Norah. *The Young Oxford Book of Archaeology*. Oxford: Oxford University Press, 1997.

Murnane, William J. *The Penguin Guide to Ancient Egypt*. New York: Penguin, 1996.

*Reeves, C. N. *Into the Mummy's Tomb*. New York: Scholastic/Madison Press, 1992.

Reeves, C.N., and Richard H. Wilkinson. *The Complete Valley of the Kings*. London: Thames & Hudson, 1996.

Siliotti, Alberto. *Guide to the Valley of the Kings*. London: Wiedenfeld & Nicolson, 1996.

Vercoutter, Jean. *The Search for Ancient Egypt*. New York: Abrams, 1992.

Weeks, Kent R. "Valley of the Kings." *National Geographic Magazine* (Sept. 1998): 2–33.

Arts and Sciences

*Howarth, Sarah. *The Pyramid Builders*. Philadelphia: Running Press, 1993.

Jean, Georges. *Writing: The Story of Alphabets and Scripts*. New York: Abrams, 1992.

*Macaulay, David. *Pyramid*. New York: Houghton Mifflin, 1975.

*Millard, Anne. *Pyramids*. New York: Kingfisher, 1996.

Morley, Jacqueline, Mark Bergin, and John James. *An Egyptian Pyramid*. New York: Peter Bedrick, 1991.

*O'Neal, Michael. *Pyramids*. San Diego, Calif.: Greenhaven, 1995.

*Perl, Lila. *Mummies, Tombs, and Treasure: Secrets of Ancient Egypt*. New York: Clarion, 1987.

Taylor, John H. *Unwrapping a Mummy*. Austin: University of Texas Press, 1995.

*Woods, Geraldine. *Science in Ancient Egypt*. New York: Franklin Watts, 1988.

Daily Life

*Caselli, Giovanni. *An Egyptian Craftsman*. New York: Peter Bedrick, 1991.

*David, Rosalie. *Growing Up in Ancient Egypt*. New York: Troll, 1994.

———.*Handbook to Life in Ancient Egypt*. New York: Facts on File, 1998.

David, Rosalie, and Rich Archbold. *Conversations with Mummies*. New York: William Morrow, 2000.

*Grant, Neil. *The Egyptians*. New York: Oxford University Press, 1993.

*Ikram, Salima. *Land and People*. Washington, D.C.: Amideast, 1997.

* Kondeatis, Christos, and Sara Maitland. *The Ancient Egypt Pack*. Boston: Bulfinch, 1996.

Lesko, Leonard H., ed. *Pharaoh's Workers: The Villagers of Deir el Medina*. Ithaca, N.Y.: Cornell University Press, 1994.

* Morley, Jacqueline. *First Facts About the Ancient Egyptians*. New York: Peter Bedrick, 1996.

Romer, John. *Ancient Lives: Daily Life in Egypt of the Pharaohs*. New York: Holt, Rinehart & Winston, 1984.

———. *People of the Nile: Everyday Life in Ancient Egypt*. New York: Crown, 1982.

Steedman, Scott, and David Antram. *Egyptian Town*. New York: Franklin Watts, 1998.

* Watson, Philip J. *Costume of Ancient Egypt*. New York: Chelsea House, 1987.

White, Jon Manchip. *Everyday Life in Ancient Egypt*. New York: Peter Bedrick, 1963.

History

Aldred, Cyril. *Egypt to the End of the Old Kingdom*. New York: Thames and Husdon, 1982.

Baines, John, and Jaromir Malek. *Atlas of Ancient Egypt*. New York: Facts on File, 1980.

Bunson, Margaret. *The Encyclopedia of Ancient Egypt*. New York: Facts on File, 1991.

Corteggiani, Jean-Pierre. *The Egypt of the Pharaohs at the Cairo Museum*. London: Scala, 1986.

* David, A. Rosalie. *The Egyptian Kingdoms*. New York: Peter Bedrick, 1988.

* Freeman, Charles. *The Legacy of Ancient Egypt*. New York: Facts on File, 1997.

* Harris, Geraldine. *Cultural Atlas for Young People: Ancient Egypt*. New York: Facts on File, 1990.

Harris, Nathaniel. *The Earliest Explorers*. Volume I of The Grolier Student Library of Explorers and Exploration. Danbury, Conn.: Grolier Educational, 1998.

* James, T. G. H. *A Short History of Ancient Egypt*. Baltimore: Johns Hopkins University Press, 1995.

Kitchen, K. A. *Pharaoh Triumphant: The Life and Times of Ramesses II*. England: Aris & Phillips, 1982.

* Koenig, Viviane, and Véronique Ageorges. *The Ancient Egyptians: Life in the Nile Valley*. Brookfield, Conn.: Millbrook Press, 1992.

Newby, P. H. *Warrior Pharaohs*. Boston: Faber and Faber, 1980.

* Odijk, Pamela. *The Egyptians*. Englewood Cliffs, N.J.: Silver Burdett, 1989.

Shaw, Ian, ed. *The Oxford History of Ancient Egypt*. New York: Oxford University Press, 2001.

Silverman, David P., ed. *Ancient Egypt*. New York: Oxford University Press, 1997.

* Smith, Brenda. *Egypt of the Pharaohs*. San Diego, Calif.: Lucent, 1996.

* Stedman, Scott. *Ancient Egypt*. New York: Dorling Kindersley, 1995.

Literature

Breasted, James Henry. *Ancient Records of Egypt*. 4 volumes. Chicago: University of Chicago Press, 1906.

Lichtheim, Miriam. *Ancient Egyptian Literature: A Book of Readings*, vols. 1–3. Berkeley: University of California Press, 1973–80.

Mythology

* Brier, Bob. *The Encyclopedia of Mummies*. New York: Facts on File, 1998.

* Cashford, Jules. *The Myth of Isis and Osiris*. Boston: Barefoot Books, 1993.

Dunand, Françoise. *Mummies: A Voyage Through Eternity*. New York: Abrams, 1994.

* Harris, Geraldine. *Gods & Pharaohs from Egyptian Mythology*. New York: Peter Bedrick, 1981.

Ions, Veronica. *Egyptian Mythology*. New York: Peter Bedrick, 1982.

Lesko, Barbara S. *The Great Goddesses of Egypt*. Norman: University of Oklahoma Press, 1999.

* Trumble, Kelly. *Cat Mummies*. New York: Clarion, 1996.

* Wilcox, Charlotte. *Mummies and Their Mysteries*. Minneapolis: Carolrhoda Books, 1992.

Rulers

Clayton, Peter A. *Chronicle of the Pharaohs: The Reign-by-Reign Record of the Rulers and Dynasties of Ancient Egypt*. London: Thames & Hudson, 1994.

Dodson, Aidan. *Monarchs of the Nile*. London: Rubicon, 1995.

Hornung, Erick. *History of Ancient Egypt*. Trans. David Lorton. Ithaca, N.Y.: Cornell University Press, 1999.

* Ikram, Salima. *The Pharaohs*. Washington, D.C.: Amideast, 1997.

Women

Hawass, Zahi. *Silent Images: Women in Pharaonic Egypt*. New York: Abrams, 2000.

Lesko, Barbara S. *The Remarkable Women of Ancient Egypt*. Providence, R.I.: Scribe, 1996.

McDonald, Fiona. *Women in Ancient Egypt*. New York: Peter Bedrick, 1999.

Watterson, Barbara. *Women in Ancient Egypt*. New York: St. Martin's, 1991.

MAGAZINES

KMT, a Modern Journal of Ancient Egypt. Published quarterly by KMT Communications, Dept. G, P.O. Box 1475, Sebastopol, CA 95973-1475. Online at http://www.egyptology.com/kmt/

* "Ancient Nubia." *CALLIOPE* (Nov./Dec. 1996): entire issue.

* "Pharaohs of Egypt." *CALLIOPE* (Sept./Oct. 1994): entire issue.

* "Queens of Egypt." *CALLIOPE* (Nov./Dec. 1991): entire issue.

* "Science and Medicine in Ancient Egypt." *CALLIOPE* (Sept./Oct. 1997): entire issue.

* "Tomb Builders." *CALLIOPE* (Sept. 2000): entire issue.

WEBSITES

Ancient Egypt

http://personalwebs.myriad.net/steveb/egypt.html

Links to dozens of websites, including The British Museum–Department of Egyptian Antiquities; The Egyptian Museum, Cairo; Australian Centre for Egyptology; "Egypt: Gift of the Nile"—Seattle Art Museum; Egyptology Resources from Cambridge University; and the Egyptian

Gallery at the University of Pennsylvania Museum of Archaeology and Anthropology

Ancient Egypt

http://www.sis.gov.eg/ancient/front.htm

Ancient Egypt section of Egypt State Information Service's website

Explores ancient Egypt through the daily activities of its people. Themes include life of ancient Egyptians, pyramids and the Sphinx, and Egyptian Treasures

The Ancient Egyptian Culture Exhibit

http://emuseum.mankato.msus.edu/prehistory/egypt

Electronic Museum run by Minnesota State University–Mankato. Themes include daily life, art, the military, architecture, hieroglyphs, religion, maps, history, archaeology, and bibliography

Explore Ancient Egypt

http://www.mfa.org/egypt/explore_ancient_egypt/index.html

Online gallery of the Egyptian Collection at the Museum of Fine Arts, Boston

Life in Ancient Egypt

www.clpgh.org/cmnh/exhibits/egypt/index.html

An introduction to the Walton Hall of Ancient Egypt at the Carnegie Museum of Natural History in Pittsburgh, Pennsylvania. Themes include the natural world, daily life, gods and religion, and funerary customs

Pyramids: The Inside Story

http://www.pbs.org/wgbh/nova/pyramid/

Maps, diagrams, and virtual tours of several pyramids

Tour Egypt

www.touregypt.net/index.htm

Official website of Egypt's Ministry of Tourism and the Egyptian Tourist Authority

Index of Ancient Egyptians by Position

Architect
Amenhotep, son of Hapu
Imhotep
Senenmut

Expedition leader and governor
Harkhuf
Weni

Landholder
Heqanakht

Military officer
Ahmose, son of Ebana
Udjahorresne

Physician
Amenhotep, son of Hapu
Imhotep
Udjahorresne

Priest
Manetho

Ruler
Ahmose I
Akhenaten (Amenhotep IV)
Amasis (Ahmose II)
Amenemhet I
Amenemhet III
Amenhotep III
Djoser
Hatshepsut
Herihor
Horemheb
Khafre
Khufu

Menes
Menkaure
Nebhepetre Mentuhotep I
Nekhtnebef (Nectanebo II)
Pepi I
Pepi II
Psamtik I
Ramesses II
Ramesses III
Senwosret I
Senwosret III
Seqenenre Tao II
Seti I
Snefru
Thutmose I
Thutmose III
Tutankhamun

Ruler's wife
Ahmose-Nefertari
Hetep-heres
Nefertari
Nefertiti
Tiye

Statesman
Hemiunu
Meketre
Pa-wer-a'a
Pepinakht
Ptahhotep
Rekhmire

Writer
Manetho
Ptahhotep

Index

References to illustrations and their captions are indicated by page numbers in **bold**.

Acknowledgments

Special thanks are owed to the staff of the John D. Rockefeller, Jr., Library at Brown University in Providence, Rhode Island, for their invaluable assistance in helping us search and locate so many of the books used in preparing *Ancient Egyptians*.

We would also like to thank the reference librarians at the main branch of the New Public Library in New Bedford, Massachusetts, and at the Southworth Library in South Dartmouth, Massachusetts, for their quick responses to our requests for information about resources and other data necessary to our research on *Ancient Egyptians*.

We are also indebted to James Henry Breasted, the author of *Ancient Records of Egypt: Historical Documents from the Earliest Times to the Persian Conquest*, for his translations and insights into the life and writings of the early Egyptians.

Picture Credits

Rosalie F. and Charles F. Baker III are the editors of the *CALLIOPE: The World History Magazine for Young People*, winner of the EdPress 1998 Golden Lamp Award and the EdPress 1998 Distinguished Achievement Award for One-Theme Issue. They are the authors of *Ancient Greeks: Creating the Classical Tradition* and *Ancient Romans: Expanding the Classical Tradition*, both part of the Oxford Profiles series; *The Classical Companion, Myths and Legends of Mount Olympos;* and *Classical Ingenuity.* Both are former teachers and administrators in public and private schools. Charles Baker is the editor of *FOOTSTEPS*, a magazine on African American history, which won the EdPress 1999 Distinguished Achievement Award for One-Theme Issue. He is also the author of *Struggle for Freedom*, 13 plays about the American Revolution for classroom performance. The Bakers live in New Bedford, Massachusetts, with their son, Chip.